COUNTRY INNS OF THE FAR WEST: CALIFORNIA

JACQUELINE KILLEEN

ROY KILLEEN
Illustrations

101 PRODUCTIONS
San Francisco

COVER DRAWING: Old Monterey Inn, Monterey. Drawing by Roy Killeen, color rendering by Sara Raffetto.

MAPS: Lynne O'Neil

Some of the drawings in this book have been reproduced from the inns' brochures with the permission of the inns, and are credited to the following artists: The Britt House, page 4, Robert Hostick; The Venice Beach House, page 15, Hipple-Sommerville Assoc.; Salisbury House, page 17, Mimi Stuart; Crown Bed & Breakfast Inn, page 22, Miller Fong; The Glenborough Inn, page 37, Donna Medley; Bath Street Inn, page 39, James Zimmerman; Union Hotel, page 43, Scott Gorsline; Rose Victorian Inn, page 45, Judith Andresen; The Jabberwock, page 55, Gloria Bottaro; The Stonehouse Inn, page 63, Nancy Taylor; Happy Landing, page 69; San Benito Hotel, page 79, Pavesich; Hermitage House, page 90, T. Anna Binkley; Spreckels Mansion, page 95, James Dowlen; The Inn on Castro, page 100, T. Kramer; Petite Auberge, page 105, Nancy Taylor; Gramma's Bed and Breakfast Inn, page 108, Steven Lustig; Olema Inn, page 114; Blackthorne Inn, page 116, Tony Lofting; The Briggs House, page 125, Lily Toppenberg; The Rupley House, page 135, Marcia O'Rourke; The Hanford House, page 141, Larry Schuman; La Residence, page 182, Casey Hobbs; Larkmead Country Inn, page 191, Marilyn Indelicato; Wine Way Inn, page 193, Chet Dippel; Grape Leaf Inn, page 202, Mike Fitzpatrick; The Haydon House, page 204, George Espinosa; Ridenhour Ranch House Inn, page 209; Headlands Inn, page 234, David Scott Meier; Whitegate Inn, page 238, Wesley Poole; Pudding Creek Inn, page 240, Susan Flanduz; Old Town Bed & Breakfast Inn, page 252, Jeff Larson.

Copyright © 1984 by 101 Productions

Some of the text and illustrations have been previously published in earlier editions of Country Inns of the Far West, copyright © 1977, 1979, 1982 by 101 Productions.

Printed and bound in the United States of America. Distributed to the book trade in the United States by The Scribner Book Companies, New York, and in Canada by John Wiley & Sons Canada Limited, Toronto.

Published by 101 Productions
834 Mission Street
San Francisco, California 94103

Library of Congress Cataloging in Publication Data
Killeen, Jacqueline.
    Country inns of the Far West--California.
    Includes index.
    1. Hotels, taverns, etc.--California--Directories.
I. Killeen, Roy.   II. Title.
TX907.K484   1984   647'.9479401   84-2318
ISBN 0-89286-231-9

CONTENTS

INTRODUCTION

This book results from a lifetime of travel in California. My parents were inveterate travelers and my earliest memories, in the 1930s, were from the back of a car exploring obscure roads as well as major highways up and down the state. Had there been B&Bs in those days we surely would have been there, but instead we sought out other unusual places that ranged from lodgings with an Italian family near the Russian River to camp grounds in the high Sierra to the luxuries of the Hotel del Coronado. In the 1940s, I got a taste of what today's inns are like from a visit to the Little River Inn in Mendocino, a stop at Benbow and a weekend at San Ysidro Ranch in the heyday of Ronald Colman, but those were about the only ones around that I recommend now. In the 1950s and 1960s my travels widened to include pensions and old palaces in Europe, bed and breakfast in England, posadas in Mexico and historic inns in New England. I wondered why there were no such pleasures in California and even dreamed of opening an inn in the Napa Valley, which then offered only a few motels.

Then in the mid 1970s the inn craze finally hit California. Historic hotels in the Mother Lode were refurbished, lumber barons' mansions in Mendocino were opened to guests, country inns started to pop up in the wine country and on the Monterey Peninsula, and in 1976 the state's first urban bed and breakfast inn opened in a renovated Victorian house in San Francisco.

Yet the pace of emerging new inns was slow, compared with today. When we published the first edition of *Country Inns of the Far West* in 1977, my co-authors and I could find only forty-eight suitable hostelries between Santa Barbara and Vancouver Island in British Columbia. And this took an exhaustive search of back roads and little towns. By 1979 the book had grown to include seventy-five inns and the 1982 edition swelled to a fat volume that described 136 places in the west coast states and Canada. We thought the inn boom had peaked, but how wrong we were. By the time we started researching this current edition, over one-hundred new inns—mostly B&Bs—had opened in California alone. It was obviously time to dissect the Pacific Northwest from California and to publish two editions of *Country Inns of the Far West,* one for each area. It was also obvious that space would not permit us to include all of the new places and so we had to be very selective. We visited almost every inn that we heard about, choosing only the best and most interesting accommodations in each area, while trying to present a variety in ambience, size and price.

What is a country inn? We define it as a state of mind, a refuge of tranquility that can be found in an urban as well as a pastoral environment. The qualities that we are looking for can be found in inns of all sizes: our selections range from four-bedroom B&Bs to a small resort hotel with one-hundred rooms, although that is exceptionally large for this book. They also range from quaint old houses and hotels gussied up with antiques to luxurious hostelries as modern as tomorrow. But they all share one trait: a dedication to personalized service and a true caring for the comfort of their guests. We consider the innkeeper's personality as important as the food and facilities that are offered, and we do have some specific standards for the latter. We require that the predominant use of the building be for the inn (as opposed to someone taking in paying guests at their home), that there be a common sitting area so you're not stuck in your room, that breakfast be served on the premises and that there be an adequate number of baths for the guest rooms, even though we do not insist on private baths. It goes without saying that cleanliness and safety are of paramont importance, as well.

I would also like to emphasize that I have personally visited each inn in this book before including it and that I periodically re-check the inns that were in the previous editions. In fact the majority of the old reviews have been rewritten for this edition. You might be surprised to learn, as I was, that some guide book authors never set foot on the premises of the inns they describe, taking their information exclusively from brochures and questionnaires that the inns fill out themselves. Other books require a fee, membership in an association or a commitment to buy a centain number of books. To be recommended herein, an inn is obliged only to maintain the highest standards for its guests.

I hope that you enjoy your journey through the inns of California as much as I have enjoyed researching it for you. I also hope that you will continue to tell me about new inns that you have discovered, as well as about any changes that have taken place in those that we have recommended.

—Jacqueline Killeen

RULES OF THE INN

Rates Due to the enormous price fluctuations of these times, I no longer quote specific rates. Instead I have categorized the inns according to the following scale as of this writing: inexpensive, under $50 for two; moderate, $50 to $75; expensive, $75 to $100; very expensive, over $100. When dinner is included in the rate, I have subtracted the price of an average dinner at that inn to arrive at the rate category.

Reservations, Deposits, Cancellations and Refunds Reservations are advised for all of the inns in this book, especially during peak travel periods. On holidays and weekends, they are often booked for months in advance. Most of the inns require a deposit of at least one night's lodging; many require a minimum stay of two nights on the weekends. In most cases your deposit will not be refunded if you cancel at the last minute; sometimes even a week's notice is required. Call or write in advance to ask about the current requirements, rates and refund policies.

Housekeeping In many of the smaller inns, guests share a community bathroom. Be sure to clean out your tub and washbasin, pick up your towels and leave the bathroom in immaculate condition for the next guest. In many of these small places, the chambermaid is actually the innkeeper; keep your room as tidy as possible.

Tipping In the larger inns, where you are presented your check at the end of each meal, tip as you would in any hotel or restaurant. In the smaller inns, where the owner does the cooking and serving, you are not required to tip. In fact most innkeepers will not accept tips and some would be insulted. If you wish to express your appreciation, send flowers or leave some wine as you would in a friend's home. You should, however, compensate the innkeeper's helpers. Some inns have a "kitty" and divide the tips among the workers; others expect you to tip individually. We recommend that, at the end of your stay, you ask the innkeeper for advice in handling this.

No Smoking Policies Many of the smaller inns do not allow smoking within the building, although in most cases guests are free to smoke outdoors on porches, patios or in the gardens. These inns have adopted this policy for important reasons: consideration of other guests and fear of fire or damage to priceless antiques. We have noted it whenever an inn does not allow smoking. Many of those who condone smoking, however, are not happy about heavy smokers; they can be annoying to other guests and the smell of their cigarettes remains in the rooms.

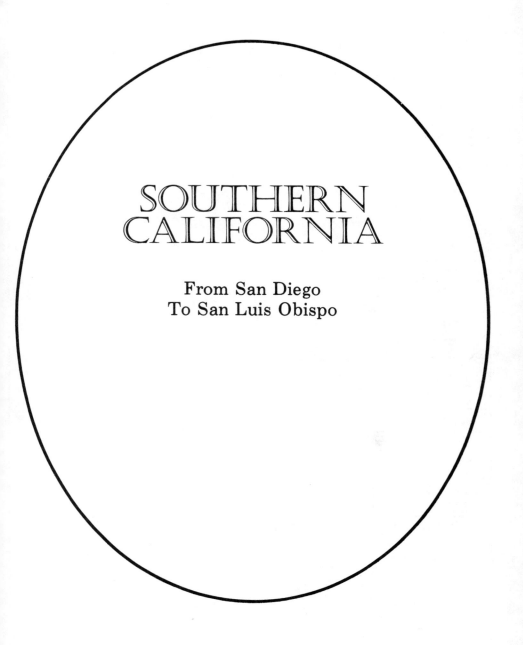

SOUTHERN CALIFORNIA

From San Diego
To San Luis Obispo

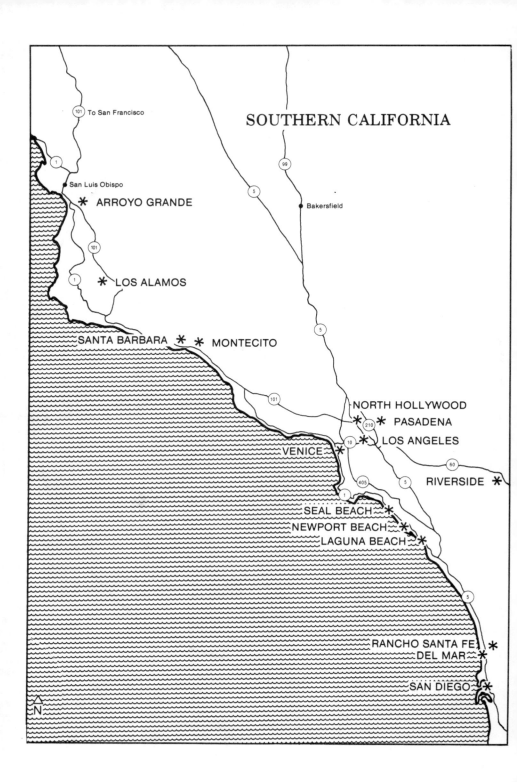

SOUTHERN CALIFORNIA

To San Francisco

San Luis Obispo

✱ ARROYO GRANDE

Bakersfield

✱ LOS ALAMOS

SANTA BARBARA ✱ ✱ MONTECITO

NORTH HOLLYWOOD
✱ ✱ PASADENA
✱ LOS ANGELES
VENICE ✱

RIVERSIDE ✱

SEAL BEACH ✱
NEWPORT BEACH ✱
LAGUNA BEACH ✱

RANCHO SANTA FE ✱
DEL MAR ✱

SAN DIEGO ✱

N

The Birthplace of California
SAN DIEGO

In 1542 the Spanish explorer Juan Rodriguez Cabrillo sailed into San Diego Bay. The first white man to set foot on California soil, he claimed the area for Spain which proceeded to ignore its new territory for over two centuries. The Spanish were looking for gold and, ironically, could see no potential in this wilderness inhabited only by poor Indians, a wilderness that one day would provide the biggest gold strike in history. Finally, in 1769 Father Junipero Serra led a group of Franciscan padres to California, founding the state's first mission at San Diego. These priests became the state's first innkeepers, building a string of twenty-one missions up the coast, spaced a day's journey apart so that travelers could find food and lodging each night.

Today San Diego is the third largest and one of the fastest growing cities in the state. Besides being a major commercial and educational center (nine institutions of higher learning are located here), the city and its adjacent communities are a year-round vacationland. Water sports—from swimming off the sun-drenched beaches to deep-sea fishing off the coast—are popular diversions. San Diego also boasts one of the finest zoos in the country and Sea World, the largest oceanarium in the world, plus countless sightseeing opportunities. These include Old Town, the original Spanish settlement with many of the old adobes intact, and the Mission San Diego de Alcala. A short drive whisks you across the border to old Mexico.

Southern California's First B&B
BRITT HOUSE
San Diego

It seems fitting that the city where California's string of missions started should give birth to southern California's first bed and breakfast inn. It was opened in 1979—several years after the B&B craze hit the northern part of the state—by designer Robert Hostick and his wife Daun Martin in a circa-1887 Queen Anne Victorian. The three-story house with its circular tower and gabled roof was built by attorney Eugene Britt; he lived there only a few years before selling to newspaper publisher E. W. Scripps, whose family owned the house for many years.

The most dramatic feature of the Britt House is a monumental entrance hall with intricate paneled wainscoting and a stairway of oak. Three stained-glass windows rise from floor to ceiling, and a filigree of spoolwork arches over the entrance to the parlor, which contains a baby grand piano.

Robert Hostick designed the interiors, opting for country charm rather than authenticity. Each room is papered in a different pattern, but color themes of blue, burgundy, rust and eggplant appear in many variations. In the nine bedrooms, periods of furnishings are mixed with considerable grace. Marble-topped Eastlake dressers and old platform rockers mingle with wicker and rattan and comfortable queen-size beds with quilted spreads. Gilt-framed "family portraits" adorn the dressers, and Hostick's own bright contemporary graphics hang on the walls. One room contains furnishings that belonged to Robert W. Waterman, governor of California from 1887 to 1891. The downstairs billiards room boasts a Civil War–vintage table, newly covered in rust felt.

Brightly colored rag dolls and stuffed animals recline around the bedrooms, and all have names. Harry the Hen inhabits the Music Room off the lower hall, and in another room, Elizabeth, a flamboyant ostrich, roosts on a velvet-canopied bed. Bouquets of silk and fresh flowers, bowls of fruit and homemade cookies are placed in all the rooms. Two rooms have private balconies. A garden cottage has a kitchenette and private bath.

Four community baths offer guests some intriguing choices of bathing. One has two "his and her" claw-legged tubs, equipped with bubble bath. Another has a sauna. All are stocked with emergency supplies of sundries travelers may have left at home: toothpaste, aspirin, needles and thread, sunburn lotion and the like.

Robert and Daun obviously have gone "the extra mile" in every detail of the Britt House, breakfast included. Daun or her assistant bakes individual loaves of a different yeast bread every day—nine-grain, orange, carrot are a few—to serve on the bedroom trays along with fresh-squeezed orange juice, shirred eggs and Viennese roast coffee. A complimentary afternoon tea is also served, consisting of tea, sherry, a trifle, shortbread and cucumber sandwiches. And to help you with dinner plans, menus have been collected from the many fine restaurants in the area. The Britt House is only two blocks from the famed Balboa Park and San Diego Zoo, and it's only a ten-minute walk to the beach and the harbor.

BRITT HOUSE, 406 Maple Street, San Diego, California 92103. Telephone: (714) 234-2926. Accommodations: nine rooms with twin or queen-size beds; one room with private bath, others share four baths with tub or shower, one with wheelchair access; no telephones; no television. Rates: moderate to expensive, breakfast included. No children under 12, except in cottage. No pets. Cards: MC, VISA. Open all year.

Getting There: From Los Angeles take Highway 405 or Highway 5 south to San Diego's Washington Street exit, proceed east to Fourth Street, turn right on Fourth to Maple.

Lovely Inn with a Shady Past
ROCK HAUS
Del Mar

Henry W. Keller was president of the South Coast Land Company which developed the beautiful beach resort of Del Mar just north of San Diego at the turn of the century. In 1910 he built a large summer home for his family on a hill overlooking the village and the Pacific. Constructed of stone and wood and surrounded by Torrey pines, the house is an elaborate version of the Craftsman style so popular in southern California during this period. After auspicious beginnings— Sunday mass was conducted in the dining room and the big name bands that came to the old Del Mar Hotel had jam sessions here—the hillside mansion became a private club in the 1920s and for the next five decades hosted almost every illicit activity imaginable. Old timers remember frequent police busts for gambling and illegal alcohol, and surmise that ladies of questionable morals frequented the establishment. In the 1950s new owners named the place Rock House Hotel and ran a boardinghouse that turned into a hippie pad, rife with the smell of marijuana in the 1960s. It was also used as a safe house for smuggling Mexicans into California.

Then in 1982 lawyer Tom Hauser and his wife Carol bought the old Rock House and after extensive renovation turned it into an inn, renaming it Rock Haus. They laughingly point to a tombstone-like rock in front of the house. "We buried the hotel's sign there," Tom says, "and with it the saga of the Rock House Hotel." This is indeed a new era for the handsome building which sits on an acre of groomed lawn and gardens. Carol has decorated the eight bedrooms to look like a 1910 summer home should, with lots of wicker and rattan, flowery comforters, mounds of ruffled pillows, little antique writing tables and some beds with canopies. Most of the upstairs rooms have fabulous ocean views, while two downstairs rooms, one with a fireplace, have private entrances.

Probably the most interesting guest room is the Whale Watch Room, a good place to bone up on the migration of the great gray whales that can be spotted all along the California coast during the winter months. These giant mammals leave their home in the Arctic and make a ten-thousand-mile round trip to have their babies in the warm lagoons off Baja California. The Hausers have placed *Moby Dick* and other works on whaleology in the room along with an 1861 chart of the whale migration and a replica of an old whalers' lodging sign, a reminder that San Diego was once a major whaling port. There's also a reminder of the inn's shady past: a paneled and mirrored headboard that once served as a false front for the area where the gambling tables were hidden off the living room.

Today this living room, with its beamed ceiling, stone fireplace and Oriental rugs on the hardwood floors, is the scene of more wholesome activities. There's a player piano, backgammon set and comfortable couches and chairs where you might want to curl up with a book from the Hausers' large library. Wine is served here in the evening and sometimes Tom conducts wine tastings in his basement cellar. A sun porch with a clear view of the Pacific is the setting for a light breakfast of fresh fruit, juice and muffins or coffeecake.

The beach and the village shops are the chief attractions of Del Mar, except in the summer months when the race track, built by Bing Crosby and Bob Hope in 1937, brings some fifty thousand horse race fans to town. The many diversions of San Diego are only a short

Rock Haus

distance away. But you might just want to while away your day at Rock Haus, it's such a lovely inn.

ROCK HAUS, 410 Fifteenth Street, Del Mar, California 92014. Telephone: (619) 481-3764. Accommodations: eight rooms with twin, queen- and king-size beds; six upstairs rooms share three baths with stall shower or tub; two downstairs rooms with private baths, stall shower; no telephones; no television. Rates: moderate to expensive, Continental breakfast included. No children. No pets. No smoking. Cards: MC, VISA. Open all year.

Getting There: From San Diego take Del Mar Heights exit off the San Diego Freeway and head west to Camino Del Mar, turn right to Fifteenth Street and turn right again. From Los Angeles take Via de la Valle exit off the San Diego Freeway and head southwest along Jimmy Durante Boulevard to the village of Del Mar, turn left on Fifteenth Street. Courtesy pickup at the Amtrak station in Del Mar.

Twenty Acres of Gardens and Eucalyptus Trees
THE INN AT RANCHO SANTA FE
Rancho Santa Fe

The very exclusive community of Rancho Santa Fe consists of elegant tile-roofed houses set among dense eucalyptus groves in the hills inland from Del Mar beach. The hub of the area is a tiny village containing exquisite shops and The Inn. A century ago, however, this was just a barren stretch of land that had been granted by the Mexican government to Juan Maria Osuna, one-time mayor of the Pueblo de San Diego. Then in 1906 the Santa Fe Railroad purchased the land from Osuna's heirs with the purpose of raising eucalyptus from Australia for railroad ties—one of the most colossal agricultural follies in California history. Over three million seedlings were planted before Santa Fe officials realized that the gnarled eucalyptus wood was totally unsuitable for ties. They recouped their investment by planting the remaining acres with citrus and by selling off the eucalyptus forests for home sites. A lovely adobe building was constructed in the Spanish style to house prospective purchasers. This is now The Inn, along with clusters of cottages scattered among twenty acres of woods, lawns, ivy-bedded walkways and gardens rife with bougainvillea, roses, magnolias and palms.

The Inn at Rancho Santa Fe

The Royce family has owned The Inn since 1958 and Daniel Royce now manages it in a very personal fashion. In the living room massive beams support a wooden ceiling that pitches some eighteen feet above the richly carpeted floor. Comfortable couches surround a fireplace, and Royce family antiques, including a large collection of old sailing ship models, adorn the walls and tables. Four dining areas offer choices ranging from an al fresco terrace to a cozy book-lined library and on balmy summer weekend nights there is dancing under the stars.

A wide range of accommodations fits almost any budget. Most rooms in the main bulding have private lanais and are simply furnished with white wicker. Many of the cottage rooms have living rooms with fireplaces and some have kitchenettes; all have private patios, terraces or decks. These units were also designed with flexibility in mind so that rooms can be opened to each other to accommodate groups or families of various sizes.

Rancho Santa Fe has all the amenities of a fine resort hotel: Three tennis courts, a swimming pool and a croquet court are located on the grounds. Guest privileges are available at two private eighteen-hole golf courses nearby. And if you seek the beach, The Inn maintains a seaside cottage with dressing rooms and showers at Del Mar which is only a few minutes away.

THE INN AT RANCHO SANTA FE, Box 869, Rancho Santa Fe, California 92067. Telephone: (619) 756-1131. Accommodations: eighty rooms, most with twin beds and some with king-size beds; private baths with tub/shower or stall shower; telephones; television; conference facilities. Rates: moderate to very expensive, no meals included. Dining rooms open for breakfast, lunch and dinner; full bar service; room service available during dining room hours. Children welcome. One dog allowed in certain rooms at extra charge. Cards: AE, CB, DC, MC, VISA. Open All year.

Getting There: From the San Diego Freeway take the Lomas Santa Fe Drive or the Via de la Valle exit and head east. Both roads lead to The Inn. For a nominal charge and with advance notice The Inn will pick up guests at the Amtrak station in Del Mar or at Lindbergh Field in San Diego.

A Tropical Paradise
HOTEL SAN MAARTEN
Laguna Beach

Seven years after he arrived in California, Father Junipero Serra founded Mission San Juan Capistrano, which is now most famous for the swallows that return on precisely the same day each year. Ten miles up the coast is the quaint artists' colony of Laguna Beach, which is especially popular in the summer months during the famed Festival of the Arts. One of the most charming of Laguna's many hostelries is a small mission-style hotel across from the beach.

In 1976 new owners remodeled and renamed the place after the Caribbean Dutch-French island of Saint Martin, also known as San Maarten. It's likely that the name was inspired by the lush tropical foliage in the central courtyard where palms, ferns, fountains and statuary ring a large swimming pool and baskets of blooming plants hang from the covered balcony above. Views of this court are glimpsed through multipaned windows in all of the guest rooms. These are decorated in a fresh country style with flowered wallpapers, quilted spreads and carved or wicker headboards. Antiques are placed in many of the rooms, but the choice pieces—marble topped dressers and mirrored armoires—are found in the hotel's four suites. These have pullman kitchens and sitting rooms with fireplaces, which unfortunately can't be used due to a city ordinance.

But a fire does burn in the lobby's hearth surrounded by good-looking leather chairs where guests may enjoy their morning croissants and coffee. Lunch and dinner are served to the public on the patio and in the hotel's restaurant which is named after Gauguin, whose paintings suggest yet another tropical island a long way from San Maarten.

HOTEL SAN MAARTEN, 696 South Coast Highway Laguna Beach, California 92651. Telephone: (714) 494-9436. Accommodations: fifty-three rooms with queen-, two queen- or king-size beds; private baths with tub/shower or stall shower; telephones; television. Rates: expensive to very expensive, Continental breakfast included; lower rates on week nights and from October through mid-June. Children welcome. No pets. Cards: AE, CB, DC, MC, VISA. Open all year.

Getting There: From San Diego, take the Highway 1 (Beach Towns) exit off the San Diego Freeway beyond San Clemente and head north.

From Los Angeles, take the Laguna Canyon Road exit from the San Diego Freeway, head west to Highway 1 and turn south. The inn is on the east side of the highway in the center of town. Off-street parking provided.

A Bit of Barbary Coast on the Beach
DORYMAN'S INN
Newport Beach

The resort towns of Newport Beach and Balboa are built on a finger of land that juts from the coast to shelter a colorful harbor dotted with tiny islands and hundreds of pleasure boats—one of the major yachting centers on the California coast. On the ocean side of this peninsula, the Newport pier thrusts into the Pacific. In 1978 real estate developer Rick Lawrence acquired an old rooming house facing the pier and after five years of renovation to the tune of two million dollars opened a classy little inn. Doryman's looks for all the world like a Barbary Coast bordello, but one patronized by bankers and silver barons, rather than boat handlers.

Two restaurants are located downstairs and from a private side door guests are whisked by elevator to the second-floor inn. Here skylights, hung with plants, and brass wall scounces shine on the hall's oak wainscoting, which is polished to a mirrored finish. Each of the ten rooms has a gas-burning fireplace, controlled by the flick of a wall switch, with antique mantels imported from Europe. "When you have five years to look for things, you can come up with ten mantels in perfect condition," comments inn manager David Stephens. Bathrooms are outfitted with skylights and sunken tubs faced with Carrara marble, some with Jacuzzi spouts. The rooms are papered with reproductions of 1880 patterns, some with hand-stenciled friezes around the top. Matching floral drapes and quilted spreads, lace curtains, down comforters and pillows trimmed with eyelet ruffles add to the romantic aura. Furnishings are mostly European antiques: Carved headboards, canopied four-posters, armoires, needlepoint chairs, rockers and gilt-edged mirrors abound. Five of the rooms have unobstructed views of the Pacific and several have French doors opening to a tiled balcony. A little sitting room also opens to this balcony. Guests may have their breakfast served here—a tray of orange juice, fresh fruit, soft-boiled eggs, breads such as pumpkin or banana and a cheesecake pastry—but most prefer the luxury and privacy of breakfast in bed.

DORYMAN'S INN, 2102 West Ocean Front, Newport Beach, California 92663. Telephone: (714) 675-7300. Accommodations: ten rooms with queen- or king-size beds; private baths with tub/shower; telephones; color television. Rates: very expensive, breakfast included. No children under 16. No pets. Cards: AE, CB, DC, MC, VISA. Open all year except Halloween Eve.

Getting There: From the San Diego Freeway take the Harbor Boulevard or Costa Mesa Boulevard exits west to Newport Beach. After crossing Highway 1 continue on Newport Boulevard to Thirty-second Street, turn left on Balboa Boulevard and turn right at the sign to Newport Pier.

Old World Aura in a Flower-Filled Setting
SEAL BEACH INN
Seal Beach

During the 1920s Seal Beach was a popular playground for the wealthy residents of Hollywood and Pasadena. The town was the last stop on an electric railway that later extended to Newport Beach. But during Seal Beach's heyday, gambling palaces, wooden bathhouses and small hotels abounded. The only one of the old hotels remaining is The Seal Beach Inn, a twenty-three-unit structure that had been neglected until Jack and Marjorie Bettenhausen discovered it in 1977. The Bettenhausens aspired to create an inn with an old-world atmosphere, reminiscent of those they had enjoyed in their travels to the Mediterranean coast of France. To the exterior they added window boxes, shutters, carved archways and blue canopies over the doorways. They paved the parking lot with brick and planted flowering shrubs all around: roses, geraniums, jasmine, camellias, hibiscus and oleander. Ornate old street lamps from Long Beach now illuminate the courtyard at night. Fountains, statues and benches from France add to the French ambience.

   To furnish the rooms Jack and Marjorie made cross-country treks, returning with truckloads of antiques and objects of art from Chicago, New Orleans and New York. The result is a busy and homey pot pourri of periods: Early American and Victorian furnishings, bentwood love seats and overstuffed hideabeds, ruffled eyelet café curtains and lace tablecloths, accessories that range from collections of orange-crate labels to Art Nouveau pieces, from Renoir prints to a wicker hatstand with a 1930s-style floppy hat. Hollywood also gets into the act: A four-poster headboard from John Barrymore's bed occupies one room; a

13

shower curtain with a nearly life-size painting of Esther Williams as a butterfly hangs in a bath; and a wood and stained-glass door from Universal Studios opens to the bridal suite that's bedecked with lace and rose satin.

The rooms range from tiny (about ten by twelve feet) to large, the latter with sitting areas and completely equipped kitchen bars. A penthouse suite has a flower-filled private deck, a large living room, a full kitchen with a breakfast nook, and two old-fashioned sleeping porches.

"The look of an inn is important," Marjorie believes, "but loving people and being hospitable are even more important." And she does these very well. Plenty of reading material is found in the downstairs library (as well as in the rooms), along with chess sets, Scrabble boards, puzzles and a decanter of sherry to sip by the fire. In the adjoining tea room a European-type breakfast is served of breads and pastries baked by a pair of European women, orange juice and Viennese or French roast coffees. Both rooms open to a patio with another touch of Hollywood—a kidney-shaped swimming pool.

Marjorie's hospitality extends to helping her guests enjoy Seal Beach. The beach is only a block from the inn, with a pier, boat excursions, fishing and a windsurfing school. The Long Beach Marina and its Seaport Village are only five blocks away. And there are shops, boutiques and eighteen restaurants in the area.

SEAL BEACH INN, 212 Fifth Street, Seal Beach, California 90740. Telephone: (213) 494-2416. Accommodations: twenty-three rooms with twin, double, queen- and king-size beds; private baths with tub/showers or stall showers; no telephones; color televisions. Rates: inexpensive to expensive, Continental breakfast included. Children welcome. No pets. Cards: AE, MC, VISA. Open all year.

Getting There: From Los Angeles take Highway 605 south to the San Diego Freeway south, take Seal Beach Boulevard exit and turn left to Highway 1; turn right and head north; turn left on Fifth Street.

THE VENICE BEACH HOUSE
Venice

At the turn of the century skeptical Californians nicknamed this beach area just outside of Los Angeles Abbot's Folly when Abbot Kinney bought a stretch of coastal marshland with the dream of re-creating Venice, Italy. He constructed canals, bathhouses, elegant hotels, boardwalks, long piers and an amusement park and encouraged art exhibitions and other cultural events. By 1906, when Sarah Bernhardt played to a full house for three nights in Venice, Angelenos had stopped scoffing at Kinney and were flocking to his new resort. One of these was Warren Wilson, wealthy publisher of the *Los Angeles Daily Journal,* who in 1911 built a spacious house in the California Craftsman style a half-block from the beach; two of Wilson's eight daughters married Kinney's sons. The Wilson family owned the property for some forty years, but meanwhile Venice was heading downhill. Oil was being drilled offshore, many of the canals were filled in, the old houses were cut up or torn down to make room for cheap apartments, the amusement park was demolished and in the 1960s hippies virtually took over the town. Kinney's dream had indeed become a folly, but today the pendulum is swinging in Venice's favor. The Marina del Rey, a fancy apartment complex, was built next door; the oil derricks are gone, leaving the beach clean and fine for swimming; and the seaside properties are now predominately upper middle-class residences.

Among those who rediscovered Venice was Philip Boesch, a young attorney from New England. He bought the old Warren house, which had been converted to apartments, just because he loved it and wanted to restore it. Several years of work later, Philip and his wife Vivian decided to turn the place into a B&B and invited her mother Elaine Burke to become the resident innkeeper. Now the handsome grey shingled house is surrounded by manicured lawns and gardens. In the wood-beamed living room the soft grey, rose and mauve hues of an enormous Oriental rug orchestrate the color scheme for much of the house. Comfortable chairs and a sofa, upholstered in shades of mauve, are set around the large brick fireplace and an adjoining sun porch offers a peek of the ocean and a breakfast buffet. This can be eaten at little tables with flowered skirts or out on the wide veranda that fronts the house. Elaine is a baker and the hot breads and muffins come from her oven; a fruit salad is usually served and sometimes apple dumplings.

Vivian deserves credit for the bedrooms' stunning decor. The walls are upholstered—not papered—with padded fabrics that match the bedspreads, an ingenious soundproofing device. In the first-floor bedroom, which boasts a piano and a garden view, the motif is mauve and rose hydrangeas printed on silk. Upstairs the most expensive room—which has a fireplace, ocean view and private sun porch—is tailored in grey wool tweed with accents of mauve. In another, the walls and a canopied bed are dressed in frilly Laura Ashley prints and is contrasted by a very masculine room resplendent with wool tartan plaids. Even the bathrooms are romantic here: One has double shower spigots, one is outfitted with a Jacuzzi tub for two, and another contains two old-fashioned tubs with gilded claws.

Whether you come to Los Angeles to play or to work, Venice is a convenient location. The inn provides bicycles for pedaling along the beach trail which extends from Santa Monica to Long Beach. There's night life aplenty in the bustling bars and bistros of neighboring Marina del Rey. Beverly Hills and Century City are about fifteen minutes away and downtown Los Angeles is a half-hour drive. As one travel-weary guest at the Venice Beach House exclaimed, "This place is wonderful. We spend nine months of the year in hotels, but this is like being at home."

THE VENICE BEACH HOUSE, 15 Thirtieth Avenue, Venice, California 90291. Telephone: (213) 823-1966. Accommodations: eight rooms with two double, queen- or king-size beds; some private and some shared baths, tub/showers; telephones and cable television available on request. Rates: moderate to very expensive. No children under 10. No pets. No smoking. Cards: AE, MC, VISA. Open all year.

Getting There: From the San Diego Freeway, take the Washington Boulevard exit south of Santa Monica and head west. Where Washington forks, follow Washington Street to the beach and turn right on Thirtieth, which is the last street before the boardwalk.

Country Charm Minutes from Downtown
SALISBURY HOUSE
Los Angeles

Early in this century—before the movie makers discovered California—Los Angeles was a sleepy town compared with boisterous San Francisco. Its affluent citizens lived several miles to the west, separated from the Pacific by ranches and citrus groves, in unpretentious houses predominately of the woodsy Craftsman style. This area, now Arlington Heights, began to decline after World War I and was further damaged when the Santa Monica Freeway cut through the middle of it. But in recent years, especially with the redevelopment of downtown and the construction of the Convention Center, Angelenos are beginning to appreciate their heritage of these fine old houses and the district is gradually being renovated. Kathleen Salisbury opened Los Angeles' first B&B here on a quiet residential street.

The two-story Craftsman house, topped with a gabled attic, was built in 1909. The downstairs is notable for its rich woodwork of dark fir, leaded glass windows and beamed ceilings, so typical of this style. Kathleen, an interior designer, has created an old-fashioned country look with a myriad of flowered papers in the Laura Ashley mode, and with her collections of Delft china displayed on plate racks and antique dolls set about here and there. The living room is homey with overstuffed couches covered with floral prints, Oriental rugs, lace cafe curtains and a wood-burning fireplace. The upstairs bedrooms are also abloom with flowery prints on the wallpapers, curtains, comforters and ruffled pillows; furnishings are European and American wood and wicker antiques. One room has an adjoining sun room with a trundle bed; it's a sitting room by day and a twin-bedded sleeping room by night. The cozy attic with a quadruple gabled roof and pine paneling also has a sitting area and a bathtub out in the room. Sherry and port are provided either in the room or in a wine rack in the hall.

Many of the Salisbury guests are business travelers and Kathleen does not send them off to a day's work hungry. Breakfast—served either in a sunny breakfast room or the formal dining room—is a hearty meal: orange juice, a fruit dish such as apple dumpling or peach and raspberry melba, homemade muffins or fruit breads, and a main course which varies from quiche to frittata to sherried crab in a pastry shell. Long-staying guests appreciate this variety as well as the proximity of downtown which is only minutes away.

SALISBURY HOUSE, 2273 West Twentieth Street, Los Angeles, California 90018. Telephone: (213) 737-7817. Accommodations: five rooms with double, queen- or king-size beds; three private baths and one shared bath with tub, tub/shower or stall shower; no telephones; television in library. Rates: inexpensive to moderate, breakfast included. Children over 10 welcome. No pets. No cards. Open all year.

Getting There: The inn is off the Santa Monica Freeway which connects downtown Los Angeles with the San Diego Freeway. Take the Western Avenue exit one block to the north and turn left on Twentieth.

Artistry in a Mediterranean Villa

LA MAIDA HOUSE

North Hollywood

This Mediterranean-style villa, surrounded by tiled patios, lush lawns and gardens, would be a sensational setting for anyone's inn. But the creativity and boundless energy of owner Megan Timothy make a stay at La Maida an exquisite experience that would be difficult to match anywhere. Megan's artistry is reflected in every aspect of the inn from the ninety-seven stained-glass windows she has designed and executed throughout the house to the sculptured pat of butter on the breakfast plate.

Antonio La Maida, an expatriate Italian, built the villa in 1926 on a large estate which has since been subdivided. The white stucco walls, red-tiled roof, arched windows, tiled patios and fountains and lavish use of fine woods and wrought iron are typical of the mansions built in Hollywood during the 1920s. The high-ceilinged living room, down a few steps from the entry hall, boasts polished oak floors, a Carrara marble fireplace and an 1881 grand piano that once belonged to band-leader Horace Heidt. An adjoining den is almost completely filled with tiers of wall-to-wall studio couches of various heights, upholstered in a rust-colored fabric and massed with pillows; one side of this unique room opens to an enclosed tiled patio, where light filters through a stained-glass ceiling onto scores of tropical plants. Glass doors open from here to the lovely gardens where fountains tinkle under the shade of a large magnolia tree and flowers bloom year round.

Four bedrooms are located upstairs, each stunningly decorated in a different style. In the largest, a canopied king-size bed is framed with rough-hewn wood and a rattan chaise, table and chairs provide a comfortable spot for the tray of pre-breakfast tea and coffee that is brought each morning. Another room is decorated with turn-of-the century furnishings, another with white wicker and the fourth opens to a balcony. All the rooms are appointed with plants, cut flowers from La Maida's gardens, complimentary toiletries, terry cloth robes and knee robes crocheted by Megan's mother. A smaller one-story villa across the street contains four suites, two with living rooms and two with private patios. Megan also owns another house two doors away with a swimming pool which may be used by the inn's guests.

Breakfast—or lunch or dinner by appointment—is served in one of three dining areas. If the group is four or less and the weather is fine, the setting might be a little second-floor balcony overlooking the garden.

For eight Megan sets the glass-topped table in a small dining room next to the enclosed downstairs patio; if guests wish to host dinners here, the den is used for the service of aperitifs. Finally a large formal dining room, lit by candlelight and a crystal chandelier, provides seating for thirty-two at round tables. Megan's talents as a cook equal her other endeavors; she runs a catering business and her recipes have appeared in many national magazines. There are no set menus ("That would be boring") and everything—even the croissants and jams—is made from scratch and far from ordinary. The breakfast juice, for example, might be orange flavored with a hint of cinnamon or blended with carrot juice or a combination of apple and celery. Dinners are custom planned to the guest's wishes and range from a simple soup-salad supper for two to an elaborate four-course feast presented with artful garnishings on gold-rimmed Limoges china. With advance notice Megan will also put up picnic baskets complete with real plates—no paper or plastic here—for jaunts to the Hollywood Bowl, which is just a few minutes away.

La Maida House is also only minutes away from Universal Studios and the NBC television studios, both of which conduct tours throughout each day. Hollywood, Beverly Hills and downtown Los Angeles are less than twenty minutes away. If you have friends or business associates in the area, be sure to give them the inn's telephone number. La Maida is so exclusive that its phone is unlisted!

LA MAIDA HOUSE, 11159 La Maida Street, North Hollywood, California 91601. Telephone: (818) 769-3857. Accommodations: eight rooms with twin, double, queen- and king-size beds; private baths with tub/shower or stall shower; no telephones; no television; air conditioned. Rates: expensive, Continental breakfast included; lunch and dinner served with advance notice at extra charge. No children under 16. No pets. No smoking. No cards.

Getting There: Take the Hollywood Freeway to the Magnolia exit in North Hollywood. Turn east on Magnolia to the first stop light and turn right on Tujunga. At the next stoplight turn left on Camarillo. Continue for three blocks and turn left on Bellflower; drive one block to La Maida.

La Maida House

A Splendid Example of the Craftsman Style

CROWN BED & BREAKFAST INN
Pasadena

Pasadena is probably most famous for its annual Rose Bowl parade. This quiet town at the base of the San Gabriel Mountains is also the home of the Norton Simon Museum of Art and the two-hundred acre Huntington Estate with its exceptional library, art gallery and botanical gardens. Architecture buffs, however, think of Pasadena as a showplace for the handsome low-slung houses designed by Greene and Greene and other practioners of the California Craftsman style, which, with its emphasis on natural woods and exposed structural elements, was a forerunner of contemporary design in America.

A splendid example of this style was designed and built in 1905 by Louis B. Easton as a speculative venture, but no one bought it for ten years! The house then served as a private residence and eventually a boardinghouse until the 1970s when it was saved from demolition by Pasadena Heritage, a non-profit group, which purchased, renovated

and sold the house, using the profits to finance subsequent preservation projects. The buyers turned the old Easton house into Pasadena's first B&B.

The entire downstairs, including one bedroom, is paneled in dark fir with large beams crossing the wooden ceilings. Oriental rugs are scattered on the polished oak floors and hand-crafted multipaned windows look out to the garden or the tree-shaded street. Furnishings are true to the period with a massive oak couch and two matching mission-style chairs surrounding a leaded glass coffee table in front of a large brick fireplace. "We couldn't afford the antique couch and chairs," confesses innkeeper Jenny Fong, "So we had them duplicated from a Craftsman pattern book." They are cushioned with a rust-colored velvet, which also covers the room's long window seat.

Upstairs four other bedrooms are papered or painted in cheerful colors and furnished with brass or wicker bedsteads, quilted eyelet or floral spreads, and ruffled pillows. Arriving guests will find bouquets of fresh flowers, a bowl of fruit and a bottle of wine awaiting them. The baths might be the best equipped in California, down to bandages and a selection of colognes; one has a washer and drier for the guests' use. Breakfast consists of orange juice, fruit, croissants or scones and cereal. You have your choice of breakfast in bed or in the downstairs dining room which opens onto a deck and garden.

CROWN BED & BREAKFAST INN, 530 South Marengo Avenue, Pasadena, California 91101. Telephone: (818) 792-4031. Accommodations: five rooms with queen-size beds or two queens; some private and some shared baths, tub/shower and stall shower; no telephones; no television. Rates: moderate, breakfast included. No children under 12. No pets. No smoking in bedrooms. Cards: MC, VISA. Open all year.

Getting There: From the north take Highway 210 or the Ventura Freeway east to Pasadena, exit at Marengo and head south to the inn. From Los Angeles, take the Harbor/Pasadena Freeway east, exit at Arroyo Parkway and proceed to California, turn right and one block later turn left at Marengo.

Fabled Landmark Saved by the City

MISSION INN
Riverside

California's missions no longer take overnight guests, but the aura of the days when they did may still be experienced at Riverside's Mission Inn. This magnificent example of Spanish-style architecture evolved from a thirteen-room adobe boardinghouse, built in 1876. In the 1880s the owners' son, Frank Miller, bought the building and embarked on an ambitious program to turn this modest hotel into one of the great resorts of the West. Over the next five decades he relentlessly added wing after wing, walkways, courtyards, fountains, bell towers, domes, galleries and chapels, all embellished with ornately carved wood and stone, stained glass, painted tiles, and religious statuary. Miller traveled widely, especially in Spain and Mexico, returning with treasures for his inn: signed Tiffany windows, valuable paintings, antique bells, carved Belgian pews, a Della Robbia wall shrine and an eighteenth-century gold-leafed altar from Mexico, around which he built a chapel dedicated to St. Francis. Eventually the hotel grew to 250 rooms surrounded by lush gardens. Its illustrious guests included Presidents William McKinley, Benjamin Harrison and William Howard Taft; Amelia Earhart, Henry Ford, John D. Rockefeller, Sarah Bernhardt and Lillian Russell. The Richard Nixons were married in the St. Francis Chapel as were the Humphrey Bogarts and the Ronald Reagans spent their honeymoon at the inn.

After Miller's death in 1935, the hotel was commercially viable until the 1950s, when a succession of owners allowed it to deteriorate; by 1976 this fabled inn was bankrupt and due to be demolished. Then the city of Riverside rescued its most beloved landmark. The Riverside Redevelopment Agency purchased the inn and turned its management over to a nonprofit Mission Inn Foundation. Individual citizens and civic groups joined the effort to restore the hotel. By 1984 most of the public rooms and seventy guest rooms or suites had been renovated.

Some rooms are quite simply, though comfortably, furnished, but the marble baseboards, massive carved wooden doors, and arched multipaned windows testify to the former grandeur of the place. Other rooms have been elaborately restored. One floor of the Cloister wing was redone as a Junior League project, with various individuals and organizations underwriting the cost of each room. One of the loveliest was revamped by the Kiwanis Club. This room has a high, beamed wood ceiling, tile floors, leaded windows of clear and stained glass, and

Mission Inn

intricately carved wooden doors and bed headboard. Wall niches contain antique artifacts, an archway sets off a small sitting area and a corridor leads to a tiny cubicle with stained-glass windows and a little writing desk.

Some of the inn's most luxurious rooms are located in a fourth-floor penthouse and open onto a tiled rooftop courtyard where plants surround a long reflecting pool. These have beamed ceilings some twenty-five feet high, fireplaces, antique furnishings and objects of art.

Many of the bedrooms, some with filigreed cast-iron balconies, face an interior court where a large fountain splashes and hummingbirds dart among the flowers, lemon trees, palms and magnolias. Meals are served here at umbrella-topped tables or in the adjoining tile-paneled dining room. The inn's cavernous music room, once the site of free organ concerts sponsored by Frank Miller, is now the setting for a popular dinner theater. Off the lobby are the beautiful gardens and a large swimming pool.

Orange groves surround the city of Riverside; California's first navel orange trees were planted here in 1873 from Brazilian cuttings. The city is also home of a University of California campus, several other colleges, and a number of museums devoted to collections of local history and anthropology, Indian culture and railroad memorabilia. But the chief attraction for visitors is the Mission Inn, where tours of its chapels and art galleries are conducted twice daily. The hordes of tourists and theatergoers are a detraction, as are the crafts sales that sometimes occupy the lobby, as is the somewhat impersonal management. But when you awaken to the tinkling of water in the fountains and the chime of the ancient bells, you can fantasize that you have really slept in an old California mission.

MISSION INN, 3649 Seventh Street, Riverside, California 92501. Telephone: (714) 784-0300. Accommodations: seventy rooms with twin, double, queen- or king-size beds; private baths with tub/shower; telephones; television in Cloister rooms. Rates: inexpensive to expensive, no meals included. Open to the public for breakfast, lunch, dinner and Sunday brunch; full bar service. Children welcome. No pets. Cards: AE, MC, VISA. Open all year.

Getting There: From Los Angeles take Highway 60 (Pomona Freeway) to Riverside. Take Rubidoux exit and go right on Mission Street, which becomes Seventh Street.

California's Own Riviera
SANTA BARBARA

In 1786 the Spanish padres founded their tenth mission at the base of the Santa Ynez Mountains, which rise from the bay at Santa Barbara. After the 1812 earthquake, the mission was rebuilt and became known as Queen of the Missions for the beauty of its Moorish-Spanish architecture and the affluence of the surrounding ranches, orchards, gardens and vineyards. The resort city of Santa Barbara still retains the aura of its Spanish heritage. Red-tile–roofed buildings and old adobes, many enclosing inner patios, grace the palm-lined streets. There are splendid beaches, and sportfishing, plus botanical and zoological gardens. Excellent restaurants abound. The Santa Barbara Museum of Art houses a number of international collections; other museums focus on local history and natural history. And a visit to the mission, one of the most beautiful and well preserved in the state, recalls the days when the padres were this city's only innkeepers.

Getting There From San Francisco or Los Angeles, Highway 101 leads directly to Santa Barbara, which is also serviced by United Airlines and Amtrak.

Over Five Hundred Acres of Privacy
SAN YSIDRO RANCH
Montecito

Among the vast holdings of Mission Santa Barbara was San Ysidro, a citrus and cattle ranch high in the Santa Ynez Mountains, with views of the oak-studded hills sloping to the Pacific far below. After the missions were secularized, new owners built rustic stone and wooden cottages among the groves of orange trees, eucalyptuses and palms, and alongside a meandering creek. By 1893, San Ysidro had become a guest ranch. The old adobe, built by the Franciscans in 1825, still stands and guests dine today in a stone building once used as a citrus packing house.

San Ysidro's first illustrious era was in the 1930s and 1940s when Ronald Colman and State Senator Alvin Weingand jointly owned the ranch. The guest book from those years reads like a combination of *Burke's Peerage* and *Who's Who* in politics, literature and show business. Sir Winston Churchill wrote part of his memoirs in a house shaded by a large magnolia tree. Somerset Maugham produced several short stories in a cottage banked by geraniums. John Galsworthy sought seclusion here to work on the *Forsyte Saga*. David Niven, Merle Oberon and Rex Harrison found life at the ranch a respite from the glitter of Hollywood. Laurence Olivier and Vivien Leigh were married in the gardens. And later John F. Kennedy brought his bride to San Ysidro for their honeymoon in an ivy-covered stone cottage.

After Colman and Weingand, San Ysidro had a succession of owners. Through years of neglect, its facilities degenerated along with its reputation. The ranch was in deplorable condition by 1976 when it was purchased by Jim Lavenson, former president of the Plaza Hotel in New York City, and his wife, Susie. The Lavensons launched a crash renovation program, painting the cottages inside and out and bringing the lush gardens back to life. Susie was—and still is—the chief decorator, charmingly furnishing the rooms with priceless family antiques from their New York home interspersed with refinished bargains culled from thrift shops and the Salvation Army.

Within a year the ranch was operating in a style equal to the Colman-Weingand days, but that wasn't enough for the Lavensons. They embarked on phase two of the rehabilitation: Two more cottages, containing five units were built, featuring soaring ceilings, fireplaces and private decks; copious tiled Jacuzzi tubs are set into the decks of three. Then, one at a time, they gutted the interiors of the older buildings, removing the low ceilings in some to expose the beamed pitch of the roof, adding modern baths with sinks set into old-fashioned sideboards or dressers, combining overly small rooms into larger spaces, rebricking hearths or adding fireplaces, rebuilding sagging decks and adding wet bars and Jacuzzis to many units. There is still more to redo—"about three years work," Susie guesses.

Old-time San Ysidro visitors might be astounded at the comforts found within the cottages today, but otherwise they would feel right at home. Except for fresh paint, the buildings' exteriors remain the same. The lovely gardens are abloom with marigolds, daisies, roses and geraniums, and the orchards are spangled with oranges, which guests are free to pick. The stables shelter fine riding horses, and the mountains that rise behind the inn offer 550 acres of isolated hiking trails. In fact privacy is a very important part of the San Ysidro tradition: The cottages are so self-contained that, with room service provided, you never need emerge—and some guests never do.

On the other hand, those looking for action will find it on the inn's three tennis courts, around the large swimming pool or in the main

San Ysidro Ranch

hacienda, which contains a piano, game tables and a chess board. Here coffee brews twenty-four hours a day and in the evening an honor bar is set up whereby guests mix their own drinks and write their own chits. Across the way, the attractive dining room has been chalking up Holiday Awards for its meals which range from hearty al fresco breakfasts to candlelit gourmet dinners. And for evening entertainment, there's an excellent pianist in the stone cellar below.

Despite all the amenities, San Ysidro is more casual and relaxed than most fancy resort hotels, with Jim Lavenson, dressed in boots and blue jeans, setting the tone. As one would expect, however, it is pricey. But now travelers on a more modest budget may enjoy the ranch's recreational facilities while staying at West Beach Inn, a modern hostelry owned by the Lavensons, overlooking Santa Barbara's yacht harbor. Meanwhile, back at the ranch . . .

SAN YSIDRO RANCH, 900 San Ysidro Lane, Montecito, California 93108. Telephone: (805) 969-5046. Accommodations: twin, queen- or king-size beds; private baths with tub/shower; telephones; no television. Rates: very expensive, no meals included; extra charges for tennis and horseback riding. Open to the public for breakfast, lunch and dinner; full bar service. Children welcome. Extra charge for pets and for boarding horses. Cards: AE, MC, VISA. Open all year.

Getting There: From Santa Barbara take Highway 101 south to Montecito; take San Ysidro Road east through Montecito Village to San Ysidro Lane.

A Facelifting for The Southland's Oldest Hotel

THE UPHAM
Santa Barbara

Over a century ago Amasa Lincoln, a transplanted Boston banker and distant cousin of Abraham Lincoln, decided that Santa Barbara needed a New England-style boardinghouse for homesick easterners. He hired the best architect in town to erect a two-story structure flanked by a columned veranda and topped with a cupola and widow's walk. In the early days the Chinese cook would send his assistant up here when the schooners landed to receive flag signals from a helper at the dock as to how many new guests would be at dinner that night. Over the years a series of owners added two other two-story buildings and four garden cottages to the Upham. In the past few decades the place has been a bit run- down, but nevertheless Santa Barbara natives and visitors alike regarded southern California's oldest continuously operated hotel with fondness and respect.

Then in 1982 Carl Johnson, a local developer who had just finished renovating the Hotel St. Helena, bought The Upham and hired Tom Brooks, one of the St. Helena's designers, to work his magic on the interiors. The first-floor public rooms have been reconstructed to house a cheerful sun porch furnished with rattan where wine is poured in the evening and a large lobby with a fireplace surrounded by velvet-covered love seats. Along one side a row of tables, skirted with a flowered print, looks into the gardens. A Continental breakfast is served to hotel guests here and an adjoining dining room alongside the veranda is open to the public for lunch and dinner.

In the guest rooms and cottages Brooks has mixed antiques—four-poster beds, old writing desks and armoires from England—with bold, sophisticated color schemes, quilted spreads of contemporary designs (often striped or geometric patterns) and white wide-louvered shutters. Earth colors—sand, brick and chocolate brown—contrast with the navy-blue carpeting found throughout. Some of the cottages have sitting rooms, fireplaces, private decks and Jaccuzi tubs. These units are reached by pathways through gardens which bloom with pansies, roses, camelias and birds-of-paradise. The setting is countrylike, yet The Upham is only a block away from the smart shops and restaurants of State Street.

THE UPHAM, 1404 De la Vina Street, Santa Barbara, California 93101. Telephone: (805) 962-0058. Accommodations: fifty rooms with two double, queen- or king-size beds; private baths with tub or tub/shower; color television concealed in armoires; telephones. Rates: expensive, Continental breakfast included. Children welcome. No pets. Cards: MC, VISA. Open all year.

Getting There: From the north take Mission Street exit from Highway 101 and head east to De la Vina, proceed to Sala and turn left one-half block to the hotel's carriage entrance. From the south, exit from Highway 101 at State Street, turn right to Sala and turn left.

The Enchantment of the Côte d'Azur
EL ENCANTO HOTEL
Santa Barbara

High in the hills above Santa Barbara's old mission, this gracious Mediterranean-style hotel offers breathtaking views of the city, the Pacific Ocean and the Channel Islands. The main building was built in 1915 to provide student-faculty housing for the University of California campus that was originally located across the way. Over the years bungalows and stucco villas were built in the surrounding ten acres of lush tropical gardens. El Encanto has been operated as a hotel since the mid-1930s, but Eric Friden, who bought it in 1977, has imparted the enchantment of an auberge on the French Riviera.

Friden, a former developer of franchises for Hilton, restored the hotel and redecorated it in French country style. Window boxes filled with geraniums flank the canopied entryway. The public rooms, are a visual symphony, orchestrated with many different fabrics in shades of rust and blue, natural woods and an abundance of plants. A spacious lounge is filled with chairs of wicker and rattan cushioned in a variety of patterns. Fireplaces and love seats upholstered in floral prints grace the cozy living room and adjoining library. And in the dining room, flowered wallpaper harmonizes with provincial-patterned chinaware; ceiling fans slowly revolve overhead and large windows frame the dramatic view. Meals are also served outside under Cinzano umbrellas on two levels of terraces. The setting alone would make one want to dine here, but lately the talent of a young chef from Provence is attracting Santa Barbara's most discriminating epicures. Even Julia Child is a regular guest.

El Encanto's gardens are planted with bougainvillea, hibiscus, banana trees, pines and palms. Bird-of-paradise and petunias border the brick walkways that lead to the guest cottages. All of the units have now been extensively remodeled with modern tiled baths and new carpeting. Many have spa tubs, wet bars and refrigerators and the most lavish have fireplaces, and private balconies or patios, some with tiled fountains. In 1978 Friden constructed a two-story building of contemporary design that contains another twenty two-room units. These have corner fireplaces, wet bars, and balconies or patios, but the bedrooms are smaller than in the older buildings. Part of the enchantment of El Encanto is a turned-down bed at night and a small decanter of Armagnac placed beside the bed.

El Encanto Hotel

All guests may share in the use of the tennis courts and the swimming pool and in the pleasure of strolling in the beautiful grounds. Here you encounter joyful surprises: a swing set in a little lawn surrounded by a blaze of cyclamen and lillies, a grape arbor enclosing a lily-filled reflecting pool. Whether a guest at El Encanto or not, every visitor to Santa Barbara should at least come here for a drink at sunset. Looking down on the tile-roofed town and the sea beyond, you would truly think you were on the Côte d'Azur, rather than the coast of California.

EL ENCANTO HOTEL AND GARDEN VILLAS, 1900 Lasuen Road, Santa Barbara, California, 93103. Telephone: (805) 687-5000. Accommodations: one hundred rooms with two double or king-size beds; private baths, with tub/shower; telephones; color television. Rates: very expensive, no meals included. Open to the public for breakfast, lunch, dinner and Sunday brunch; full bar service. Children welcome. No pets. Cards: AE, MC, VISA. Open all year.

Getting There: From Highway 101, take Mission Exit east; when road ends at Laguna, turn left at the Mission, then turn right on Los Olivos; where road forks, take right fork, Alameda Padre Serra; from here follow signs to El Encanto.

A Spanish Colonial Jewel
VILLA ROSA
Santa Barbara

Santa Barbara architecture immediately brings to mind white Spanish-style buildings embellished with ornate wooden balconies, wrought-iron grillwork, red tile roofs, arched windows and interior patios filled with fountains and tropical foliage. A classic of this style has now been turned into an inn and it's only a half block from the beach. Four Santa Barbarans—architect Mark Kirkhart, builder Robert Young and their wives—are responsible for the half-million dollar renovation project that transformed this run-down fifty-year-old apartment house into a jewel of a little hotel.

The exterior design was already there but the inside was virtually rebuilt and strikingly decorated in a contemporary southwestern fashion. Desert hues of slate, sand and rosy terra cotta are used throughout and the sturdy mission-style furniture was manufactured in

Santa Fe. Couches and chairs are upholstered in handsome wool tweeds, beds are covered with woven spreads and rosy sheets, and Navajo blankets are hung on many of the walls. Some of the seventeen guest units are one- or two-story suites, several with fireplaces and kitchenettes. Other rooms have mullioned glass doors opening to private balconies—some with an ocean view—or to the large interior courtyard.

Here a swimming pool and spa are set among a melange of palm trees, banana groves and pots of colorful flowers. Also opening to the patio is the lovely living room with its high beamed ceiling and wood-burning fireplace faced with tile. Adjoining is a cozy lounge where a Continental breakfast is served and wine and cheese are offered in the evening. The Villa Rosa bids each guest good night by placing a long-stemmed red rose on the pillow of the turned-down bed.

VILLA ROSA, 15 Chapala Street, Santa Barbara, California 93101. Telephone: (805) 966-0851. Accommodations: seventeen rooms with queen- or king-size beds; private baths with tub/shower; telephones; no television. Rates: expensive to very expensive, Continental breakfast included. No children under 14. No pets. Cards: AE, MC, VISA. Open all year.

Getting There: Exit from Highway 101 at Chapala and head toward the beach.

Bed and Breakfast a Block from the Beach
THE OLD YACHT CLUB INN
Santa Barbara

The Old Yacht Club Inn was the first of Santa Barbara's B&Bs. The two-story bungalow was built in 1912, facing the beach, and for a while served as temporary headquarters for the Santa Barbara Yacht Club, which had washed out to sea in a storm. Thus the name, though nothing else is nautical here. The house was moved a block inland from the beach in the 1920s and is now decorated with homey, country-style furnishings. The large living room–dining area has a fireplace and a bookcase stocked with a set of the Harvard Classics. Big windows look out onto a wide front porch, lawn and gardens. Innkeeper Nancy Donaldson loves to cook and puts a lot of effort into the breakfasts. She usually serves an omelet (perhaps zucchini or spinach) or French toast, in addition to home-baked breads, and fruit and juice. She will also cook a five-course dinner (with advance notice) for her guests.

The four upstairs bedrooms are decorated primarily in warm shades of rose and gold, with plaid or print spreads and matching draperies edging the lace-curtained windows. Fresh flowers and decanters of sherry are set on the tables. In the two front rooms, French doors open to a private balcony where you can hear the ocean, though it's obscured from view. A fifth bedroom with a sitting area and private bath is located downstairs.

Recently the Old Yacht Club's four owners acquired the house next door and each decorated one guest room there to reflect her own background, using family memorabilia. The Hitchcock House, as it is called, is operated separately from Old Yacht Club and might be preferred by those looking for privacy: Each bedroom has its own bath and outside entrance. In the mornings, the innkeepers deliver breakfast baskets to the door which many guests like to take out to the rear garden or down to the beach, less than a block away.

THE OLD YACHT CLUB INN, 431 Corona Del Mar, Santa Barbara, California 93103. Telephone: (805) 962-1277. Accommodations: five bedrooms within the inn with double, queen- or king-size beds; one with private bath, four rooms with sinks share two baths with tub/shower or stall shower; four rooms in Hitchcock House with queen- or king-size beds and private baths with tub/shower or shower; no telephones; no television. Rates: moderate to expensive, breakfast included, dinner (with advance notice) extra. Children over 14 welcome. No pets. Cards: MC, VISA. Open all year.

Getting There: From the south take Cabrillo Boulevard exit off Highway 101 toward the beach; just past the Sheraton Hotel, turn right on Corona Del Mar. From the north, take second State Street exit off 101 to the right; turn left on Cabrillo and turn left on Corona del Mar.

Proud of its Personal Services

THE GLENBOROUGH INN

Santa Barbara

A number of Santa Barbara's other B&Bs are located within a few blocks of each other in a residential area close to the downtown shops, restaurants and museums, and an easy bike ride from the mission. Glenborough was the first of these inns to open. Innkeepers Jo Ann Bell and Pat Hardy have decorated the turn-of-the-century house in an old-fashioned style. The small, formal parlor has a velvet-upholstered settee pulled up to a Franklin stove. An old Victrola is stocked with records. Most of the four upstairs bedrooms are furnished with antiques: brass or oak or four-poster beds, patchwork or velvet quilts, marble-topped chests, wickerware and curtains of old textiles, crochet, knitting or lace. Glenborough also offers quarters in a restored 1880s Victorian cottage across the street. Each unit here has its private entrance and two have sitting rooms with fireplaces. These rooms are also decorated in the style of the nineteenth century.

Jo Ann and Pat take pride in the small personal touches they provide: flowers, plants, and decanters of purified water in the rooms;

beds turned down at night with a mint on the pillow; towels and soap changed twice daily. Each breakfast tray is set with a silver coffeepot, a lace mat, a linen napkin, homemade coffeecake or nut bread, a fruit plate and juice. You may have this in your room or out in the pretty gardens in back of both houses. Behind the rear lawn of the main house is a Jacuzzi, completely fenced for privacy, that may also be used by guests staying in the cottage. They are also invited for a glass of wine in Glenborough's parlor each night.

THE GLENBOROUGH INN, 1327 Bath Street, Santa Barbara, California 93101. Telephone: (805) 966-0589. Accommodations: four rooms with double or queen-size beds and two shared baths with tub/shower in main house; four rooms with double or queen-size beds and private baths in cottage; no telephones; no television. Rates: moderate to expensive, Continental breakfast included. Children over 12 welcome. No pets. Smoking discouraged. Cards: MC, VISA. Open all year.

Getting There: Take Carrillo exit off Highway 101 and head east to Bath; turn left.

Bed, Breakfast and Fantastic Baths
BATH STREET INN
Santa Barbara

Four blocks up the street from Glenborough, The Bath Street Inn occupies an 1873 three-story house with a gabled roof. Innkeepers Susan Brown and Nancy Stover have kept the vintage charm of the place, while rebuilding the rear to focus on the lovely gardens and views of the Santa Ynez Mountains.

Some Victorian overtones remain in the attractive living room, where wine is poured afternoons in front of a big fireplace and leaded glass doors open to a shady side garden. There is a choice of several spots to enjoy your morning meal of juice, fruits and croissants: a sunny deck and garden behind the house, an intimate breakfast area adjoining the kitchen or a formal dining room that seats twelve and is also used for small conferences. A rotisserie, hibachi, refrigerator and dishes are furnished for guests who want to play backyard chef; they must provide only their food. Susan and Nancy will cater dinners for special groups.

Books, decanters of port, and flowers are in all the bedrooms. Four rooms occupy the second floor, three other bedrooms nestle under the top-floor eaves, the beds set in alcoves draped with floral patterns that match the spreads and window curtains. The third floor also has a common room for use by all guests. It's equipped with love seats, games and puzzles; nothing fancy, but as Susan says, "It's a place where you can relax and put your feet on the table."

The Bath Street Inn should really be classified as a BBB&B: bed, breakfast, bath and bicycles. The baths here are very special, with basins set into Victorian dressers; and two have gigantic claw-footed tubs where you can soak with a view of the mountains after a bike tour of town. Bicycles are provided with the compliments of the house.

BATH STREET INN, 1720 Bath Street, Santa Barbara, California 93101. Telephone: (805) 682-9680. Accommodations: twin, queen- or king-size beds; private baths with tub or stall shower; no telephones; no television. Rates: moderate to expensive, Continental breakfast included. Children over 14 sometimes accepted midweek. No pets. Cards: MC, VISA. Open all year.

Getting There: Take Carrillo exit off Highway 101 and head east to Bath; turn left.

Sun-Splashed Victorian with Ocean Views

THE PARSONAGE
Santa Barbara

In 1892 the Trinity Episcopal Church built a splendid Queen Anne residence on a hillside above Santa Barbara for a parsonage. The good reverend must have worshipped the sun along with his professed deity, because—unlike most Victorians—the house is splashed with light through a multitude of large windows of both clear and leaded glass. When interior designer Hilde Michelmore bought the place in 1981, it had been completely renovated for an inn, but her decorating talents and an impressive collection of Chinese rugs make the sunny rooms truly sparkle.

Each room derives its theme and color scheme from its rug. In the living room, for example, a green and lilac floral motif is echoed in the upholstery of an oversize couch. On days when the sun is not pouring in from the corner windows, a fire burns in the hearth and also in the formal dining room with its large glassed-in bay. Here or on a spacious outside deck, Hilde serves a large breakfast that includes scrambled eggs or French toast or quiche and nut or date breads.

Two of the upstairs guest rooms offer picturesque views of the city and ocean. One of these adjoins a private solarium with three walls of glass and an enormous bathroom. The bedrooms contain turn-of-the-century furnishings—armoires, draped or canopied beds, marble-topped pieces and, as downstairs, the handsome rugs.

At this writing Hilde was one-upping the inn's original renovator by adding private baths for all the rooms and waiting for her building permit to add two suites and a widow's walk to the third floor. The views from there should be spectacular.

THE PARSONAGE, 1600 Olive Street, Santa Barbara, California 93101. Telephone: (805) 962-9336. Accommodations: four rooms (two more planned) with twin, queen- or king-size beds; private baths with tub/shower or stall shower; no telephones; television in living room. Rates: moderate to expensive, breakfast included. Children over 14 welcome. No pets. Smoking discouraged. No cards. Open all year.

Getting There: From the north, take Mission Street exit from Highway 101 east to Olive Street and turn right. From the south, take Laguna Street exit across town to Arrellaga Street and turn right to Olive.

The Parsonage

Just Like Great Grandmother's House
RED ROSE INN
Santa Barbara

A border of red roses around the lawn inspired the name for one of Santa Barbara's newest and smallest B&Bs. The four-bedroom Victorian, built in 1886, was opened to guests in 1973 by a young couple, Neile and Rick Ifland, after one year of restoration. Inside, the inn's name is echoed by a single red rose in a stained-glass window and by the fresh roses placed in the guest rooms. Otherwise the color scheme is blue and white throughout, reflected in a bevy of floral wallpapers, quilted, crocheted and patchwork spreads. Among the nineteenth-century furnishings are armoires (containing terry cloth robes for the guests) and a bed that supposedly belonged to Abraham Lincoln. Each of the rooms is named after one of the Iflands' great grandmothers.

You may have breakfast—orange juice, fresh fruits, homemade breads, muffins and jam—in a number of places: in your room, by fireside in the dining room, in a tiny breakfast nook off the blue-and-white tiled kitchen, or in the back garden which has a deck, flagstone patio and a lawn shaded by a huge avocado tree. Bicycles are provided for exploring the nearby shops. Wine and cheese are served in the parlor each evening. And when you retire, your bed is turned down with a mint on the ruffled pillow.

RED ROSE INN, 1416 Castillo, Santa Barbara, California 93101. Telephone: (805) 966-1470. Accommodations: four rooms with double or queen-size beds; two private baths and one shared bath with tub/shower; no telephones; no television. Rates: moderate, Continental breakfast included. Children allowed week nights only. No pets. No smoking. Cards: MC, VISA. Open all year.

Getting There: From the north take Mission exit from Highway 101, from the south take Arrellaga exit, head east to Castillo and turn right.

Stagecoach Stop with the Spirit of 1880

UNION HOTEL
Los Alamos

In the sleepy little agricultural town of Los Alamos, Dick and Teri Langdon, with a dedicated staff, have re-created the spirit of 1880 in the Union Hotel. The original hotel was built of wood that year and served as a Wells Fargo stagecoach stop until it burned down in 1886. In the early 1900s the hotel was reconstructed in Indian adobe and in the 1960s modernized to remove whatever traces of antiquity were left. When Dick Langdon bought the hotel in 1972, he dismantled twelve old barns and rebuilt the hotel's facade exactly as it appeared in an 1884 photograph. Inside, decades of paint were stripped to reveal the original woodwork and brass and rooms were papered with colorful Victorian prints.

Dick spent a year traveling the United States to find antiques. In the high-ceilinged downstairs parlor, a pair of two-centuries-old Egyptian burial urns found in Alabama flank an intricately chiseled fireplace mantel from a mansion in Pasadena. A coffee table was constructed from an oak-framed copper bathtub. There's an 1885 Singer sewing machine, chandeliers from Lee J. Cobb's home, and the hotel's original safe, blackened on one side from an early shooting. Swinging doors, from a bordello in New Orleans, lead into a saloon with a 150-year-old bar of solid African mahogany.

43

The large dining room contains furnishings and gaslights from a plantation in Mississippi. Tables are set with lace cloths and an array of old chinaware, no two dishes quite alike. Meals are family-style country cooking with some recipes derived from a nineteenth-century cookbook that Teri found: for dinner, tureens of soup, corn bread, platters of beef and country-baked chicken; for breakfast, apple pancakes and sausage or bacon and eggs served with potatoes and cinnamon rolls.

Upstairs, the fourteen rooms contain some beds that could be museum pieces: a two-hundred-year-old Australian brass and cast-iron bedstead with insets of cloisonne, and an original Murphy bed, concealed in a mahogany armoire. Vintage patchwork quilts and crocheted spreads serve as covers, and even the bedside Bibles are circa 1880.

In and out of the hotel, Dick has created a flurry of old-time activity for his guests. An upstairs parlor houses a Brunswick pool table inlaid with ivory. The yard is now an 1880s park, equipped with old-fashioned street lights and park benches, brick walkways, and (with a nod to the present) a swimming pool, and a Jacuzzi concealed under the floor of a Victorian gazebo. After dinner guests gather in the saloon for complimentary wine and popcorn. And after breakfast each morning guests are shown the sights of Los Alamos in a 1918 touring car.

Langdon has never stopped improving his hotel during his twelve years of ownership. From a town forty miles away he has moved an 1864 three-story Victorian house to Los Alamos to be restored for an additional ten guest rooms. He also has acquired two cabins next to the hotel which he plans to turn into romantic honeymoon cottages, complete with king-size beds, Jacuzzis, fur rugs and fireplaces. And eventually in back there will be a racquetball court disguised as a barn.

The area around Los Alamos has its own attractions. Many guests enjoy touring the eight local wineries or taking a picnic basket, prepared by the hotel, to nearby Zaca Lake. Solvang, a re-creation of a Danish Village, is not far away. And if the 1880s become too much, you can always slip back another century by visiting the area's two missions: La Purisima Concepcion and Santa Inez.

UNION HOTEL, 362 Bell Street (P.O. Box 616), Los Alamos, California 93440. Telephone: (805) 344-2744. Accommodations: fourteen rooms with twin, double or king-size beds; some private baths with tub/shower; shared baths with tubs and showers; no television; no telephones. Rates: moderate to expensive, breakfast included. Open to the public for dinner; full bar service. No children. No pets. No cards. Open all year, Friday, Saturday and Sunday only; also open Thanksgiving.

ROSE VICTORIAN INN
Arroyo Grande

When Queen Elizabeth II visited California in 1973, Diana and Ross Cox invited her to be a guest at their Rose Victorian Inn. Her Majesty never slept here, but a framed letter of regret from Buckingham Palace now hangs in the inn. Actually the queen would have felt quite at home in the surroundings emanating from her great great grandmother's era. The towered stick-Eastlake house was built in 1885 for Charles Pitkin, who owned five hundred acres of orchards and farmland in this lush agricultural valley near Pismo Beach. The Coxes have painted the house in four shades of rose and landscaped the grounds with two hundred rose bushes that trail from an arbor and surround a lawn and a large gazebo—a popular spot for weddings.

The only Pitkin possession remaining is a pump organ in the front parlor, while a square rosewood piano, which once belonged to General John Fremont, occupies a place of honor in the sun-splashed rear

parlor. Each of the six bedrooms is named after a variety of rose and decorated accordingly with vivid colors and floral papers. Tropicana, for example, is papered in an orange and white pattern and decorated with white wicker and a white quilted spread. The rooms are light and sunny with views of the farmlands and on clear days a glimpse of the ocean. Several bunkhouses and a carriage house behind the gardens are presently being converted for additional guest units.

Breakfast is a sit-down affair in the formal dining room which is papered with a paisley silk of burgundy and gold and boasts a lovely Italian chandelier of crystal. The meal is hearty—eggs Benedict or Florentine or croissants stuffed with meaty fillings—rotated to give variety. A building behind the inn houses a restaurant that is open to the public for dinner and Sunday brunch. A huge century-old mahogany bar from the Gold Country dominates one end of the room. Windows along one wall look out to the rose gardens, and the tables, set with rose-rimmed china, are cheered by a fire from a brick hearth. Dinners include a relish tray, soup, salad, vegetables fresh from the inn's garden and a selection from seventeen entrées that range from seafood to steaks grilled over an oak barbecue to Continental specialties of the English chef. "Most people say we have the best food in the county," Diana says with pride. Dinner is included in the price of a room here and the Coxes also throw in preprandial wine and hors d'oeuvre served to inn guests in the parlor. No one ever complained of hunger at the Rose Victorian Inn.

No one complains of boredom either. There is excellent surfing and sportfishing at nearby Pismo Beach and tastings at the wineries in the area. The town of San Luis Obispo with its many shops and old mission is only fifteen miles away.

ROSE VICTORIAN INN, 789 Valley Road, Arroyo Grande, California 93420. Telephone: (805) 481-5566. Accommodations: six rooms with queen- or king-size beds, some with an additional single, in main house; private and shared baths with tub/shower; four rooms with private baths in bunkhouses; no telephones; no television. Rates: moderate, breakfast and dinner included. Restaurant open to the public for dinner Thursday through Sunday and for Sunday brunch. Children over 16 welcome; younger children sometimes allowed. No pets. No smoking, except in restaurant. Cards: AE, MC, VISA. Open all year.

Getting There: Take the Arroyo Grande exit from Highway 101, turn left at Fair Oaks and turn left on Valley Road.

CENTRAL COAST

From Big Sur
Through the Monterey Peninsula
To Half Moon Bay

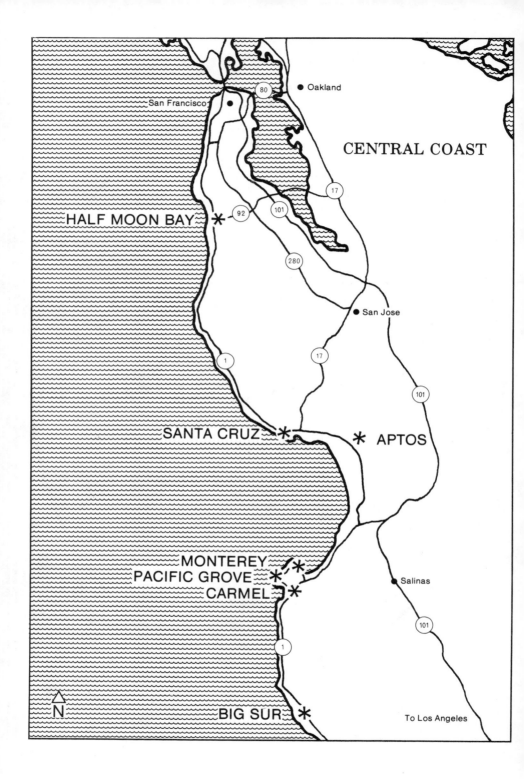

Total Luxury and a Spectacular Site
VENTANA INN
Big Sur

Between San Simeon, where Hearst built his castle, and Monterey, the Santa Lucia Mountains rise precipitously above the incessantly pounding Pacific surf. Today Highway 1 traverses this rugged terrain across high bridges and along niches blasted out of the cliffs. The Spanish missionaries found this section of the coast impassable and detoured inland. But this very remoteness appealed to one of the first settlers, a Yankee sea captain with the unlikely name of Juan Bautista Roger Cooper who landed his cargoes at the mouth of Big Sur River to avoid paying customs duties to the Mexicans in Monterey. The struggles of the homesteaders who later tried to farm this land inspired the poetry of Robinson Jeffers. But it was another writer who shaped the destiny of Big Sur. Henry Miller moved here in 1944, seeking the serenity of the coastal mountains after his expatriate days in Paris. Other artists followed, and for the next decade or so Big Sur was a hardworking bohemian community.

Only recently has the traveler to Big Sur been able to sleep in style. In 1975, the Ventana Inn was built on a meadow twelve hundred feet above the Pacific. The contemporary architecture is spectacular, with soaring ceilings, giant beams, unexpected angles and planes. From every room there are views of the mountains, the meadow or the ocean far below. The rooms are paneled with knotty cedar and handsomely appointed with wicker furniture, hand-painted headboards, patchwork quilts from Nova Scotia and window seats tucked in alcoves. All have private balconies or patios and luxurious carpeted baths. Some have Franklin stoves and individual hot tubs. There are also two-story units with kitchenettes and living rooms.

A fire in the lobby helps remove the chill from the morning fogs that often shroud the Santa Lucia range. Here guests receive a light breakfast: freshly squeezed orange juice, breads and pastries from Ventana's own bakery, assorted fruits and coffee. In the afternoon wine and cheese are served. Across the meadow on another hilltop is the Ventana's restaurant, which offers a diverse selection of lunch and dinner dishes.

There is a large swimming pool at Ventana, plus Japanese hot baths, a sauna and a Jacuzzi. There are hiking trails in the mountains above and down the road is Nepenthe, a restaurant and bar of intriguing design, built around a cabin that Orson Welles once bought for Rita Hayworth (although they never lived there). Today on a sunny afternoon the broad deck is crowded with locals and visitors sipping wine or beer, while enjoying the recorded classical music and a breathtaking view of the coast.

VENTANA INN, Big Sur, California 93920. Telephone: (408) 667-2331. Accommodations: forty rooms with queen-size, two queens or king-size beds; private baths with tub/shower; television; telephones. Rates: very expensive, Continental breakfast included. Restaurant open to the public for lunch and dinner; full bar service. Small children discouraged. No pets. Cards: AE, DC, MC, VISA. Open all year.

Getting There: From San Francisco, follow directions to Monterey and take Highway 1 south. From Los Angeles, take Highway 101 to San Luis Obispo and Highway 1 north. The inn is south of the village of Big Sur and just north of Nepenthe. During the rainy season Highway 1 is sometimes closed; you should check before taking this route.

Rich in History and Scenic Beauty
MONTEREY PENINSULA
Monterey, Carmel and Pacific Grove

In 1770 Father Junipero Serra founded Mission San Carlos in Monterey, the second in California's chain of missions. The following year he moved the mission to Carmel, and later returned here to spend his last years. The Spanish military expedition that Serra accompanied had established a presidio in Monterey. In 1775 Spain designated Monterey as the capital of California, and so it remained through the Mexican rule until the American flag was raised over the Customhouse in 1846.

Monterey had become a cultivated town, where the Spanish citizens and their families lived auspiciously in two-story adobe casas with roofs of red tile. Then the Yankees discovered the abundance of whales offshore and turned this sedate Spanish community into a bustling whaling port. Sardine fishing brought added prosperity and west of town, Cannery Row was built and later immortalized in the works of John Steinbeck. Today many of the old adobes are open to the public or house restaurants and shops. And after the sardines had all but disappeared, Cannery Row was converted into a complex of shops and dining places.

Steinbeck was not the only writer beguiled by this lovely peninsula. Robert Louis Stevenson lived in Monterey in 1879. Then after the turn of the century a group of writers and artists settled in Carmel. Edward Weston, Maynard Dixon, Ambrose Bierce, Don Blanding, Lincoln Steffens and Robinson Jeffers lived here over the years. Although Carmel is built in a potpourri of architectural styles—from Victorian and half-timbered cottage to neo-Spanish—new construction or remodeling is strictly controlled to preserve the woodsy, village-like quality of the picturesque streets.

Pacific Grove is vastly different from Monterey and Carmel. Founded in the 1870s by the Methodist Church to the west of Monterey, the town became famous for its summertime religious conferences and was known as the Chautauqua of the West, an educational tradition that's kept alive today at the Asilomar Conference grounds. The city's streets and its rocky coast are lined with large Victorians that were built to house the conference attendees and later vacationers as the town gained favor as a summer resort. Today many of these stately old mansions are being converted to inns, and with a growing number of good restaurants and shops, Pacific Grove is again making a strong bid for the tourist business.

Few places in the West offer such diverse recreational facilities as the Monterey Peninsula. There are eight public and four private golf courses. Sailboats may be chartered in Monterey Bay. Skin diving, scuba diving, fishing, tennis, polo matches—they're all here. Then there is the spectacular shoreline to explore from the cypress-bordered white sand dunes of Carmel to the rocky coves and hidden beaches of Lovers Point. Carmel is a shopper's paradise with a plethora of crafts, jewelry, clothing and antique stores. It's a sightseer's mecca, too, with choices that include reliving history at the old mission or viewing the palatial mansions along Pebble Beach's famed Seventeen-Mile Drive. The Monterey Peninsula probably has more restaurants per capita than any other area of the West.

Getting There: From San Francisco take Highway 101 to the Monterey Peninsula cut-off, north of Salinas; in Castroville this joins Highway 1, which goes through Monterey to Carmel. For a longer and more scenic route from San Francisco, take Highway 280 to San Jose, Highway 17 through Los Gatos to Santa Cruz, and Highway 1 south to Monterey. From Los Angeles, take Highway 101 to Salinas and Highway 68 to Monterey; or for a more scenic but much longer drive, leave Highway 101 at San Luis Obispo and take Highway 1 through Morro Bay and the Big Sur to Carmel.

The Perfect Inn
OLD MONTEREY INN
Monterey

When Ann and Gene Swett decided to open their elegant Tudor-style home for bed and breakfast, they vowed they would make it the perfect inn. And they have succeeded, down to every detail. Built in 1929 by Carmel Martin, a former mayor of Monterey, the half-timbered house sits on an oak-studded hillside surrounded by an acre of beautiful gardens. Begonias, fuschias and hydrangeas abound, along with twenty-eight varieties of roses. The wooded banks of a creek are rampant with ivy, ferns and rhododendrons.

The interior of the house (where the Swetts raised six children, now grown and gone) is decorated with impeccable taste. Bedrooms are equipped with comfortable places to sit—wicker chairs or upholstered love seats or perhaps a chaise—and with books and magazines to read. Plants and well-chosen pieces of bric-a-brac make the house look homey but not cluttered. Bathrooms are well stocked with bubble bath and essentials you might have left at home, like toothpaste and razor blades. Downstairs a large refrigerator is filled with soft drinks and fruit juices, compliments of the house, and a pot of coffee is always ready.

Woodburning fireplaces enhance most of the ten bedrooms. The most spectacular of these is the Library, which has floor-to-ceiling shelves of books, and a private balcony with a chaise. A king-size bed occupies a niche with windows on all sides. There is no need for window shades here; the limbs of a massive gnarled oak provide all the privacy you need. On the third floor, tucked under the eaves, are two enchanting rooms with fireplaces, half-timbered walls, and skylights in the slanted ceilings. And behind the inn is another fireplace unit: a two-room shuttered cottage dressed up in plaid and flowered patterns of lime and green. A sitting room with a dramatic skylight is furnished with wickerware; up a few steps is a cozy bedroom with a window seat overlooking the garden.

In the evenings a fire also burns in the lovely high-ceilinged living room, where sherry is served with crackers, cream cheese and assorted condiments such as chutney, fresh salsa and jalapeña jelly. A table is set up for backgammon or dominoes. And to help you choose from the peninsula's many restaurants, there's a book in which previous guests have written critiques of their local dining experiences.

In the morning you may have a breakfast tray brought to your room, or you may join the other guests in the formally appointed dining

Old Monterey Inn

room beside yet another fire. Breakfast starts with a glass of orange juice with banana slices floating on top, and a plate of melon followed by a basket of freshly baked muffins or cheese puffs or popovers.

Though it's a temptation to while away the day here in the lovely gardens, the Swetts have prepared another treat for their guests: a picnic kit composed of a basket with plates, silverware, a tablecloth and napkins, glasses, a corkscrew, salt and pepper, plus a fact sheet on ideas for picnic sites and the most scenic ways to get there. You have to provide the food, but the kit also contains a guide to the best delis and markets in the area. Shopping here is half the fun.

OLD MONTEREY INN, 500 Martin Street, Monterey, California 93940. Telephone: (408) 375-8284. Accommodations: ten rooms with twin, queen- or king-size beds; private baths with tub/shower or shower only; no telephones; no television. Rates: expensive to very expensive, Continental breakfast included. No children. No pets. No cards. Open all year.

Getting There: Take Munras exit off of Highway 1 and turn left on Soledad Drive. Turn right on Pacific and turn left on Martin Street.

Tulgey Wood, Borogrove and Bay Views Too
THE JABBERWOCK
Monterey

Razzleberry flabjous might be on the morning menu and you'll sleep in room called Tulgey Wood or Borogrove with views of the garden or Monterey Bay. All this nonsense comes from The Jabberwock poem in *Alice in Wonderland.* But you won't need a looking glass to enjoy this place, though the binoculars or telescopes placed in the view rooms do help spot the seals and sea otters that bark in the bay. This towered and turreted house on the hllside four blocks above Cannery Row was built in 1911, served as a Catholic convent for fifty years and later as the headquarters for the local church of Scientology, before Jim and Barbara Allen bought it for an inn in 1982. They chose the name Jabberwock because Jim loved the sound of it. "When I was a kid, that's the only poem I ever learned," he admits.

The five charming guest rooms are decorated with flowered papers, antique furniture, goosedown quilts and ruffled pillows, on which a little handmade sachet of potpourri is placed. Bathrobes are provided in case you left yours at home. The Toves, a downstairs bedroom, has an especially striking headboard and matching dresser of burled walnut and opens to a private brick patio, while Borogrove offers the best view, along with a fireplace and sitting area. There are plenty of other places to relax in, however. A homey living room cheered by a brick fireplace, a glassed-in veranda with comfortable rattan chairs for reading and tables for puzzles or games, or the garden, filled with ferns, roses, begonias, dahlias and iris.

Jim, a former Los Angeles fireman, is a gregarious host and, if time permits, likes to take guests sightseeing in his old English cab. Barbara brings to the inn years of hotel experience, including stints as executive housekeeper at Los Angeles' Biltmore and Hyatt Regency hotels. Together they pamper their guests. A big Continental breakfast is served at fireside in the dining room with Jabberwock names for the day's dish etched in reverse on glass. At five o'clock a bell bids you to sherry and hors d'oeuvre. At any time of night or day you may help yourself to complimentary soft drinks from a refrigerator dubbed "The Tum Tum Tree." And when you retire with cookies, milk and a Lewis Carroll volume on the bedside table, you'll truly think you are in Wonderland.

THE JABBERWOCK, 598 Laine Street, Monterey, California 93940. Telephone: (408) 372-4777. Accommodations: five rooms with queen- or king-size beds; two rooms have private baths with showers; others share two baths with tub/shower and shower; no telephones; no television. Rates: expensive, breakfast included. No cards. No younger children. No pets. Open all year.

Getting There: From San Francisco take Del Monte Avenue off Highway 1 into Monterey, following signs to Cannery Row through the tunnel to Lighthouse Avenue. Turn left on Hoffman to Laine, and turn left again. From Carmel take the Munras Avenue exit off of Highway 1, turn left on Soledad and right on Pacific Street which leads to Lighthouse Avenue. Pick-up service at Monterey airport by advance arrangement.

The House That Never Stops Growing
THE GOSBY HOUSE INN
Pacific Grove

To the west of Monterey, Pacific Grove was founded in 1875 as a Methodist educational camp, similar to the Chautauqua settlement in New York, and later became a stopping point on the Chautauqua circuit and a summer resort for wealthy Californians. To house this influx of visitors, many handsome Victorians were built around the town. One of these was originally constructed in a rather simple style by J. F. Gosby in 1887, but as his guest register grew, so did the house—in both size and architectural complexity. The large Queen Anne tower that now distinguishes the house was built to spite his neighbor, who had built an intricately ornamented Queen Anne next door.

These traditions of hospitality, improvement and growth have been carried on by the Gosby's present owners, banker Roger Post and real estate developer William Patterson. After an extensive renovation, they opened the inn in 1977 and have never stopped improving it. Over the years more units (two with kitchens and fireplaces) were added in rear buildings opening to a pretty garden and in early 1984 the interior was overhauled to provide private baths and fireplaces in most of the rooms. Post and Patterson also acquired an adjoining house (another former Chautauqua retreat) which will add six more rooms with fireplaces to the complex.

The Gosby's rooms are designed in turn-of-the-century style with flowered wallpapers, antique furniture and ruffled muslin curtains.

The Carriage House at the Gosby House

Bowls of fresh fruit and silk flowers are placed in the rooms. There's always a gracious innkeeper (dressed in old-fashioned attire) on duty to brew a cup of tea or chocolate any time of the day or help you with restaurant reservations or sightseeing plans. Sherry and hot-spiced cider are served in the evening and a Continental breakfast in the morning—either in the parlor or in an adjoining meeting and game room with a fireplace. And when you retire, there's another touch of Gosby hospitality: a turned-down bed with a mint on the pillow.

THE GOSBY HOUSE INN, 643 Lighthouse Avenue, Pacific Grove, California 93950. Telephone: (408) 375-1287. Accommodations: twenty-three rooms with double, two double, or queen-size beds; private baths with tub/shower or stall shower in all but two rooms, which share bath; no telephones; no television. Rates: moderate to very expensive, Continental breakfast included. Children under 12 discouraged. No pets. No smoking. No cards. Open all year.

Getting There: From Highway 1, take the Pebble Beach/17-Mile Drive turnoff. Turn right onto Highway 68, which leads to Pacific Grove. Turn left at Lighthouse Avenue and proceed three blocks to the inn.

Million Dollar Restoration Project
THE CENTRELLA
Pacific Grove

The Centrella, like the Gosby House, came into being during the building boom of the 1880s when the tents of the religious encampments were being replaced by hotels and rooming houses. The hotel was built by the Beighle family to accommodate the overflow of lodgers they had been taking in at their home; within years it had doubled in size, so popular was Pacific Grove. Until recently in this century, however, vacationers ignored Pacific Grove in favor of Carmel and Monterey and what was left of the Centrella's comforts was enjoyed by winos and transients. Then in 1982 an investment group was formed to save the old hotel and over a million dollars was poured into the restoration.

Today the twenty-seven guest rooms sparkle with Laura Ashley prints, Axminster carpeting from England, and turn-of-the-century style furnishings, which have earned the hotel several design awards. To the side and rear of the main building, separated by a flower-filled garden, are cottages that contain two-room suites with fireplaces and wet bars. Two other suites with dormered windows and gabled roofs occupy the top floor of the building.

The large lobby is dominated by a floor-to-ceiling stone fireplace flanked by comfortable couches and chairs. Sherry and hors d'oeuvre are served here in the evening and in the morning a large buffet is set out: fruit juices, cereal, fruit bread and pastries, yogurt, cream cheese and fresh fruit. You have a choice of joining other guests at round tables for six in the lobby or having an intimate repast at little tables for two in the adjoining sun porch overlooking the garden. In the fall you may even spot one of the giant orange and black Monarch butterflies during their annual migration to Pacific Grove.

THE CENTRELLA, 612 Central Avenue (P.O. Box 884), Pacific Grove, California 93950. Telephone: (408) 372-3372. Accommodations: twenty-seven rooms with twin, queen- or king-size beds; all but two rooms have private baths with tub or shower; direct-dial telephones; color television in cottages. Rates: moderate to very expensive, breakfast included. Children under 13 allowed in cottages only. No pets. Cards: AE, MC, VISA. Open all year.

Getting There: From Highway 1, take Highway 68 west to Pacific Grove. From Forest Avenue, turn left on Central.

A Fairy Tale Setting on Monterey Bay
THE GREEN GABLES INN
Pacific Grove

The advent of the railway to Pacific Grove brought affluent vacationers who erected elaborate homes along the craggy coast of Monterey Bay. One of these showplaces—a half-timbered mansion of many gables— was built in 1888 by William Lacy who sold it shortly thereafter to a judge from Monterey for a summer home. Roger and Sally Post (co-owners of The Gosby House) resided here for ten years, opening several of the rooms to overnight guests for a few months during the summer. Then in 1983 they turned the entire building and an adjacent carriage house into one of the area's most exquisite inns.

It's a dazzling setting with breathtaking views of the water and mountains beyond, glimpsed from windows, which are crafted in a myriad of sizes and shapes into a seemingly endless number of alcoves, dormers and bays. From window seats or love seats in the upstairs

59

bedrooms you can watch the sea otters at play, the seals sunning on rocks that protrude from the bay or occasionally a passing whale. But the most spectacular feature of these rooms are the sloping beamed ceilings that pitch every which way. One of the rooms, originally a chapel, is entered through a quadruple set of carved doors and distinguished by a stunning rib-vaulted ceiling. The Posts have appointed the guest rooms generously: soft quilts and a plethora of pillows on the beds, antique writing tables, bowls of fruit, plants, books and magazines. Only two bedrooms have private baths, but a caddy of soap and towels, plus robes are provided for those that share. On the lower floor, there's a two-room suite with a fireplace edged with Delft tiles and a sofa that makes up into an extra bed.

More alcoves and bays embellish the living room, where a fireplace rimmed with stained glass soars to a twelve-foot ceiling which is bordered by a sculptured frieze, painted bright blue. In the dining room a crystal chandelier is suspended from a graceful medallion over a formal table. There's a fireplace here, too, and a dramatic view through windows framed with latticework. A sit-down breakfast combines a substantial main course—crêpes or Belgian waffles or frittatas—with fresh fruits, juices, granola and muffins.

A patio behind the house is planted with azaleas and impatiens. Beyond that a carriage house contains four more rooms. These don't have the fairy-tale ambience of the main house, but they do provide more privacy, along with fireplaces and modern baths.

THE GREEN GABLES INN, 104 Fifth Street, Pacific Grove, California 93950. Telephone: (408) 375-2095. Accommodations: ten rooms with double and queen-size beds, some with trundle beds; two rooms with tub or shower, carriage house rooms have private baths with stall shower; no telephones; no television. Rates: expensive to very expensive, breakfast included. Children over 12 welcome. No pets. No cards. Open all year.

Getting There: From Highway 1 take Highway 68 west to Pacific Grove, continue on Forest Avenue to Ocean View Boulevard, then turn right to Fifth Street.

Green Gables Inn

Victorian Ambience in the Heart of Town
PINE INN
Carmel

In 1902, the year after Queen Victoria's death, Pine Inn opened its doors, bringing all the gaudiness of the Victorian era to Carmel. The town was then a quiet refuge for artists and writers. But at the turn of the century Carmel had also been discovered by land developers who built Pine Inn to house prospective purchasers of lots, which cost $250 apiece! As the land boom prospered and Carmel grew, so did Pine Inn. The old Carmelo Hotel was moved from another location to serve as an annex; new wings were added haphazardly until the inn occupied most of a block by 1960. At that time Pine Inn was purchased by the McKee family who have carefully maintained its Victorian ambience.

Pine Inn is located on Ocean Avenue, Carmel's heavily trafficked thoroughfare. Yet a step inside is a step into the past. The original building houses the lobby and a bevy of dining rooms decorated with deep-red carpeting, flocked and flowered wallpapers, massive wooden sideboards, electrified gas lamps. There is also a cozy bar with stained-glass windows, marble-topped tables and a cast-iron fireplace—marvelous for a drink on a foggy day. A large brick patio was covered with a glass dome a few years back and converted into a gardenlike dining area.

The inn has forty-nine bedrooms, of which no two are alike. Those in the older part of the inn are small, but have the most historic charm. They are decorated in *fin de siècle* style with chintz wallpapers, white shutters and wainscotings, marble-topped wooden chests and brass bedsteads. In the newer additions, the rooms are larger and the furnishings are more modern and luxurious. An ornately furnished penthouse suite with fireplace opens to a private patio and will accommodate eight.

PINE INN, Ocean Avenue (P.O. Box 250), Carmel, California 93921. Telephone: (408) 624-3890. Accommodations: forty-nine rooms with twin, double queen- or king-size beds; private baths with tub/shower; telephones; color television. Rates: moderate to expensive, no meals included. Open to the public for breakfast, lunch and dinner; full bar service. Facilities for small conferences up to 50. Children welcome. No pets. Cards: AE, MC, VISA. Open all year.

THE STONEHOUSE INN
Carmel

Among those who nourished Carmel as an artists' colony was an expatriate San Franciscan known as Nana Foster. In 1906 she built a house of hand-hewn stone on the sand dunes above the beach and invited the prominent writers of the era to be her guests. Today the inn's bedrooms bear the names of some of the literati who stayed there—Jack London, Mary Austin and others who were most likely visitors as well, such as Robinson Jeffers and Sinclair Lewis. Even though the view of the ocean is obscured by the houses and trees that now surround the inn, the feeling of early Carmel remains.

Literary ghosts, however, are not the only inhabitants of this charming retreat. A seven-foot Raggedy Ann doll reclines on a shelf by the massive stone fireplace and flocks of stuffed, ceramic and wooden ducks and geese occupy nearly every nook and cranny of the large living room and the cozy glassed-in sun porch. They even march up the stairs to the four guest rooms that nestle under the gabled and dormered roof. These and all other rooms throughout the house have the white-painted board and batten walls so typical of early Carmel houses. They are appointed with antiques, quilted spreads, ruffled curtains, a bevy of

pillows, silk flowers and bowls of fruit. Downstairs are two other bedrooms, one with its own porch.

A sit-down breakfast is served in the tile-floored dining room where multi-paned windows on three sides look into gardens and foliage. There is usually a hot bread and pastry, plus juice, fresh fruit and granola. Coffee, tea and hot chocolate are offered all day, sherry and hot cider in the evening. If you detect some similarity in service to Gosby House or Green Gables in Pacific Grove, it's no coincidence. Stonehouse and Gosby are owned and operated by the same people with the same high standards of innkeeping.

THE STONEHOUSE INN, Eighth below Monte Verde (P.O. Box 2517), Carmel, California 93921. Telephone: (408) 624-4569. Accommodations: six rooms with double and queen-size beds; three shared baths, tub/shower or stall shower; no telephones; no television. Rates: moderate, Continental breakfast included. Children over 12 welcome. No pets. No smoking. No cards. Open all year.

Getting There: Off Ocean Avenue turn south on Monte Verde. Turn right on Eighth.

A Poetic Flower-Filled Hideaway
VAGABOND HOUSE
Carmel

Don Blanding lived here in the 1940s, but no one is certain if his poem *Vagabond's House* was named for the inn, or if the inn was later named for the poem. Nevertheless Vagabond House is a poetic hideaway with rooms looking through treetops into a stone courtyard filled with rhododendrons, camelias, azaleas and roses. In the center, baskets of ferns, begonias and fuchsias hang from the branches of a large oak.

Vagabond House was originally built in 1941 for efficiency apartments when Carmel's population suddenly swelled from the influx of military personnel to Fort Ord. Later it became an inn and is presently owned by Dennis and Karen Levett.

The rooms are large and charmingly furnished with Early American maple, pieces of wicker, quilted bedspreads, and antique pendulum clocks, books and flowers. Most of the rooms have fireplaces and all have refrigerators or kitchenettes, a holdover from apartment house

Vagabond House

days. A decanter of cream sherry is placed in each room, plus a coffee pot and freshly ground coffee.

Off the patio is a large common room with a fireplace and a collection of English hunt prints. A substantial buffet breakfast is laid out here in the mornings: freshly squeezed orange juice, muffins and currant rolls with strawberry jam, a fruit basket, hard-cooked eggs and cheeses. No one goes hungry here, even the squirrels. A big sack of peanuts is provided so you can feed the friendly little creatures that congregate on the patio and window ledge.

The Levetts also own Lincoln Green Inn, a group of four cottages set among gardens on the far side of town near the Carmel River. Each has a living room with fireplace, separate bedroom and full kitchen. There is no common room or food service at Lincoln Green, but guests are welcome to take their breakfast at Vagabond House. Reservations may also be made through Vagabond House.

VAGABOND HOUSE, Fourth and Dolores (P.O. Box 2747), Carmel, California 93921. Telephone: (408) 624-7738. Accommodations: twelve rooms with two doubles, queen- or king-size beds; private baths, some with tub/shower, some with shower only; no telephones; color television. Rates: moderate to expensive, breakfast included. No children under 12. Pets welcome. Cards: MC, VISA. Open all year.

Getting There: From Ocean Avenue turn north on Dolores. Free pickup at Monterey Airport.

Privacy and the Sound of the Surf
SAN ANTONIO HOUSE
Carmel

This three-story shingled house was built in 1907 as a private residence, and during its early years served as a studio and weekend retreat for artists and writers from the San Francisco Bay Area. In the 1930s Lincoln Steffens lived next door and played host to a continuous flow of the literati of his day. In 1950, the handsome old house, set back from the street by a spacious lawn, became a guest house. It is presently owned by Vagabond House proprietors Dennis and Karen Levett. The accommodations consist of two- and three-room suites, each with its own patio or garden. All of the units have fireplaces and, like Vagabond House, coffee and a decanter of cream sherry are supplied. One suite

66

San Antonio House

has a full kitchen and the others have refrigerators. In the morning, the newspaper is at your door and when you're ready for breakfast, just pick up the phone. The resident innkeeper will bring you a tray laden with the same goodies that are served at Vagabond House. San Antonio House is a place for people who seek complete privacy and the sound of the surf. It's only a block away from Carmel's beautiful beach.

SAN ANTONIO HOUSE, San Antonio between Seventh and Ocean (P.O. Box 3683), Carmel, California 93921. Telephone: (408) 624-4334. Accommodations: queen-size and one single bed in each unit; private baths with tub/shower; telephones; color television. Rates: expensive, breakfast included. No children under 12. Pets welcome. Cards: MC, VISA. Open all year.

Getting There: Take Ocean Avenue to San Antonio and turn south.

Loving Care for Lazy Vacationers
HAPPY LANDING
Carmel

This pretty little inn has been a happy landing indeed for its management team. Owners Bob Alberson and Dick Stewart had been partners in several retail businesses in San Francisco and often vacationed at the inn. Then they decided to give up shopkeeping for innkeeping and bought the place in 1981. Two years later they lured innkeeper Jewell Brown away from Vagabond House to do what she does best: taking care of guests. All three of them pour a constant stream of loving care and enthusiasm into Happy Landing.

Built in 1925, the inn consists of three buildings with high pitched ceilings surrounding a central garden where flagstone paths meander through courtyards and beds of flowers, ferns and banana trees to a gazebo and small reflection pool. One guest room and a common room with an enormous stone fireplace occupy the main building. The smaller structures each contain two bedrooms and a two-room suite. Some of the units have fireplaces and all have private entrances to the garden and are handsomely furnished with antiques. Bowls of fresh flowers and a decanter of cream sherry are placed in the rooms.

The breakfast routine at Happy Landing is unique. When you awake, you open your curtains as a signal for Jewell to bring to your room a tray laden with juice, fresh fruit, hot breads and beverage, plus the morning paper. Breakfast is served at what Jewell calls "Carmel time"—from 8:30 until any time of the day. "People come here on vacation and they have a right to sleep as late as they want."

HAPPY LANDING, Monte Verde between Fifth and Sixth (P.O. Box 2619), Carmel, California 93921. Telephone: (408) 624-7917. Accommodations: seven rooms with double, queen- or king-size beds; private baths with shower or tub/shower; no telephones; color television. Rates: moderate to expensive, Continental breakfast included. Small children discouraged. Small pets permitted. Smoking discouraged. Cards: AE, MC, VISA. Open all year.

Getting There: Turn north off Ocean Avenue on Monte Verde.

In the French Provincial Style
NORMANDY INN
Carmel

On the south side of Ocean Avenue is a French Provincial complex of buildings designed and built by architect Robert Stanton, and decorated by his wife Virginia, former party editor of *House Beautiful,* and managed by the Stantons' son, Samuel. After graduating from UC Berkeley, Stanton worked for architect Wallace Neff on a number of Hollywood homes, including Douglas Fairbanks's Pickfair, and the Fredric March home, which inspired his interest in French Provincial design. Stanton moved to Carmel to practice architecture, and built the Normandy Inn in 1937. Over the years newer and larger units were added, and a group of cottages were built across the street. Today the Normandy has forty-eight units clustered around gardens banked with pots of blooming flowers and a kidney-shaped pool.

The older rooms have the atmosphere of a French country inn. Many have corner fireplaces adorned with painted tiles. Multi-paned windows look out to the trees and gardens, or occasionally offer a glimpse of the ocean beyond. There are shuttered alcoves and beds tucked into niches in the wall. The newer units have more luxurious appointments such as king-size beds and large picture windows, but lack some of the charm of the older rooms. The cottages across the way are centered around a brick patio; there are fireplaces and kitchenettes in most of these.

In the mornings the Normandy serves guests juice, coffee and orange muffins in a quaint country dining room filled with pots of flowers. Here Virginia Stanton has installed her fine collection of antique Quimper plates from France.

NORMANDY INN, Ocean Avenue (P.O. Box 1706), Carmel, California 93921. Telephone: (408) 624-3825. Accommodations: forty-eight rooms with twin, double or king-size beds; private baths, some tub/shower, some shower only; telephones; television in newer rooms. Rates: moderate to expensive, Continental breakfast included. Children welcome. No pets. No cards. Open all year.

Normandy Inn

SEA VIEW INN
Carmel

The Sea View has been operated as an inn since the mid-1920s, but Marshall and Diane Hydorn, the present owners, think the three-story shingled house was probably built just after the turn of the century. Two of the early innkeepers here, the Misses Olive and Pearl Stout, advertised rooms for three dollars a night. Hydorn speculates that this included meals as well! Located three blocks from the ocean on a quiet residential street, the inn was obviously named for its view; however, over the years large pines have grown up around the house, allowing only a peek at the sea from upstairs rooms today.

The inn maintains the aura of Carmel in the twenties. The board and batten walls have been painted white, and the solid, comfortable furnishings of previous owners are mixed with the Hydorn's antiques. The homey living room has a large brick fireplace, shuttered windows and three tables where the Hydorns serve a morning spread of juices, dry cereals, English muffins and homemade coffeecake. Sherry and wine are offered in the evening.

The bedrooms have a country charm, with four-posters or wicker bedsteads, and quilted spreads. A burled armoire in one room, a rocker in another, marble-topped dressers here and there, are interspersed with pieces of no discernable lineage. In some rooms a studio couch is cozily placed in an alcove; in others there are window seats by the dormered windows. Over the years this inn has developed a loyal clientele. Recently, to the Hydorn's delight, a couple who had honeymooned at Sea View returned for their fiftieth anniversary.

SEA VIEW INN, Camino Real at Eleventh (P.O. Box 4138), Carmel, California 93921. Telephone: (408) 624-8778. Accommodations: eight rooms with twin, queen- or king-size beds, some with additional studio couch; private or shared baths with tub/shower or shower only; no telephones; no television. Rates: inexpensive to moderate, breakfast included. Children over 12 welcome. No pets. Cards: MC, VISA. Open all year.

Getting There: From Ocean Avenue, turn south on Camino Real.

Sea Views for an International Clientele
SANDPIPER INN
Carmel

Graeme and Irene Mackenzie, who bought the Sandpiper Inn in 1975, are no starry-eyed novices to the tasks of innkeeping. Rarely will you encounter a small inn managed so professionally. Born in Scotland, Mackenzie graduated from Lausanne Hotel School and did postgraduate work at Cornell University. He brings to Carmel over twenty years of experience in some of the finest hotels in Europe, Bermuda, Hong Kong, the United States and Canada.

The Sandpiper Inn, located on Carmel Point just fifty yards from the beach, has been in operation since 1929. The Mackenzies completely refurbished it, adding many antiques: a mixture of American country, French and English pieces. Quilted flowered spreads cover the new king- and queen-size beds, and bowls of fresh flowers are on the tables. Some of the rooms have wood-burning fireplaces and many have views of Carmel Bay and Pebble Beach. The Mackenzies added full modern baths to all of the fifteen rroms and rebuilt two small cottages behind the inn.

George Washington never slept here, nor did any other American president, but Graeme Mackenzie jokingly points to a bed that President Ford slept in while staying at a home in Pebble Beach. There was no king-size bed in the guest room, but the Sandpiper graciously lent one of theirs for Ford's comfort.

The Mackenzies' guest book, however, does list the presidents of many corporations, along with an international clientele representing sixty-six countries. In the evening, around the stone fireplace in the spacious living room, you are likely to hear many languages. Graeme and Irene are both multilingual, (she is a former United Nations interpreter), which helps the foreign visitors feel at home. At five o'clock sherry is served and ice and mixes are provided if you want to bring some stronger spirits.

To one side of the living room is a cozy library with a writing desk and shelves stocked with books. At the end of the living room is a long table where a breakfast of orange juice, hot Danish pastries and coffee is served. Guests are invited to help themselves to coffee in the kitchen at any time.

Flower gardens surround the inn, with brick patios for sunning. Ten-speed bicycles are available for peddling along the cypress-studded drive that fronts Carmel's glorious beach. Graeme is happy to suggest restaurants and tours of the excellent Monterey County wineries and to introduce guests to most of the famous golf and tennis clubs on the peninsula.

SANDPIPER INN, 2408 Bay View Avenue at Martin, Carmel, California 93923. Telephone: (408) 624-6433. Accommodations: seventeen rooms with queen-or king-size beds with an additional single bed in some rooms; private baths with tub/shower or shower only; no telephones; television in living room. Rates: moderate to expensive, Continental breakfast included. Children over 12 welcome. No pets. Credit cards: MC, VISA. Open all year.

Getting There: Take Ocean Avenue to Scenic Avenue and proceed south along the beach to the end; seventy yards beyond the stop sign in the middle of the road, turn left at Martin.

APPLE LANE INN
Aptos

North of Monterey, Highway 1 follows the shore of Monterey Bay from Watsonville (Artichoke Capital of the World) through the seaside resort towns of Aptos, Capitola and Soquel to Santa Cruz. Over one hundred years ago San Franciscans started discovering these beaches and building summer houses here. Other settlers came to farm. One of these was J. Farrel who in 1875 built a handsome three-story farmhouse on a hill above Aptos surrounded by 160 acres of apple trees, vineyards and pasture land. Ninety years later the house and two acres of the land were acquired for a family home by Peter Farquhar, who renovated the house over a period of eighteen years, then turned it into an inn.

Peter, his wife Barbara and their cat Ptolomy live in the rear of the house and rent the four upstairs bedrooms to guests. Peter stripped the woodwork of the large parlor to its natural redwood and furnished the room with family antiques, Oriental rugs, Victorian loveseats, an unusual vicar's chair and a player piano. A brick fireplace is flanked by floor-to-ceiling bookcases that give a clue to some of Peter's diverse interests: volumes, including first editions, on geography (he teaches the subject at nearby Cabrillo College), travel, and mountaineering (he climbed Mt. Everest to 18,000 feet with the 1983 United States team). Bottles of sherry from a nearby winery are set out in the parlor and breakfast is also served here: fruit juice, a fresh fruit platter, home baked nut breads and blueberry muffins, sometimes soft-boiled eggs. A basement cider room and wine cellar, also open to Apple Lane guests, house wine presses and casks (winemaking is another of Peter's hobbies). There's a checker set, dart board and a pull-down screen on which Peter sometimes projects slides of his climbs and travels (he's also an avid photographer).

The bedrooms look like they belong in a country farmhouse with old-fashioned furnishings—brass or wooden bedsteads, pretty printed wallpapers, dried flower arrangements, quilted spreads, wickerware—and views of the trees and hills. The only contemporary touch is an Ansel Adams photograph in each room. The second-story bedrooms have private half baths and share the use of a wood-paneled bathroom as large as most bedrooms. The third-story rooms have whitewashed ceilings that expose the pitched, beamed roof, and sinks built into antique dressers; these rooms share a bath with a skylight.

Apple Lane Inn

In front of the house is a brick patio surrounded by a grape arbor, lemon and apple trees. It's quiet and secluded up here on the hillside, but a walk down the tree-shaded lane will bring you to a health spa and racquetball club that offers swimming and a hot tub. The many beaches that stud the bay are only a short distance away and the area abounds with good restaurants. Just up the street is Cabrillo College, site of the renowned Cabrillo Music Festival in August.

APPLE LANE INN, 6265 Soquel Drive, Aptos, California 95003. Telephone: (408) 475-6868. Accommodations: four rooms with double, two double or queen-size beds; two rooms with private half baths share tub/shower, two rooms share bath with tub; no telephones; television in cider room. Rates: moderate, breakfast included. No children under 12. No pets. No smoking in bedrooms. Cards: MC, VISA. Open all year.

Getting There: From Highway 1, south of Santa Cruz, take Park Avenue exit to the east. Turn right on Soquel Drive. The inn is on the east side of the road, before you reach Cabrillo College.

Reminder of a Bygone Era
CHATEAU VICTORIAN
Santa Cruz

In 1791 the Spanish padres erected the Santa Cruz Mission at the north end of Monterey Bay. By the 1890s the town had become the queen of the seaside resorts, noted for its boardwalk, casino and fashionable homes on the hill behind the beach. In this century, however, the town's status as a resort declined; the old Victorians near the beach were turned into cheap rooming houses or replaced by boxlike motels; and the boardwalk became best known for its giant amusement park, annual Miss California pageants and shoddy clientele. Then in the 1960s the construction of a University of California campus on the hills behind the city infused a new life into Santa Cruz, including a gigantic downtown renovation. Now an effort is being made to reclaim the beach area by restoring the run-down Victorians for bed and breakfast inns.

One of these, a block from the boardwalk, is Chateau Victorian. Today, with its exterior freshly painted in burnt-orange with black trim, the elegant house seems out of place among the nondescript hotels around it. And once inside, you are treated to every luxury a country inn can offer. The owners—Franz Benjamin and Dan and Diane Christiansen—spent over a year on the renovation, adding modern tiled baths and plush burgundy carpeting throughout. Five of the seven bedrooms have wood-burning fireplaces, some with marble facades. One room has a marvelous canopied four-poster, while brass or iron bedsteads are used in other rooms. Springlike Laura Ashley prints adorn the walls, bedding, curtains and shades and the rooms are appointed with comfortable wing or lounge chairs, plants and flowers. Three of the bedrooms have private entrances from a flower-filled brick patio in the rear; two of these are actually in a separate building that has Oriental rugs on Mexican tile floors and a pine-paneled ceiling.

Franz Benjamin, a former engineer and realtor from Menlo Park, is resident manager. Becoming an innkeeper was the farthest thing from his mind when his partners got the idea of starting a B&B in the house, which they had owned for some years. But he loves his new profession and he loves Santa Cruz, taking pride in serving products of the area: sherry from local wineries; croissants and bagels from nearby bakeries, with marmalades and assorted jams; platters of fresh seasonal fruit. Breakfast is served at little tables covered with burgundy and white striped cloths in the living room or, on balmy days, out on a secluded deck. Benjamin is also a good guide to the activities of the area. Even if the nearby boardwalk is too honky-tonk for your taste, there are many other beaches along the bay, plus pier-fishing facilities and deep-sea charters. Stream fishing, hiking and nature trails are found in the redwood forested Santa Cruz Mountains that rise behind the town. And just six miles north of town, a steam-powered narrow-gauge railroad provides a scenic ride through the big trees and, like Chateau Victorian, is another reminder of a bygone era.

CHATEAU VICTORIAN, 118 First Street, Santa Cruz, California 95060. Telephone: (408) 458-9458. Accommodations: seven rooms with queen-size beds; private baths with tub/shower or shower; no telephones; no television. Rates, moderate to expensive, Continental breakfast included. No children. No pets. No smoking. Cards: AE, MC, VISA. Open all year.

Getting There: From Highway 1 take Ocean into Santa Cruz. Turn right on Barson and left on Campbell, which becomes Riverside after it crosses the river. Turn right on Second, left on Cliff and right on First.

Country Charm in a Tiny Hotel

SAN BENITO HOUSE
Half Moon Bay

Some thirty miles south of downtown San Francisco, the coastal village of Half Moon Bay is surrounded by flower nurseries and fields of artichokes and pumpkins—a blaze of orange in the fall. Beaches and the fishing harbor of Princeton are nearby. The town's Main Street is lined with turn-of-the-century street lights and buildings. One of these structures is a small hotel built by Estanislaus Zabella, who married into the Miramontez family, holders of the original Spanish land grant. Known for years as the Mosconi Hotel, the name was changed in the 1930s to Dominic's. For years, despite the run-down condition of the place, huge bargain-priced, family-style Italian dinners attracted drivers from the San Francisco Bay Area.

Then in 1976, Carol Mickelsen, a local schoolteacher, embarked on a three-year restoration project to turn the old hotel into a European-style inn, naming it San Benito after the original name of Half Moon Bay. Now the little hotel is resplendent with fresh paint and refinished redwood paneling and beams. The old corner saloon is outfitted with a mammoth bar, nineteenth-century decor and etched-glass swinging doors that lead to the dining room. Here butcher-block tables, covered with paisley cloths, are set with pretty china and bouquets of daisies, marigolds and whatever else is blooming in the

large flower garden next to the inn. French doors open to a wide deck banked with more flowers.

The food at San Benito House is still bringing diners from all over the area, but now for its quality. Carol was a serious student of cooking before she took over the inn, and lately has studied with such noted chefs as Roger Vergé and the Troisgros brothers in the south of France and Guiliano Bugialli in Florence. Thus it's not surprising that the menus at San Benito tend toward country French and northern Italian. The seafood of Half Moon bay is emphasized, as is local produce; artichoke and pumpkin soups are among the specialties. And many of the vegetables come from the inn's gardens.

After checking in, guests are given a key to the front door. Inside, a hall and stairway, stunningly decorated in blue and white, lead to eight bedrooms, two suites and a sauna. These rooms contain a charming potpourri of furnishings: antique wooden chests, flowery comforters, some Italian lamps, paintings and artifacts from local flea markets, baskets of flowers, bric-a-brac or vases on wall brackets, a floor-to-ceiling headboard made from paneled double doors in one room, a rose-patterned canopy in another. Most of the rooms have private baths, decorated in great style with oil paintings, old chandeliers and bouquets of flowers, with stained-glass partitions behind the claw-legged tubs. The windows, bedecked with boxes of geraniums or impatiens, view the mountains, the ocean or the inn's garden.

San Benito House serves a complimentary breakfast of homemade whole-wheat bread, fresh fruit compote, juice and coffee. On Sunday mornings, when the dining room is open to the public, overnight guests may order the full breakfast at a discounted price. Carol's creative cooking and constantly changing menu are incentives for taking all your meals at the inn, but if you wish a change, there are several good seafood restaurants nearby.

SAN BENITO HOUSE, 356 Main Street, Half Moon Bay, California 94019. Telephone: (415) 726-3425. Accommodations: seven rooms with double or king-size beds; private and shared bath with tubs; no telephones; no television. Rates: inexpensive to moderate, Continental breakfast included. Open to the public for lunch, dinner and Sunday breakfast; full bar service. Children welcome. No pets. Cards: AE, MC, VISA. Open all year.

Getting There: From San Francisco take Highway 280 south to Highway 92 and head west; when you reach Main Street turn left. From Monterey, Highway 1 to San Francisco passes through Half Moon Bay.

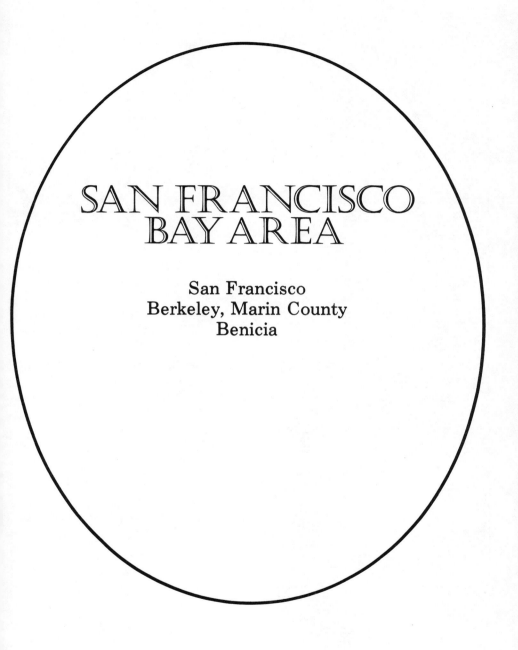

SAN FRANCISCO BAY AREA

San Francisco
Berkeley, Marin County
Benicia

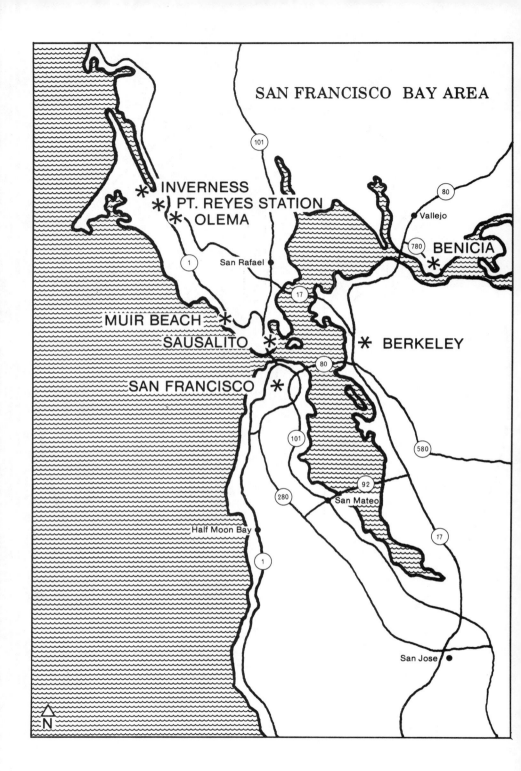

SAN FRANCISCO BAY AREA

INVERNESS
PT. REYES STATION
OLEMA

Vallejo

BENICIA

San Rafael

MUIR BEACH
SAUSALITO

BERKELEY

SAN FRANCISCO

Half Moon Bay

San Mateo

San Jose

N

A Conglomerate of Colorful Neighborhoods
SAN FRANCISCO

San Francisco is the needle's eye through which the threads of California history have converged. Spanish missionaries first brought Western culture here in 1776. But it was the fortunes in gold from the Mother Lode in the 1850s and later the silver from the Comstock that built the magnificent city by the Golden Gate. To her teeming port came the European immigrants who planted California's fertile valleys with grapes and returned their wines to San Francisco's splendid tables. And from the redwood forests to the north came the lumber for the houses that soon covered her hills and valleys. The fire of 1906 obliterated most of the Victorian houses east of Van Ness Avenue, but many thousands of Victorians still impart a nineteenth-century aura to the outlying neighborhoods. A 1976 survey of only nine districts cataloged over thirteen thousand extant Victorian structures; Pacific Heights and Cow Hollow were not even included.

Today San Francisco is a city of intimate neighborhoods, each with a distinctive character that is usually missed by visitors who stay at the downtown hotels. But now a number of small hostelries have opened in the neighborhoods, many in Victorians. These offer the charm and hospitality of a country inn, while being only ten or fifteen minutes from the heart of San Francisco.

Getting There: The quickest routes to the inns of San Francisco will vary depending on what part of the city you are coming from. If you're not familiar with the city, your first purchase should be a street map. For the sake of simplicity here, directions to each inn are given from Van Ness Avenue. If you are entering the city from the east or south, follow the freeway signs to the Golden Gate Bridge until you come to the Van Ness exit. If you are entering via the Golden Gate Bridge, follow the signs to downtown and Lombard. Go east on Lombard to Van Ness and turn right.

A Touch of England off Union Street

BED & BREAKFAST INN

San Francisco

San Francisco's first urban inn occupies two brightly painted Italianate houses in a cul-de-sac off Union Street. Long before the bed and breakfast craze swept San Francisco, Marily and Robert Kavanaugh dreamed of opening a guest house patterned after England's B&Bs. Finally in 1976 they found the perfect building, a former boardinghouse, remodeled it with extraordinary flair, and decorated it with family heirlooms from England, combined with vividly colored contemporary accents. Two years later they purchased the house next door and added three other units.

The Bed and Breakfast Inn is a place for romance, and its *pièce de résistance* is a room in the second house called Celebration. Here a queen-size bed reposes in an alcove papered and curtained with a dainty blue and white Laura Ashley print. A love seat upholstered in blue velvet occupies a little sitting area. And beyond a divider containing pots of blooming flowers is a sunken double bathtub surrounded by brown-tinted mirrors. Downstairs is a suite named Mandalay that is decorated with grass cloth, rattan furniture, a Burmese-style ceiling fan, and sheer draperies emulating mosquito netting around the queen-size bed. On awakening, one would expect to see the dawn come up "like thunder outer China 'crost the Bay."

Next door the Victorian first restored by the Kavanaughs houses the breakfast area, a library and four bedrooms, each with a distinctive name and color theme inspired by boldly patterned quilts. Green Park and Kensington Garden open to a flower-filled deck behind the inn. A fifth unit on the top floor was formerly the Kavanaughs' living quarters. This penthouse suite has a living room, a dining area, a full kitchen and a latticed terrace filled with plants. A spiral staircase leads up to a bedroom loft that, like Celebration, is outfitted with a double bathtub.

Marily welcomes her guests with the warmth of an old friend. Upon your arrival you are offered sherry from a crystal decanter on a silver tray in the sitting/breakfast room. A Windsor table is set with Copeland china that belonged to Marily's grandmother. English country prints are on the wall. There's a white wicker settee with deep cushions covered in a floral print. Flowers and plants are everywhere; a spinning wheel is in the corner. Downstairs the cozy library contains a game table for backgammon, cards or puzzles, a color television and a leather-bound collection of the works of Dickens.

The Bed and Breakfast Inn

In all the rooms, Marily's gracious touches are found. A bouquet of fresh spring flowers on the nightstand. A bowl of fruit and selection of current magazines on a table. Beds turned down to reveal the pretty printed sheets and pillowcases. And on each pillow—a fortune cookie.

Breakfast is as important as the beds here. Marily serves juice, freshly ground coffee, hot croissants or occasionally "sticky buns" on her antique flowered chinaware. Some guests prefer to be served in the breakfast room or outdoors on umbrella-covered tables in the flower-filled garden. But Marily prefers to pamper you with a breakfast tray in bed.

The Bed and Breakfast inn is located in San Francisco's Cow Hollow district, named for the dairy farms that once covered the area. The neighborhood is a treasure trove of Victorian architecture, notably along Union Street where the colorfully painted old houses have been turned into fashionable shops, bars and restaurants. A bus line leads directly to downtown San Francisco.

THE BED AND BREAKFAST INN, 4 Charlton Court (off Union between Buchanan and Laguna), San Francisco, California 94123. Telephone: (415) 921-9784. Accommodations: ten rooms with twin, double, queen- or king-size beds; shared half-baths with tub/shower or shower only; private baths with shower or double tub; telephones and television in suites. Rates: moderate to very expensive, Continental breakfast included. Children discouraged. Pets discouraged. No cards. Open all year.

Getting There: From Van Ness, turn west on Union Street to Charlton Court and turn left.

Sophistication in the Heart of North Beach
WASHINGTON SQUARE INN
San Francisco

While the affluent citizens of San Francisco were building their palatial residences on Nob Hill and Pacific Heights, the working-class immigrants settled in North Beach. The city's ethnic mix is particularly mirrored in Washington Square, a small park at the base of Telegraph Hill. This square started out ignobly in the 1840s as the potato patch of Juana Briones, the Hill's first settler, and was later dubbed the "Spanish Lot." In 1849 the area around the park became known as "Little Chile," when the gold rush lured an influx of Chilean settlers here. Later came the Italians, who moored their fishing boats at the nearby wharves, and then the Chinese, whose homes and shops have spread into North Beach from neighboring Chinatown. Today in the early mornings office workers walk their dogs in Washington Square, while runners jog and middle-aged Chinese faithfully perform their graceful tai chi exercises. Later in the day, elderly Italian gentlemen take over the park benches, reading *Italo-Americana*. At noontime, residents of Casa Costanzo, an Italian home for the aged on the south side of the square, observe the limousines lined up below, bringing well-heeled lunchers to the Fior d'Italia. Meanwhile, on the square's western perimeter, once the site of a Russian Orthodox church, the Washington Square Bar and Grill attracts a younger, sophisticated mix of literary types; and the Pagoda Theatre advertises Chinese-language movies. Chimes peal across the park from the imposing tower of SS. Peter and Paul Catholic Church on the square's northern boundary. And on the east side, with a view of the park and Russian Hill beyond, is the Washington Square Inn.

Until 1978 this two-story corner building housed a drugstore, medical offices and run-down apartments. After being condemned, the building was totally refurbished and charmingly decorated by Nan Rosenblatt, one of the new owners. An antique French desk and brass chandeliers accent the informal lobby where a Continental breakfast of freshly squeezed orange juice, croissants and scones is served beside an intricately carved fireplace. In the late afternoon, tea is offered, with cucumber sandwiches and shortbread cookies. Guests may also purchase a bottle of wine from the inn's cellar of California varietals and champagnes.

The inn's fifteen bedrooms are individually decorated with bright French florals and chinoiserie; each is coordinated around a different color. Antique armoires, dressers and tables are scattered about; most of the beds are draped with colorful canopies. Three of the rooms are large bedroom-sitting room combinations with sofa beds that make them suitable for families of four. The others vary from spacious to small. The front rooms overlooking the square are, of course, the best. Here, from a seat by the bay window you may observe the colorful goings-on in the park.

Washington Square is midway between downtown San Francisco and Fisherman's Wharf—a short bus ride or a ten-minute walk from each. There is, however, much to see and do in the immediate vicinity. A block away is upper Grant Avenue—the center of the Beat movement of the 1950s and now the site of a conglomeration of crafts shops, antique stores, coffeehouses and so forth; a few blocks south, Grant leads into Chinatown. Strollers will delight in exploring the picturesque lanes hidden behind the main streets of Telegraph and Russian hills.

Since most of the pleasures of San Francisco are accessible by foot or bus to Washington Square, you really don't need an automobile; in fact parking is the nemesis of the area. If you wish to wander farther afield, the inn's manager will arrange a car rental or just about anything else to enhance your visit—theater tickets, a tour, a stenographer or a picnic.

WASHINGTON SQUARE INN, 1660 Stockton Street, San Francisco, California 94133. Telephone: (415) 981-4220. Accommodations: fifteen rooms with twin, double, queen- or king-size beds; private and shared baths with tub or shower or tub/shower; telephones; televisions on request at no charge. Rates: moderate to very expensive, Continental breakfast and tea included. Children welcome. No pets. Cards: AE, MC, VISA. Open all year.

Getting There: From Van Ness, take Union Street east to Stockton and turn left.

Stately Mansion in Pacific Heights
JACKSON COURT
San Francisco

Pacific Heights is San Francisco's most exclusive residential district. Two inns in this area offer the amenities of an elegant home to guests who plan an extended stay in San Francisco for business or pleasure. The first to open was Jackson Court, located in a lovely old mansion that had disintegrated to a cheap rooming house before it was refurbished by interior designer Suzanne Brangham in 1978. You enter the inn through a plant-filled courtyard shared by an adjacent twin house. In the gracious living room with its dark ceiling beams and wooden wainscoting, a fire bids welcome under a monumental mantelpiece of carved Italian marble flanked by cinnamon velvet love seats. Sherry is served here in the evening.

The hospitable feeling is emphasized by a "welcome home" sign on the wall of the staircase that leads to the upstairs bedrooms. These are light and spacious, painted in bright colors with contrasting trims and furnished with a blend of antiques and contemporary pieces, Oriental rugs on the hardwood floors, custom-made quilts on the beds.

Several of the rooms have fireplaces and all have comfortable sitting areas, deks, color cable television and telephones with private lines. They were designed with a long stay in mind. Plants, flowers and books are scattered about.

Each of Jackson Court's three floors has a kitchen, one with a little brick fireplace. Juices, coffee or tea, croissants, muffins and jams are set out here each morning, and if you wish to cook yourself something more substantial at any time, you are free to do so if you provide the groceries. But if you want to dine out, the concierge will be happy to make your restaurant reservations, as well as obtaining your theater tickets and arranging your transportation.

The ownership of Jackson Court is through an unusual time-share program, whereby investors purchase as many weeks of residency as they wish in the inn. During the rest of the year the rooms are rented out, for a minimum stay of two days. A conference room is also available for small meetings.

JACKSON COURT, 2198 Jackson Street, San Francisco, California 94115. Telephone: (415) 929-7670. Accommodations: ten rooms with twin, double and queen-size beds; private baths with showers; private-line telephones; color cable television. Rates: expensive to very expensive, Continental breakfast included. Children sometimes accepted. No pets. Cards: MC, VISA. Open all year.

Getting There: From Van Ness, head west on Jackson.

Historic Pacific Heights Victorian
HERMITAGE HOUSE
San Francisco

This seventeen-room, four-story Greek Revival mansion is sited a block away from Pacific heights's Lafayette Park in an area studded with Victorians. The house was built at the turn of the century for Judge Charles Slack and was maintained as a single-family residence until the 1970s when it served as a drug rehabilitation center. In 1978 Ted and Marian Binkley bought the place for an inn. Their motivation was unusual: They had enjoyed meeting interesting people while staying at European inns and felt they could add another dimension to their lives by greeting visitors to San Francisco. As is nearby Jackson Court, Hermitage House is geared for guests who stay a while and higher rates are charged for less than three nights.

The carved detailing in the redwood beams, pillars and stairway scrolls of the entrance hall is exceptionally fine, as are the carved mantel and the inlaid floors of the large living room with its graceful curved bay. A decanter of wine is set by the fireside here in the evenings. Marian has decorated a cozy breakfast room with mauve and white chintz wallpaper and matching cloths on little round tables. Magnificent leaded glass cabinets line the walls of this room and the adjoining formal dining room, where a buffet of juices, fruits, croissants and cold cereals is laid out each morning. As at Jackson Court, guests are invited to use the old-fashioned kitchen to prepare heartier breakfasts or other meals on the vintage 1900 Wedgewood stove.

Five of the bedrooms have working fireplaces, and wherever possible sitting areas and desks are provided. The bedrooms are cheerfully papered with chintz or floral patterns, beds are brass or four-postered or canopied, and each is stacked with as many as a dozen pillows of various patterns, sizes and shapes. Comfort is the byword here. The most unusual room is Judge Slack's former study under the eaves on the top floor. Paneled in redwood with a gabled ceiling, the room is lined with bookshelves and has a large stone fireplace. A desk has been placed in a dormered window with a southern view of the city towards Twin Peaks.

With private-line telephones and direct bus service to Nob Hill and downtown San Francisco, Hermitage House is an ideal head-

quarters for people on the go. But it's also a place to relax. An upstairs refrigerator is filled with ice and cold drinks to take onto a little sundeck. Or you may laze in a chaise in the sunny western garden.

HERMITAGE HOUSE, 2224 Sacramento Street, San Francisco, California 94115. Telephone: (415) 921-5515. Accommodations: ten rooms with twin, double, queen- or king-size beds, studio couches in some rooms as well; private and shared baths with tub or shower; private-line telephones on request; television on request. Rates: moderate to expensive, breakfast included. Children discouraged. No pets. Cards: MC, VISA. Open all year.

Getting There: From Van Ness, head west on Sacramento.

The Legacy of a Silver King
THE QUEEN ANNE
San Francisco

In 1890 Senator James G. Fair used part of the fortune he had amassed from his Comstock silver holdings to erect a towered, turreted and gabled structure near Pacific Heights to house Miss Mary Lake's School for young Girls. Gymnasiums, classrooms and dormitories for sixty-five boarders were provided. Fair spared no costs on the interior, installing stained-glass windows, English oak paneling and a monumental staircase of Spanish cedar. The school closed nine years later and an exclusive gentlemen's club, the Cosmos, moved into the four-story Queen Anne. In the 1920s the Episcopal Diocese purchased the building as a home for young working women: The Girl's Friendly Society Lodge. After World War II, new owners converted it to a residence club for men and women.

Finally, in 1980, an investment group purchased the former girls' school, and after extensive renovation opened it as a small luxury hotel. A newly installed elevator gives access to the forty-nine guest rooms on the upper floors. These rooms have been papered or painted and decorated with English antiques. Some bedrooms have fireplaces and wet bars. All have private baths with telephones! A Continental breakfast of juice, croissants and coffee is served in the bedroom or in the first-floor parlor and drawing room, where the original fireplace rises from floor to ceiling. Afternoon tea and sherry are also offered here.

THE QUEEN ANNE, 1590 Sutter Street, San Francisco, California 94109. Telephone: (415) 441-2828. Accommodations: forty-nine rooms with queen-, double queen- or king-size beds; private baths with tub/shower; telephones; color television. Rates: expensive to very expensive, Continental breakfast included. Children welcome. No pets. Cards: AE, CB, DC, MC, VISA. Open all year.

Getting There: From Van Ness head west on Sutter.

In the Style of the 1890s
VICTORIAN INN ON THE PARK
San Francisco

In the 1890s many wealthy San Franciscans built their mansions along the Panhandle, a wooded, grassy plot one block wide and eight blocks long leading to Golden Gate Park. One of these houses—an ornate four-story Victorian with an open Belvedere tower—was built in 1897 by a local lumberman for his son Thomas Clunie, who later became a state senator and United States congressman. In more recent years the house was occupied by a cult group that believed in rebirthing, a rite that took place in a hot tub in the basement! Now the house itself has been reborn under the aegis of Lisa and William Benau who have faithfully restored its turn-of-the-century splendor for an inn.

Clunie lavished the wares of his lumber business on the house. The parquet floors are inlaid with oak, mahogany and redwood, the entry hall is intricately paneled in mahogany and the dining room has oak wainscotings with an unusual spooled plate rack. Lisa, an attorney who also operates a small antiques business with her mother, has furnished the inn with authentic period pieces: velvet upholstered Queen Anne chair and sofa in the parlor, brass and carved wood headboards in the bedrooms, marble-topped sinks in the baths. Six guest rooms occupy the second floor. The largest has a fireplace and view of the Panhandle from the curved bay of the tower. The smallest is a light-splashed glassed-in porch with a sunken tub in the bath. And the most unusual is decorated in Art Deco style with accents of stained glass and posters. At this writing the Benaus are remodeling the top-floor ballroom into four other rooms, one of which will have as its private deck the open tower with its view of San Francisco. Another two bedrooms will be built in the basement. They're not certain what they will do with the hot tub.

Victorian Inn on the Park

The lovely white-tiled fireplace in the parlor is the gathering spot for a glass of wine in the evenings, and sometimes tastings of California and imported wines are conducted. Breakfast, served in your room or in the dining room, consists of fresh fruit, orange juice, flaky croissants and homemade breads. If guests wish, the Benaus will arrange catered dinners or allow the use of a small library for private meetings, which makes the inn attractive for business travelers.

With the Panhandle parkway at its front door, this inn is also popular with walkers and joggers. Golden Gate Park, the largest man-made park in the world, is only seven blocks away. At its entrance bicycles can be rented for exploring one-thousand acres of flower-filled meadows, woods, streams and lakes. The park is also the site of the de Young and Asian Art museums, the California Academy of Sciences and the Japanese Tea Garden.

VICTORIAN INN ON THE PARK, 301 Lyon Street, San Francisco, California 94117. Telephone: (415) 931-1830. Accommodations: six rooms with twin or queen-size beds (another six rooms being added); private baths with tub/shower or stall shower; telephones upon request; color television in library. Rates: expensive, Continental breakfast included. Small children discouraged. No pets. Smoking discouraged. Cards: AE, MC, VISA. Open all year.

Getting There: From Van Ness Avenue, take Fell Street west to Lyon. The inn is on the corner.

Turn-of-the-Century Haight Ashbury Showplace
THE SPRECKELS MANSION
San Francisco

The Haight Ashbury district has become again a quiet residential neighborhood after enduring a turbulent notoriety in the 1960s as the blossoming place for San Francisco's flower children. This area on the northern slopes of Twin Peaks was countryside until the 1890s, when a flurry of building activity made it a popular suburb. Today some twelve hundred relics of Victorian architecture line its streets. One of these houses, a splendid example of the Colonial Revival style, was built in 1898 for Richard Spreckels, superintendent of the Western Sugar Refinery owned by his uncle, sugar baron Claus Spreckels.

The stately mansion, facing the heavily wooded Buena Vista Park, was well maintained as a single-family residence until 1979 when

Jeffrey Ross and Johathan Shannon turned it into a spectacular inn. "The house has had a way of adapting to the times and attracting artistic people," Ross observes. Ambrose Bierce and Jack London supposedly worked in the top-floor ballroom at one time. And during the 1960s the producer for the Grateful Dead rock band owned the house and used the old ballroom as a recording studio.

Ross (an architect, interior designer and restorer of historic **buildings) and Shannon (a designer of women's evening wear) did not** intend to become innkeepers. When they heard the Spreckels house was threatened by a developer's scheme, they decided to save the building and possibly convert it into apartments. Then they saw the interior, with an amazing amount of its original embellishments intact: seven fireplaces, some with rare detailing such as a tortoise-shell tile hearth in the master bedroom; hand-painted Meissen chandeliers; museum-quality windows of leaded stained glass, many with Art

Nouveau overtones; embossed wall coverings with gilt friezes; Corinthian columns in the hall and parlor. Ross and Shannon decided to preserve the residential character of the mansion by making it an inn.

They surmised that their guests would not feel comfortable in the stiff decor of the Victorian era and used their skills as designers to blend French and English turn-of-the-century antiques with pieces from other periods, including contemporary furnishings. All of the rooms have sitting areas with wing chairs, and throughout are fanciful touches. The bed in the spacious former parlor, for example, is set in a columned alcove with a canopy swooping up to the Corinthian capitals. Many of the bedrooms—and even the master bathroom—have fireplaces, and most look out either to Buena Vista Park or west over Golden Gate Park to the ocean.

The third-floor ballroom is now a stunning two-bedroom suite, decorated with contemporary furniture and Oriental accessories. A gabled redwood ceiling rises some thirty feet over the living room, where sofas covered with navy-blue suede flank the large fireplace. Raised sitting areas in two large dormers command spectacular views of the city, Golden Gate Park, the ocean and the Marin headlands. A tiled bar-kitchen at one end of this room and a commodious table at the other make this unit suitable for small conferences.

Next door to the mansion is a handsome Edwardian building that was built as a guest house around 1900. Ross and Shannon also acquired this as part of their inn. The pride of the music room, now a common salon for guests, is an extraordinary baby grand piano, built in Paris circa 1890, with every surface covered with Art Nouveau designs fashioned from inlaid woods.

The upstairs bedrooms are designed to inspire fantasies. Entering the very Edwardian English Rose, one would not be surprised to find Sherlock Holmes sitting in the black wing chair in front of the brick fireplace. In Sunset Suite, where a view of the ocean is framed by stained-glass panels, the decor is reminiscent of a room in the French countryside. Gypsy Hideaway has a view and a fireplace, and a paisley-draped, -canopied and -covered bed that will make you think you've been abducted by a gypsy caravan. And the many skylights in Stargazers' Suite encourage flights of fancy to outer space; this suite also has a magnificent western view and an unusual fireplace.

In the mornings trays of juice, croissants and coffee are brought to the rooms at Spreckels Mansion. In the evenings wine is served in the library of the main house. From here it's a pleasant stroll past rows of colorful Victorians to Haight Street, where the former hippie hangouts are being transformed into nice shops and restaurants.

THE SPRECKELS MANSION, 737 Buena Vista West, San Francisco 94117. Telephone: (415) 861-3008. Accommodations: ten rooms with queen-size beds; some shared baths, mostly private baths with tub and/or shower; telephones; no television. Rates: expensive to very expensive, Continental breakfast included. Children sometimes accepted. No pets. Cards: AE, MC, VISA. Open all year.

Getting There: From Van Ness go west on Market to Haight and head west to Buena Vista West.

French Chateau on Alamo Square
THE ARCHBISHOP'S MANSION
San Francisco

In 1851 the City of San Francisco annexed the farmlands west of Van Ness Avenue between the Haight-Ashbury hills and Pacific Heights. This area, known as the Western Addition, was a popular suburb in the 1880s and 1890s and, as it was spared from the great fire of 1906, it still contains hundreds of Victorian houses. Some of the most beautiful examples of these picturesque buildings face Alamo Square, a small park on a sloping hillside. On its north side stands a stately three-story mansion with a slate mansard roof which looks like a manor house in the French countryside. It was built in 1904 as a residence for Archbishop Patrick Riodan and for four decades he and his successors entertained Catholic dignitaries from all over the world in the imposing first-floor reception rooms. Pope Pius XII stayed here in the mid 1930s when he was still a cardinal.

In recent decades the Alamo Square district sharply declined. The archbishop's home became a boys' school and in the 1970s was used as a half-way house by a local hospital. But the area was recently designated as a historic preservation district and the fine old buildings around the square are mostly restored. Five now shelter inns, of which the most spectacular is The Archbishop's Mansion, another exquisite creation of Jonathan Shannon and Jeffrey Ross, owners of The Spreckels Mansion.

In the grand hall a splendid brass chandelier from France hangs from the coffered mahogany ceiling. Fourteen-foot high redwood columns with intricately carved capitals flank the base of a three-story stair crowned with an oval dome of stained glass. In the formal parlor the triple-vaulted ceiling is painted with a motif derived from a Louis

XIV carpet, an embellishment added by Shannon and Ross. A sitting room across the hall boasts gold fleur-de-lis stenciled above the paneled wainscoting. Wood-burning fireplaces, most with mirrored and carved mantels, enhance almost every room of the house, including all but two of the fifteen guest units.

Shannon and Ross resisted the temptation to use a clerical theme in decorating The Archbishop's Mansion. Instead they named the rooms and suites after romantic nineteenth-century operas, since the San Francisco Opera House is only six blocks away. They also nixed Victorian decor, opting for museum-quality French furnishings that reflect the Second Empire style of the house. One of the most impressive pieces came from a castle in the south of France—a massive four-poster bed with cherubs carved on its walnut canopy and headboard. "If that doesn't get you to heaven, nothing will," Ross quips. A bedstead with ivory inlays of Japanese ladies sets the theme for Madame Butterfly's room and a neo-Egyptian sleigh bed with inlaid sphinxes graces Aida's boudoir. A chaise upholstered in silver velvet reclines on a base of gilded silver swans in Der Rosenkavalier's enormous bath-sitting room. And there's also a chaise—plus a fireplace and free-standing tub—in Carmen's bathroom. In the third-floor rooms the mansard dormers are fitted with window seats for a peek at the square or the city's hills and skyscrapers rising above the neighboring rooftops. The archbishop's chapel, which was also located here, now serves as a spacious meeting room.

Shannon and Ross are making a strong bid for the conference business and for weddings and receptions, which may be held in the gracious lower rooms. But to make sure that the inn's guests are not disturbed by these goings-on, a large sitting room on the second floor, facing the square, has been allocated for their exclusive use.

A Continental buffet breakfast is served in the enormous dining room which is papered in silk patterned with ivory fleur-de-lis. This room, which can seat sixty-five, and a smaller dining room, which seats twelve, may be used for catered dinners by guests at The Archbishop's Mansion and at the other inns surrounding Alamo Square. This recalls an early tradition of this house when His Excellency offered hospitality after the 1906 fire to the homeless San Franciscans who camped in the square.

THE ARCHBISHOP'S MANSION, 100 Fulton Street, San Francisco, 94117. Telephone: (415) 563-7872. Accommodations: fifteen rooms with queen- or two queen-size beds; private baths with tubs and showers or stall showers; direct-dial telephones; television available on request. Rates: expensive to very expensive, Continental breakfast included. Children discouraged. No pets. No smoking in most public rooms. Cards: AE, MC, VISA. Open all year.

Getting There: From Van Ness Avenue head west on Fell to Steiner and turn right to Fulton; the inn is on the corner. Offstreet parking for eight cars; nearby church lots available for valet parking during receptions.

A House Full of Art and Heart
THE INN ON CASTRO
San Francisco

Castro Village, where Market Street begins its ascent over Twin Peaks, is the center of San Francisco's large gay community—several bustling blocks of bars, discos, shops and restaurants. But The Inn on Castro, a half block up the hill from the village, is by no means all gay. "We have a mixed clientele and we like it that way," says owner Joel Roman, a talented artist and designer from New York. Straights, gays, singles, couples and families find their way to the inn and most of them return, because it's a very special place. The building was two Victorian flats when Joel took it over, but by the time he finished remodeling the only hint of the past was the facade. Inside, streamlined contemporary furnishings are accented with a riot of color from Joel's own paintings and numerous collections of brightly hued glass, pillows and whatnot.

The five guest rooms are located on the first floor. Each has a vivid color scheme picked up from a painting and a fanciful treatment of the high ceilings. The front room has a green tiled fireplace, eight paper parasols hanging from the ceiling, a windowed bay full of plants and the tones of green, lime and gold from a large gouache reflected in a Haitian cotton bedspread, masses of pillows, and rattan and wicker furniture. A second room, with brilliant gold, yellow and red emanating from a pineapple painting, hosts a bevy of papier-mâché parrots sitting on hanging perches. A rear room offers a view of San Francisco from a plant-filled bay and Chinese coolie hats dangle above. Another unit looks into a small greenhouse and is highlighted by a pink, grey and white striped canopy that extends up a raspberry colored wall and across the ceiling. Behind the first floor is a sheltered deck.

Joel lives upstairs, sharing his living and dining rooms with his guests. These rooms are decorated in brown and white to provide a neutral background for Joel's paintings and the constantly changing color schemes he achieves by switching around his collections of glass and pillows. (He admits to having about three hundred pillows stashed away.) A low modular couch of tufted brown mohair extends around the living room, with a break only for a fireplace and doors, turning the entire room into a large conversation pit. Joel encourages his guests to drop in here any time for a chat or tips on enjoying San Francisco, offered with coffee, tea, wine or a drink. The dining room is dominated by a large oval table, designed by Eero Saarinen, and Eames chairs. A Continental breakfast is served here on different dishes every day. Joel has been collecting china for twenty years and you could eat here for twenty-three days and never see the same plates. The dining room also houses yet another collection: heart-shaped boxes in a variety of sizes and colors. He started with twenty, but returning guests keep bringing them and he now has over two hundred. And what an appropriate gift for this house that's all heart.

THE INN ON CASTRO, 321 Castro Street, San Francisco, California 94114. Telephone: (415) 861-0321. Accommodations: five rooms with single, twin, queen- or king-size beds; three shared baths with tub/shower

or shower; telephones on request; no television. Rates: moderate, Continental breakfast included. Well-behaved children welcome, but only one at a time. No pets. Smoking permitted on first floor only. Cards: AE, MC, VISA.

Getting There: From Van Ness head west on Market to Castro and turn right.

A Convenient Spot for Business Travelers
THE WILLOWS INN
San Francisco

Window boxes filled with geraniums distinguish this three-story building from its look-alike neighbors near the bustling intersection of Church and upper Market. The inn occupies the top two floors above a restaurant, but at the top of the stairs, a stand of pussy willows in the reception area ushers you into a peaceful world.

The Willows derives its name from the unusual furniture of bent willow wood made especially for the inn and found throughout in the form of headboards, sofas, chaises and chairs. The graceful willoware gives a countryish look to this hostelry near the heart of the city, as do the Laura Ashley prints that bloom in pastel shades of lilac, blue, peach and green on the walls, bedspreads and ruffled pillows of every room. Wooden shutters, bouquets of dried and fresh flowers, and serigraphs by Graciela Boulanger complete the setting. There are no private baths, but each room is outfitted with a wash basin and a terry cloth bathrobe for the trip down the hall.

Complimentary wine is poured each evening in the small parlor. You may have your morning orange juice, coffee and croissants here, but most guests prefer service in their rooms. The pretty tray is done in pink and comes with a carnation and the morning paper. At night a turned-down bed, a mint and a brandy greet you.

Propietors Rachmael ben Avram and Gerard Lespinette cater to the business traveler. The Muni underground streetcar stops at the inn's front door and will whisk you downtown in minutes. A limousine service to the Moscone and Trade Show centers is provided for visiting exhibitors and buyers as well. The innkeepers will line up car rentals, restaurant reservations, secretarial and duplicating services, and almost anything else you might require. It's like having an office staff away from home. Many business travelers will also find they have a lot

101

in common with their genial hosts, for French-born Gerard was a banker in Paris before coming to this country five years ago and innkeeping is Rachmael's third career. He formerly was active in the theater as a stage and company director and most recently served as the national director of the Gucci stores. Their lives changed, however, several years ago when a friend casually commented: "You like to entertain so much, I see you as innkeepers." They agreed and they love it.

THE WILLOWS INN, 710 Fourteenth Street, San Francisco, California 94114. Telephone: (415) 431-4770. Accommodations: eleven rooms with double or queen-size beds; four shared shower rooms, some with tub/shower, and four shared lavatories; direct-dial telephones; no television. Rates: moderate, Continental breakfast included. Children over eight welcome. No pets. Cards: AE, DC, MC, VISA. Open all year.

Getting There: From Van Ness Avenue take Market Street west to the intersection of Church and Fourteenth; turn right on Fourteenth. Offstreet parking provided for a nominal charge.

Italianate Mansion in the Sunny Mission
THE INN SAN FRANCISCO
San Francisco

In 1776 the Spanish chose the flattest and warmest part of San Francisco as a site for Mission Dolores and its surrounding farmlands. The area was ignored by later settlers until the 1860s when a streetcar line connected the boom town of San Francisco with the sunny fields to the south and amusement parks, a race track and fashionable homes lured gold-rich San Franciscans to the Mission. In this century, however, the affluent moved to the hills of the north and abandoned the area "South of the Slot" to working-class residents and a growing number of Latin American immigrants. But the pendulum again swung to the Mission in the 1960s when a new generation of San Franciscans discovered the bargain-priced Victorians there and the blue skies that bless the district when most of the city is shrouded by fog.

Among the newcomers were Tony Kramedas and Joel Daily, who bought an 1872 three-story Italianate mansion that had been covered in stucco, stripped of its moldings and converted to a hotel. After two years of extensive renovation, which included an authentic reconstruction of the ornate facade, Tony and Joel opened the mansion as an inn in

The Inn San Francisco

1980. Inside they refinished the fine redwood paneling and wainscotings and restored the carved fireplaces in the double parlors with their fourteen-foot ceilings. Here inn guests are treated to a morning buffet of pastries, hard-cooked eggs and tropical fruits.

Tony and Joel have provided many spots to relax. In the rear of the building the old kitchen has been converted into an informal sitting room with comfortable couches, cable television, tables stacked with magazines, restaurant menus, backgammon boards, a chess set and whatnot. Behind is a glass-domed garden room where a Jacuzzi hot tub bubbles away. A spiral staircase winds from the top floor of the inn to a large roof deck which commands a panoramic view of San Francisco and the mountains of Marin County beyond.

The inn's fifteen guest rooms were upgraded considerably in early 1984 with the addition of private baths to most and the replacement of chenile bedspreads with quilted comforters and ruffled pillows. The master bedroom has twelve-foot ceilings, a working fireplace, a sunken tub and a sunny bay window. Another room has a queen-size bed with a ladder leading up to a loft-bed above it—perfect for families. Some of the third-floor rooms have skylights and views of downtown San Francisco. Even with all of the work they have done so far, Tony and Joel are busy planning future improvements for their inn. They have acquired the house next door which has a big yard where they intend to install a swimming pool. "We keep working on it. We never stop," they say.

Despite all the renovation that is going on, the Mission District today is still a mixed neighborhood, economically and ethnically. The brightly painted restored Victorians along South Van Ness are interspersed with run-down buildings and commercial properties, and a block away on Mission Street you are likely to hear more Spanish than English. But the area is only minutes from downtown by bus or BART and it does have the best weather in the city.

THE INN SAN FRANCISCO, 943 South Van Ness Avenue, San Francisco, California 94110. Telephone: (415) 641-0188. Accommodations: fifteen rooms with double, queen-size or two queen-size beds, rollaways available; eleven rooms with private baths, four shared baths, tub/showers, tubs and stall showers; direct-dial telephones; color television on request. Rates: inexpensive to moderate, breakfast included. Children over 14 welcome. No pets. Cards: AE, MC, VISA. Open all year.

Getting There: Take Van Ness Avenue south across Market where it becomes South Van Ness. Parking garage across the street from inn.

PETITE AUBERGE

San Francisco

Half way up Nob Hill from Union Square this small hotel offers the ambience of a French country inn and every personalized service you can imagine. Flowers pop from window boxes and ruffled muslin curtains peek through the windows of the ornate Baroque facade. An attendant will park your car and a houseman will escort you to your room, where the scent of potpourri fills the air and a flick of a switch will start a gas flame in a tiled fireplace. Eighteen of the twenty-six rooms have fireplaces, but all are richly appointed with countryish flowered wallpapers, quilted spreads, antique writing desks, comfortable chairs, plants, bowls of fresh fruit, and armoires that conceal color television sets. There is one suite with a Jacuzzi and a private deck.

In the late afternoon you can join the other guests around the fireplace in the lounge for complimentary sherry or tea accompanied with a spread of cheese balls, crudités with a dip and sweet pastries. The concierge will take care of your dinner or theater reservations. At night, when you return to your room, your bed will be turned down and a rose, a Swiss chocolate candy and a poem will be on the pillow. And don't forget to leave your shoes outside your door. When you awake in

the morning, they will be shined and the day's paper placed alongside. As you freshen up for the day, you'll find special soaps and lotions, shampoos and bubble bath in the modern, tiled bathrooms. Breakfast is taken at little tables in a room that opens to a small courtyard, filled with potted flowers, plants and the twitter of birds. Here a buffet is laden with fruit juices, breads, pastries, muffins, cereals, granola, cheese and a main dish that changes daily, sometimes a soufflé or frittata or quiche.

Petite Auberge is another superb example of the inns operated by the Post-Patterson group, owners of the Gosby House et al on the Monterey Peninsula. As manager Karen Tropper puts it, "Our business is to take care of people." They do.

PETITE AUBERGE, 863 Bush Street, San Francisco, California 94108. Telephone: (415) 928-6000. Accommodations: twenty-six rooms with queen-size beds; private baths with tub/shower or stall shower; direct-dial telephones; color television. Rates: expensive to very expensive, breakfast included. Children welcome. No pets. Smoking permitted in guest rooms only. Cards: AE, MC, VISA. Open all year.

Getting There: From Van Ness Avenue head east on Bush.

Luxurious Haven Near the Theaters and Shops
THE INN AT UNION SQUARE
San Francisco

For those who want to stay in the heart of San Francisco, the Inn at Union Square offers a personalized alternative to the commercial hotels. One-half block from the Square and its elegant shops, the inn had been a sixty-room transient hotel, vacant for some years, when it was renovated in 1980 by interior designer Nan Rosenblatt, owner of the Washington Square Inn. She cut the number of guest units to twenty-nine, creating some two-room suites from the smaller rooms and a luxurious sixth-floor suite with a fireplace, wet bar, whirlpool bath and sauna.

The decor and service at Union Square is very similar to Washington Square. The bedrooms are furnished with English antiques; bright fabrics drape the beds and cover the goose-down pillows. Fresh flowers are set in the rooms. Each floor has a little lobby, with a fireplace, where an English tea is served in the afternoons, along with hors d'oeuvre. Bottles of wine may be purchased from the inn. A Continental breakfast—croissants, juice, fruit and coffee—is served by this fireside or in the rooms.

Also, as at Washington Square, the Inn at Union Square has a concierge to take care of restaurant reservations, theater tickets and the like. Valet parking is available at the door.

THE INN AT UNION SQUARE, 440 Post Street, San Francisco, California 94102. Telephone: (415) 397-3510. Accommodations: twenty-seven rooms with twin, queen- or king-size beds; private baths with tub/shower; telephones; color television. Rates: Expensive to very expensive, Continental breakfast included. Children welcome. No pets. Cards: AE, MC, VISA. Open all year.

Getting There: From Van Ness go east on Post Street.

TLC in a Tudor Mansion
GRAMMA'S BED AND BREAKFAST INN
Berkeley

There is no real gramma here, but a large portrait of the owner's grandmother, Elizabeth Taber, hangs in the stairwell. She was an Irish immigrant who ran a boardinghouse in Boston. Steven and Kathy Lustig decided to dedicate their inn to her and to instigate some grandmotherly practices such as keeping a cookie jar freshly stocked at all times.

Gramma's is located in a splendid turn-of-the-century Tudor-style mansion, a five-minute walk away from Berkeley's UC campus. Constructed by builder J. A. Marshall as his residence, the house later served as a convalescent home before the Lustigs purchased it for an inn. Most of the original beautiful detailing of the lower floor remains intact, such as the intricately inlaid hardwood floors and foliated plaster friezes. In the living room a graceful bay of leaded clear glass windows looks out to the big trees that screen the inn from busy Telegraph Avenue. Beige velveteen upholstered sofas are pulled up to the painted tile fireplace. In the rear is a second sitting room and a large breakfast area with enormous windows opening to a broad deck and bountiful gardens where a fountain bubbles away.

All of the nineteen bedrooms are papered with floral patterns and the brass or carved-wood bedsteads have handmade patchwork quilts, the work of a local quiltmaker. Rooms in the main house range from small to quite large, with sitting areas and window seats. One room has a private deck. The nicest accommodations, however, are in the reconstructed servants' quarters at the rear of the garden. These rooms all have tiled fireplaces, and windows on two sides.

For breakfast Gramma's serves some of the best granola in town, along with fresh fruits, home-baked breads, scrambled eggs and French roast coffee. On Sundays the public is invited in for an elaborate champagne brunch that includes buffets of cold dishes, hot dishes and desserts, all prepared with great care. For inn guests, complimentary coffee and tea are available all day; wine and cheese are served in the evening Monday through Friday. And if you want to entertain at Gramma's, a greenhouse room will seat up to twenty-five for dinner.

GRAMMA'S BED AND BREAKFAST INN, 2740 Telegraph Avenue, Berkeley, California 94705. Telephone: (415) 549-2145. Accommodations: nineteen rooms with twin, double, queen- or king-size beds; private baths with tub and/or shower; telephones; television on request. Rates: moderate to expensive, breakfast included. Open to the public for Sunday brunch. No children under six. No pets. Cards: AE, MC, VISA.

Getting There: From San Francisco cross Bay Bridge and follow signs to Berkeley via Highway 80. Take Ashby Avenue exit east to Telegraph Avenue and turn left.

A Cascade of Cottages above the Bay
CASA MADRONA HOTEL
Sausalito

Just across the Golden Gate Bridge from San Francisco is the colorful town of Sausalito, once a Portuguese fishing village and now a chic residential community where houses cling to the steep wooded hills that rise from the bay. On one of these hillsides overlooking the harbor a stately mansion was built in 1885 for a private residence. Over the years it has metamorphosed as a hotel, bordello, beatnik boarding house, European-style pension and finally, under the ownership of John Mays, as one of the state's most elegant inns.

After buying the property in 1978 Mays restored the rooms in the mansion, decorating them in turn-of-the-century style according to different themes—one reminiscent of a bordello, another with a nautical touch and so forth. Next, he renovated three adjoining cabins for guest rooms. Then in 1983 he took the plunge—literally—and constructed a cluster of cottages that cascade down the bank from the mansion to the street that fronts the bay. Each is different with peaked roofs, dormers, bays, gables and decks and although brand new, they look like they have been there forever. Mays commissioned sixteen interior designers and gave each a free hand to decorate one of the rooms, resulting in enormously different interiors for the cottages, with a mix of styles ranging from Oriental to Victorian to art nouveau. One room emulates a country French chateau, another an Italian villa, another a New England summer retreat. The most unusual might be a Parisian artist's loft with skylights and a raised platform fully equipped with an easel, canvas and paints; paintings by former inhabitants of this room are hung on the walls.

Architecturally, each unit is also unique. No two are the same size and shape and none is a box: bays protrude here and there, skylighted ceilings slope at various angles and raised platforms hold beds or sitting areas. Almost all of the rooms have working fireplaces, most have private decks or balconies and all have dazzling views of the bay. The little amenities are not forgotten here either. Refrigerators are stocked with fruit juice and mineral water, bathrooms are supplied with hand lotion and a staff member is assigned full time to keep fresh flowers in the rooms.

A buffet breakfast of juice, fruits, yogurt and croissants is served in the charming dining room of the old mansion. Copies of the *Los Angeles Times, New York Times* and the *San Francisco Chronicle* are also provided. This room, with its magnificent views of the yacht harbor and Belvedere Island, is open to the public in the evening when a French chef takes over for a nouvelle cuisine-style dinner. Or, if you want to do your own lunch or dinner picnic style, there are several large decks equipped with tables and barbecue grills.

Many of Casa Madrona's guests are actually visitors to San Francisco who prefer getting away from the city life. Sausalito itself offers much to do with its quaint shops, crafts galleries, coffeehouses and restaurants that line the shore. And when it's time to commute to San Francisco, there's the beauty of a thirty-minute ride by ferry boat across the bay.

CASA MADRONA, 801 Bridgeway, Sausalito, California 94965. Telephone: (415) 332-0502. Accommodations: thirty-two rooms or suites with twin, double, queen- or king-size beds, rollaway beds and Japanese futon mats available; all rooms but two have private baths with tub/shower, stall shower or tub; three-room suite suitable for small conferences; telephones; color television on request. Rates: moderate to very expensive, breakfast included. Restaurant open to the public for dinner. Children welcome. No pets. Cards: AE, CB, DC, MC, VISA. Open all year.

Getting There: From San Francisco take Highway 101 north across the Golden Gate Bridge. Take the Alexander Avenue exit and follow into center of town which becomes Bridgeway. Marin Airporter service from San Francisco International Airport to Sausalito, where hotel will pick up guests. Daily ferry boat service from Sausalito to Fisherman's Wharf or the Ferry Building in San Francisco.

An English Pub on the Pacific
PELICAN INN
Muir Beach

In Marin County, Highway 1 crosses the coastal range and plunges down the western slopes of Mount Tamalpais to Muir Beach. At the foot of this grade, encircled by coastal wilderness and bordered by the Pacific Ocean, is a very civilized bit of Old England. Pelican Inn is the creation of British-born Charles Felix, who is descended from four generations of pubkeepers in Surrey, England. According to Felix, the inn's name is derived from Sir Francis Drake's ship (originally called

Pelican Inn

Pelican and later rechristened *Golden Hinde*), which was beached in Marin County "some four hundred years ago to claim California for Queen Elizabeth I and her descendants forever."

To help carry out this mandate, Felix purchased the Muir Beach property on the edge of the Golden Gate National Recreational Area and constructed a replica of a sixteenth-century English farmhouse. The white stucco building, crisscrossed with wooden beams, is surrounded by well-tended lawns, jasmine, and honeysuckle vines. Felix (a San Francisco advertising executive), his wife Brenda and two of their children have an apartment in the inn. The rest of the building houses six guest bedrooms, all with private baths, and a popular pub/restaurant.

On weekends the wood-paneled bar is jam-packed with locals and city folk who come here to enjoy a pint of beer and hearty pub grub: shepherd pies, Scotch eggs and the like. Thursday through Sunday evenings, a piano player adds to the conviviality. The adjoining dimly lit, low-ceilinged dining room is furnished with wooden tables and Felix's family antiques from Surrey. A huge inglenook (walk-in fireplace) of brick contains seats, a priest hole (hiding place) and a chamber for smoking hams. On Saturday and Sunday, a buffet lunch is served and in the evenings there is a formal dinner menu which of course includes roast beef with Yorkshire pudding and an English mixed grill. Beyond the dining room an enclosed patio with a fireplace accommodates the usual overflow of diners; during quieter times of the day guests like to relax here with a glass of wine or a cup of tea. Breakfast, served downstairs or in the bedrooms is big: juice, eggs and bangers (sausages) and homemade bread.

In contrast to this hub of activity downstairs, the upstairs bedrooms are serene and romantic, with initials of honeymooners and other couples who have inhabited the rooms carved into the beamed ceilings. The unusually high beds are canopied with brocade and covered with custom-made comforters. Oriental rugs, English antiques, pewter pots filled with fresh flowers and a decanter of cream sherry complete the decor. The leaded-pane windows (brought from England) offer vistas of the surrounding countryside, and some rooms have their own private balconies.

Felix admits that superstition is his great idiosyncrasy: "Witches and the little folk are all kept at bay." To keep the "evil eye" away, he buried bones and iron under the hearth. Pieces of holly on the doors protect the rooms from witches. And over each bed he has hung a stone with a hole in it "to insure no rickets in case of pregnancy."

THE PELICAN INN, Muir Beach, California 94965. Telephone: (415) 383-6000. Accommodations: queen-size beds; private baths with showers; no telephones; no television. Rates: expensive, full breakfast included. Open to the public for lunch and dinner. Rollaway bed provided for children at extra charge. No pets. Cards: MC, VISA. Open all year.

Getting There: From San Francisco take Highway 101 beyond Sausalito to the Mill Valley–Stinson Beach cut-off. From there take Highway 1 through Mill Valley (follow the signs to Stinson Beach) over the mountains to Muir Beach.

A Mecca for Nature Lovers
POINT REYES AREA
Olema, Point Reyes Station and Inverness

The San Andreas Fault runs down the center of Tomales Bay, a long fingerlike inlet that separates Point Reyes Peninsula from the mainland. A railroad once ran along the east shore of the bay, bearing cargoes of lumber from the northern timberlands. Today Highway 1 follows its tracks, carrying carloads of Sunday drivers to the little seafood houses around the town of Marshall to feast on the bay's gastronomic gift to California: oysters. The west side of the bay shelters the village of Inverness, a popular weekend and summer resort. Beyond this is the Point Reyes National Seashore: seventy thousand acres of coastal wilderness with magnificent hiking trails and beautiful beaches. Here a model village has been built, typical of those inhabited by the Miwok Indians who once dwelled on these shores. And here is the harbor that supposedly sheltered Sir Francis Drake's *Golden Hinde* during his expedition to the Pacific in 1579. Point Reyes is one of the best spots for bird watching in the country: Over four hundred species have been observed in the park. On weekends the park rangers conduct nature walks along the beaches and lectures in the visitors centers at Bear Valley and Drakes Beach.

Getting There: From San Francisco take Highway 101 north to the San Anselmo turn-off; continue on Sir Francis Drake Boulevard (Highway 17) through Fairfax to Olema and Inverness.

The New Cuisine in a Century-Old Hotel

OLEMA INN
Olema

In the mid-nineteenth century Olema was a lively vacation spot and commercial center for the surrounding ranches and dairy farms. The town boasted three hotels and a racetrack and was even a candidate for the county seat. About all that's left is one of the century-old hotels, recently restored and rechristened the Olema Inn. For decades this two-story American Colonial building was known as Nelson's Hotel and attracted visitors from throughout the state, including such celebrities as John Steinbeck and Jack London. Then after a stint as an army barracks during World War II, the hotel was allowed to deteriorate and was almost demolished in 1973. At that time Sausalito architect Gene Wedell heard of its plight and headed a restoration project that lasted seven years.

Today three upstairs bedrooms with country-style furnishings and a common room are used by overnight guests. But it's the cooking of chef Drew Spangler that is luring guests from near and far. She is a practioner of the new California cuisine and the menu sparkles with items like oysters from Drakes Bay baked with a lemon-garlic topping; a savory tart of leeks and goat cheese from Sonoma; a salad of smoked trout with red onions, apples and pecans; linguini tossed with chives, pecans and cream; braised rabbit with shallots and cornichons; and grilled prawns with a cilantro- and mint-seasoned tomato sauce.

Lunch and dinner are served in two handsome high-ceilinged dining rooms or out on a rear deck. These rooms and an adjoining library-bar are also a showplace for works of local artists in changing exhibitions organized by the inn's co-owner Donn Downing, who was

formerly associated with the Vorpal Gallery in San Francisco. There is live music on Friday, Saturday and Sunday nights and periodically wine tastings are conducted. Something is always going on at Olema Inn.

OLEMA INN, 10,000 Sir Francis Drake Boulevard, Olema, California 94950. Telephone: (415) 663-8441. Accommodations: three rooms with queen-size beds; one private bath, one shared bath, tub/showers; no telephones; no television. Rates: moderate, Continental breakfast included. Restaurant open to the public for lunch, dinner and Sunday brunch; full bar service. Children welcome. No pets. Cards: MC, VISA. Open all year.

English Gardens in the Wilderness
HOLLY TREE INN
Point Reyes Station

Located in a secluded nineteen acres of forest, this inn is named for the manicured holly trees that combine with English boxwood and lilac to form a hedge around the spacious lawn with its flower-covered stone wishing well. Owners Diane and Tom Balogh live downstairs in the two-story ranch house. Upstairs guests have their own large living room, papered in blue and white Laura Ashley prints, with comfortable overstuffed sofas and chairs upholstered in matching fabrics arranged around a brick fireplace. Another copper-hooded fireplace warms the adjoining dining room where breakfast is served: fresh fruits and juices, cheese, croissants and coffeecake. These rooms open to a private deck sheltered by a flowery hillside. Four bedrooms, decorated with antiques, quilted bedspreads and ruffled curtains, offer views of the woodsy surroundings.

HOLLY TREE INN, 3 Silverhills Road (P.O. Box 642), Point Reyes Station, California 94956. Telephone: (415) 663-1554. Accommodations: four rooms with double or king-size beds; two private baths with shower, one shared bath with tub/shower; no telephones; no television. Rates: moderate, breakfast included. Children welcome. No pets. No cards. Open all year.

Getting There: From Highway 101 take Sir Francis Drake Boulevard west. Beyond Point Reyes Station turn left onto Bear Valley Road; take first right onto Silverhills Road and look for Holly Tree Inn sign.

Romantic, Treetop Hideaway
BLACKTHORNE INN
Inverness

Here is an inn for young-at-heart romantics. The nucleus of Blackthorne is a tiny cabin, built during the 1930s on a steep forested hillside near Inverness. Then in 1975 patent attorney Bill Wigert designed an amazing structure above it, using beams from the piers in San Francisco and gigantic doors salvaged from the Southern Pacific depot. An eight-sided tower with a spiral staircase rises from the cabin through two floors flanked with decks to an octagonal eagle's nest room topped by a platform that peeks out of the treetops some seventy feet

above the ground. Bridges connect the tower rooms to hillside walkways banked with rhododendrons and to another deck with a hot tub, cold tub and bath house.

Two small bedrooms are located in the original cabin. Above it is a glass-walled solarium and the living room with its dramatic, skylighted A-frame ceiling of rough hewn wood. A walk-in stone fireplace shelters a cast-iron stove and pillows, often occupied by the inn's cats. Oriental rugs on burnished wood floors, comfortable sofas and chairs, and a decanter of sherry add to the gracious aura. Here a breakfast is served of orange juice, fruit salad, granola and yogurt.

A climb up the spiral staircase brings you to two other bedrooms with arched windows and pitched ceilings, cozily furnished with quilted bedspreads and ruffled pillows. Balconies from one of these overlook both the deck and the living room. At the top of Blackthorne is the eagle's nest. Its eight sides are enclosed by multipaned floor-to-ceiling windows that look out to oak, redwood and bay trees, its skylight offers a view of the stars, and a ladder leads up to the rooftop deck. The eagle's nest's only furnishing is a Japanese-style bed—a huge mattress on the carpeted floor. This is not exactly your conventional inn.

BLACKTHORNE INN, 266 Vallejo Avenue (P.O. Box 712), Inverness, California 94937. Telephone: (415) 663-8621. Accommodations: five rooms with double or queen-size beds; two shared baths within the inn, one in outside bath house, all with showers; no telephones; no television. Rates: moderate, breakfast included. Children permitted on occasion. No pets. Cards: AE, MC, VISA. Open all year.

Getting There: From Highway 101 take Sir Francis Drake Boulevard through Olema towards Inverness. Turn left on Vallejo Avenue, at the Inverness Park Grocery two miles south of Inverness.

Peaceful Is the Word Here
TEN INVERNESS WAY
Inverness

A tranquil, homelike setting for those who want to get away from it all is provided in this spacious redwood-shingled house, built as a residence in 1904. Designer-contractor Stephen Kimball and writer Mary Davies remodeled the building for a bed and breakfast inn in 1980. A new partner, Ruth Kalter, is resident innkeeper. A large fir-paneled living

Ten Inverness Way

room, furnished with antiques and an Oriental rug, is a restful spot for reading during the day, but livelier in the evening when guests gather for sherry around the big stone fireplace—especially if there's someone who wants to play the player piano. A full breakfast is served in the adjoining dining room cheered by a large Danish fireplace. There's always fruit, perhaps a half grapefruit, and goodies such as quiche or banana pancakes with apricot sauce, or French toast made from homemade bread. Upstairs the five bedrooms, paneled with white carsiding, are furnished with handmade patchwork quilts and rag rugs. And there are always bowls of flowers cut from the gardens that surround the inn. It was rumored that a ghost once inhabited this house, but Stephen and Mary had the local Episcopal priest bless each room with holy water when the inn opened. Only good spirits live here now. As Mary says, "Peaceful is the word most often used to describe our place."

TEN INVERNESS WAY, 10 Inverness Way, Inverness, California 94937. Telephone: (415) 669-1648. Accommodations: five rooms with twin and double beds; two shared baths with shower, tub/shower; no telephones; no television. Rates: moderate, breakfast included. Children sometimes welcome. No pets. No cards. Open all year.

Getting There: From San Francisco take Highway 101 north to the Sir Francis Drake Boulevard exit and contine through Olema to Inverness. Once in the village, turn left at the Inverness Inn Restaurant.

A Return to the Nineteenth Century
THE UNION HOTEL
Benicia

Benicia was founded in 1846 on the Carquinez Straits, where the Sacramento and San Joaquin rivers flow into San Francisco Bay. During the gold rush the city's strategic location brought such prosperity that the town rivaled San Francisco as a commercial center and for a year in the 1850s Benicia was the capital of California. It was also the site of a major United States Army arsenal and so noted for its educational institutions that it was dubbed "Athens of California." Then history and commerce bypassed Benicia, resulting in a rare phenomenon—an entire nineteenth-century town largely intact, possessing some of the most significant buildings of California's early history. Today Benicia is enjoying a renaissance, while its buildings are being

119

restored. One of these is The Union Hotel, built in 1882 not far from the water's edge.

The interior of the three-story hotel was actually rebuilt to provide comforts like modern tiled bathrooms, all with Jacuzzi tubs. Each of the twelve guest rooms is decorated around a different theme. There's Louis le Mad with tufted, gilted pseudo French furnishings, Four Poster with a high Queen Anne canopy bed, Mei Ling with Chinese Chippendale, 1932 with metallic Art Deco pieces, Summer Skies with lilac walls and white wickerware, and so forth. Many of the rooms have lovely views of Carquinez Bay and the bridge that arches over the straits. All are scented with potpourri.

A bar and dining room occupy the first floor, separated from the street by floor-to-ceiling windows of stained and leaded glass. A handcarved 1886 bar lines one wall of the saloon which is furnished with armchairs and loveseats around low marble-topped tables. When the hotel reopened in 1980, a seasonal menu of regional American dishes brought unqualified kudos from restaurant critics. A new chef has instigated a simpler, unchanging menu that is as American as the chili, pan-fried chicken, steaks and pork chops now offered. Hotel guests receive a complimentary Continental breakfast of orange juice, cream biscuits and coffee and those wishing a heartier meal may order from an extensive à la carte selection of waffles, buttermilk pancakes, eggs and bacon.

The town of Benicia sponsors many special events such as an old-fashioned Fourth of July parade and picnic, a peddlers fair that brings over three hundred antique dealers to town in August, and a handicraft fair in September. Year-round attractions include antique hunting in the many shops, fishing, bird watching, picnicking and strolling around the historic buildings of this nineteenth-century town.

THE UNION HOTEL, 401 First Street, Benicia, California 94510. Telephone: (707) 746-0100. Accommodations: twelve rooms with queen- or king-size beds; private baths with Jacuzzi tub/showers; telephones; color television. Rates: moderate to expensive, Continental breakfast included; lower rates on week nights and a special rate that includes dinner. Children welcome. No pets. Cards: AE, DC, MC, VISA. Open all year.

Getting There: From San Francisco, take Highway 80 northeast to Vallejo. Take the turn-off to Benicia and exit at Second Street. Proceed to Military and turn right to the first stop light which is First Street. Turn left and drive through town to the hotel.

GOLD COUNTRY

Sacramento
The Mother Lode
Across the High Sierra
To Virginia City

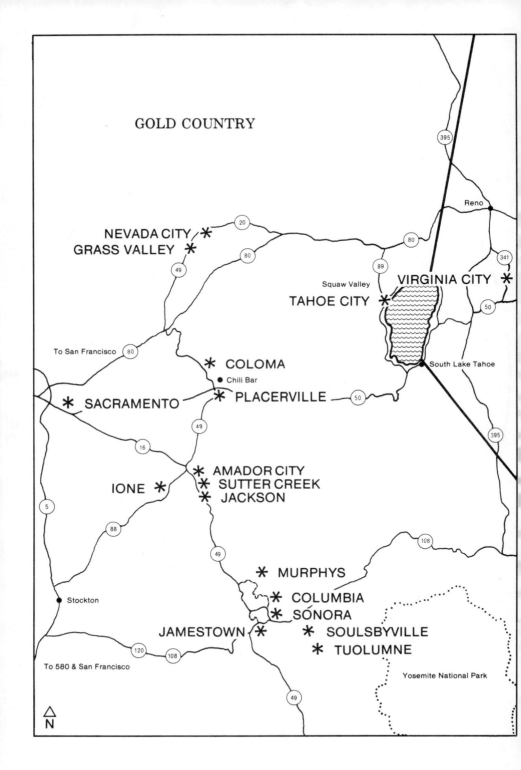

GOLD COUNTRY

NEVADA CITY
GRASS VALLEY

VIRGINIA CITY

Reno

Squaw Valley
TAHOE CITY

South Lake Tahoe

To San Francisco

COLOMA
Chili Bar

SACRAMENTO   PLACERVILLE

AMADOR CITY
SUTTER CREEK
IONE   JACKSON

Stockton

MURPHYS
COLUMBIA
SÓNORA
JAMESTOWN   SOULSBYVILLE
TUOLUMNE

To 580 & San Francisco

Yosemite National Park

N

The Gateway to the Gold Country
SACRAMENTO

In 1839, when California was still part of Mexico, a Swiss adventurer named John Sutter obtained a Mexican land grant to establish the colony of Nuevo Helvetia at the spot where the American River flows from the Sierras into the Sacramento River. Here, the present site of Sacramento, he built Sutter's Fort with timber extracted from the nearby mountains. Then on January 24, 1848 at one of Sutter's sawmills in Coloma, James W. Marshall found some glittering specks in the mill tailrace. These turned out to be gold and the destiny of California was forever changed. Marshall rushed back to Sacramento to share his discovery with Sutter who agreed to keep the strike a secret. But the news leaked out and within the next decade some hundred thousand prospectors came to the Mother Lode, taking $550 million in ore from her rich veins.

Neither Sutter, who lost his holdings and was bankrupt by 1852, nor Marshall, who died a pauper, ever prospered from the Sierra mines. Among those who really struck it rich from the gold rush were the merchants of Sacramento, where the miners came to spend their diggings. Four of the wealthiest shopkeepers—Charles Crocker, C. P. Huntington, Mark Hopkins and Leland Stanford—later turned their profits into gigantic fortunes by starting the Central Pacific and Southern Pacific railroads. In 1854 Sacramento became the capital of California and later the western terminus for the Pony Express.

Today the colorful early history of this city has been recaptured in Old Sacramento, a restoration and reconstruction of the old town along the river front. Here wooden sidewalks lead by the Huntington Hopkins Hardware Store, Pony Express terminus and the old Wells Fargo Office, plus a bevy of restaurants and shops. Other tourist attractions in Sacramento include the Crocker Art Gallery, the Railroad Museum, the reconstruction of Sutter's Fort, river boat cruises and, of course, the Capitol itself and the many Victorian mansions that were built nearby. In a quiet area just east of the Capitol several of these older homes have been turned into inns.

Getting There: From San Francisco Highway 80 leads to Sacramento; from Los Angeles, take Highway 5. Sacramento is served by Amtrak and a number of airlines, including AirCal, PSA, United and Western.

THE BRIGGS HOUSE
Sacramento

Four dedicated women brought the bed and breakfast concept to Sacramento in 1981 when they bought a lovely 1901 Colonial Revival home near the Capitol and within weeks had transformed it into an inn. Their aim was to provide an old-fashioned homelike ambience for two types of clientele: the increasing number of tourists attracted by Old Sacramento and business or professional travelers. The owners furnished the place with family antiques: Oriental rugs on the hardwood floors, lace curtains, crocheted, patchwork or quilted bedspreads and pretty printed sheets. A downstairs bedroom has a woodburning fireplace, one of the upstairs units has a private sundeck and out back there's a rustic garden cottage with a fully equipped kitchen. The rooms are filled with fresh flowers and touches that make this a very special place: **engraved stationery, little sachets and terry cloth bathrobes for the guests' use and hardbound diaries in each room where tenants record their impressions of the inn or their adventures in Sacramento.**

The day begins with a full breakfast served on antique china either in your room, in the parlor or in the pretty rear garden which is planted with camelias, firs and orange trees. In season, oranges from these trees provide the freshly squeezed juice for the morning meal. Croissants and homemade breads and jams are also served, along with the cook's daily creations—things like frittatas and baked apples with cinnamon sauce. At night there's no lack of things to do at Briggs House. Wine, fruit and nuts are served before the fire in the early evening. A hot tub, an unusual sauna set in a wine cask, and a big hammock offer relaxation in the garden. And if you want to take a spin on a bicycle, the inn will provide that too.

Briggs House also presents an ongoing series of special events and theme weekends: fireside poetry readings, chess or backgammon evenings, quiltmaking seminars, musical entertainment, Sunday tea and crumpets, a photography weekend and an antiques lovers weekend, to name a few. There's a nominal charge for some of the sessions, but they are staged by professionals as is everything else at this superb inn.

BRIGGS HOUSE, 2209 Capitol Avenue, Sacramento, California 95816. Telephone: (916) 441-3214. Accommodations: five rooms with twin, double or king-size beds; two rooms have private baths, three share two baths, tub/showers and stall showers; cottage with full kitchen and private bath sleeps four; telephones in some rooms; no television; air conditioned. Rates: moderate, breakfast included; lower rates on week nights. Younger children welcome in garden cottage. No pets. Cards: AE, MC, VISA. Open all year. Advance schedule of special events available upon request. Parlor available to guests for meetings or social events by special arrangement.

Getting There: Take 15th Street exit from Highway 80, turn right to 16th Street, turn left and stay on 16th until you reach Capitol Avenue. Turn right on Capitol.

Crystal and Stained Glass Everywhere
AMBER HOUSE
Sacramento

Long before Sacramento's bed and breakfast craze was born, Robert O'Neil and Bill McOmber toured the inns of California, gleaning ideas for their own place and studying the art of innmanship. Then in 1981 the search for the right real estate ended with the purchase of a two-story craftsman house, built in 1905. They opened Amber House just a few months after the Briggs House came into being. There's a handsome library downstairs and a lovely living room with beamed ceilings, Oriental rugs and a brick fireplace. A dining room, with an interesting collection of forty crystal or cut-glass candlesticks, is the site of a generous breakfast—usually quiche or frittata along with homemade pastries, fresh fruit and juice—served on Limoges china.

Throughout the inn you find fresh flowers, Baccarat vases and leaded stained-glass creations, the work of Robert whose profession was glassmaking before he took up innkeeping. Upstairs, the bedrooms are furnished with antiques. In the two that share a huge common bath, robes are provided for the guests. But possibly the most interesting room of the entire house is the private bath off the room called Lindworth. Here a skylight illuminates a seventy-year-old porcelain tub with brass fixtures and ivory handles. A sliding tray across the tub is appointed with bubble bath and reading materials—you might just want to bring in the complimentary bottle of wine you'll find in your room and soak away the evening. Other complimentary touches of Amber House include use of their bicycles and pick-up service at the airport limousine terminals and the Amtrak station.

AMBER HOUSE, 1315 Twenty-Second Street, Sacramento, California 95816. Telephone: (916) 444-8085. Accommodations: four rooms with double beds; two share a bath with stall shower, two have private baths; no telephones; no television; air conditioned. Rates: moderate, breakfast included. No children. No pets. No smoking. Cards: AE, MC, VISA. Open all year.

Getting There: Take Capitol Avenue east to Twenty-Second Street and turn right.

Where the Gold Rush Began
EL DORADO COUNTY
Coloma and Placerville

Within months of James Marshall's discovery of gold at Coloma in January, 1848, thousands of fortune hunters were roaming the nearby mountains and rivers seeking *el dorado* (the gilt). One of the most popular camps, about seven miles south of Coloma, was named Dry Diggings because the miners had to tote the gravel that contained the ore to water for washing. But many of the rough and tough adventurers who inhabited the camp found an easier way to get their gold: Murder and robbery became so rampant that a vigilante committee was formed to hang the culprits. And as the hangings increased the camp became known as Hangtown until a more respectable group of citizens changed it to Placerville.

In the early years of the gold rush both Coloma and Placerville thrived, and they became engaged in a heated rivalry for the county seat. Coloma, which had grown to a city of over ten thousand inhabitants within a few years of the gold strike, won out at first, but in 1857, after several heated elections, the county government was moved to Placerville, which was then the third largest city in California. Meanwhile, the gold in El Dorado County was being depleted and the fickle prospectors had moved on to the vast mines to the south and north. Placerville managed to prosper as a government and commercial center, but by 1868 Coloma had dwindled to a population of two hundred, among them a bitter and impoverished James Marshall, who survived by occasionally working as a gardener.

Coloma today, barely a speck on the map, is best known for its historic park that contains the reconstruction of Sutter's Mill where the gold was first discovered. Placerville, still a thriving town, contains a number of historic buildings and the old Gold Bug mine which is open to the public. Nearby attractions include white water river rafting, a number of prize-winning wineries and Apple Hill® Farms, an association of forty-four independent apple growers whose farms on a mountain ridge east of Placerville are open to the public. In addition to selling apples, other fruits, vegetables and preserves, many of the farms have arts and crafts stores, bake shops and sandwich bars. Higher in the mountains a number of ski areas are located.

A Three-Generation Family Affair
VINEYARD HOUSE
Coloma

In 1885, five years after James Marshall's death, a large bronze monument was erected in his honor over the place of his burial and thousands of people flocked to Coloma for the dedication ceremonies. The highlight of these festivities was an elaborate ten-course banquet for two thousand guests at Vineyard House, the home of Robert Chalmers, an extravagant local vintner. Chalmers had built the house in 1878 as an elaborate residence for himself and his bride, a young widow, on vineyards she had inherited from her late husband, Martin Allhoff. Chalmers improved the original winery, built in 1866, and developed the vineyards to five hundred producing acres. The house had nineteen rooms with nine fireplaces, and he spent the then exorbitant sum of fifteen thousand dollars on furnishings. Later he had a special wing added for the Marshall Monument banquet.

In his later life Chalmers allegedly became insane and locked himself in the basement where he starved to death. (There is some evidence, however, that he actually died elsewhere.) After Chalmers's death, his ghost was rumored to haunt the house, which fell into disrepair. The vineyards withered away and the old winery crumbled into ruins.

The Vineyard House was being operated as a run-down hotel and restaurant when it was discovered by Gary Herrera, an Oakland restaurateur who wanted to escape the metropolitan rat race. In 1975, Gary bought the property in partnership with his brother and sister-in-law, Frank and Darlene Herrera, and a friend, David Van-Buskirk.

Thus began a gigantic, do-it-yourself restoration project. The four of them stripped floors and balustrades to the natural wood, papered walls, and hauled long-since forgotten pieces of period furniture down from the attic and refurbished them.

The dining rooms are filled with relics of yesteryear. In one, fire burns in a Franklin stove; genuine kerosene-burning lamps flicker on tables topped with brown and white checkered cloths. The dishes and flatware are a mishmash of patterns such as one might have inherited from a myriad of aunts. (Actually some of the chinaware came with the house, but much of it has come from doting customers who turn up with "grandma's dishes.")

Vineyard House

The food is old-fashioned country cookery. Not always perfect, but always hearty and homemade. Pots of soup and big bowls of salad are set on the table and you serve yourself. The bread is freshly baked. Entrées include rib-sticking fare such as simmering chicken topped with a two-inch layer of dumplings and gravy. Vineyard House does not serve a complete breakfast, but coffee and homemade dessert breads are available for overnight guests.

Upstairs seven bedrooms have been renovated. "We will probably never be finished," Darlene observes. "There is always something to do." Each room is different, some with brass bedsteads, others with massive Victorian headboards. Homemade quilts top the beds.

The Vineyard House is very much a family operation, complete with a real grandma. Darlene Herrera's mother lives in the house and helps make the desserts. Her younger brother runs the gift shop. Her two sons are the "bellboys." And, as Darlene expresses it, "Everybody who comes here becomes automatic family."

VINEYARD HOUSE, P.O. Box 176, Coloma, California 95613. Telephone: (916) 622-2217. Accommodations: seven rooms with double and king-size beds; one community bath with tile shower; no telephones; no television. Rates: inexpensive to moderate, Continental breakfast included. Open to the public for dinner. Children over 16 welcome. No pets. Cards: AE, MC, VISA. Open all year except Mondays and Tuesdays from September to June.

Getting There: From San Francisco take Highway 80 to Sacramento, Highway 50 to Placerville, then Highway 49 north. Turn left just before Coloma at the Vineyard House sign.

Watch the White Water Rush Past
RIVER ROCK INN
Chili Bar

During the 1850s the South Fork of the American River between Coloma and Placerville was heavily populated with miners. Today, it swarms with the rafts and kayaks of white water aficionados who come from all over to enjoy the thrills of this very fast river and to see the relics of old mining camps en route. Chili Bar (a gold rush camp founded by Chilean miners) is headquarters for the river raft expeditions and just a little downstream is River Rock Inn. This contemporary stone and brick house furnished with antiques was the country home of Dorothy Irvin and her husband Norman. In 1982, with their children grown and gone, they turned it into an inn.

All the rooms front on a wide deck with spectacular views of the river, which is illuminated by floodlight at night. (The bed heights were designed to be eye level with the river.) Chaises, tables, a hot tub and potted flowers grace the deck, where breakfast is served on sunny mornings. On chilly days the morning repast is taken before a fire in the stone-walled dining room—and a bounteous meal it is. Dorothy on a typical day might serve orange juice mixed with bananas, eggs Benedict, apple crêpes, freshly baked rolls and baking powder biscuits, homemade jams and fresh fruit. In fact, one might say she is a compulsive cook. The big country kitchen is the hub of this house and there usually are cookies, pies or cakes baking in the oven—for the guests' enjoyment—while bread rises on an ancient woodburning cookstove. By special arrangement she will prepare dinners or picnic lunches for her guests.

Dorothy will also arrange for one- or two-day raft trips down the river, conducted by qualified guides. For the less adventurous, there's excellent trout and white salmon fishing on the banks near the inn. And if you're truly lazy, you can just lie on the deck and watch the white water rush by.

RIVER ROCK INN, 1756 Georgetown Drive, Placerville, California 95667. Telephone: (916) 622-7640. Accommodations: three rooms with double or queen-size beds share one bath with three lavatories and stall shower; one suite with private bath; no telephones; color television in living room; air conditioned. Rates: moderate, breakfast included. Children welcome. Pets discouraged. No cards. Open all year.

Getting There: From Placerville take Highway 49 (Coloma Road) north to the intersection of Highway 193 (Georgetown Road), which leads to Chili Bar. After crossing the American River turn left immediately on the first road, which leads to the inn.

Old Farmhouse Complete with Pastoral Setting
THE FLEMING JONES HOMESTEAD
Placerville

Among the hordes who rushed to the gold country in 1851 were Fleming Jones' parents, dairy farmers from Wisconsin. But instead of gold, they staked their claim on a homestead of ninety-seven wooded acres just east of Placerville. Fleming liked to gamble and also acquired an interest in a saloon. After a particularly good night at the tables, he arrived home with twelve hundred dollars and told his wife, Florence, to go build herself a house. She did. Descendents of the Jones family lived there until the late 1970s, and in 1980 the old farmhouse and eleven acres of the land were acquired by Janice Condit, an administrator at the University of California in Santa Barbara and a former State Department interpreter. She had decided to become an innkeeper.

Janice's inn mirrors her interests in cooking, antiques, farming and California wines. You enter through the farmhouse kitchen, rife with the aroma of freshly baked bread or simmering preserves of fruit from the pear, apple and fig trees in her orchards. A homey parlor is furnished with a Morris rocker, an overstuffed sofa and tables laden with magazines on farming, wine and Californiana. In the adjoining dining room guests gather for breakfast around a massive oak table with carved griffin feet. On gold-rimmed Haviland and Limoges china, Janice serves an "expanded" Continental breakfast of fresh fruit or baked apples, two or three kinds of homemade fruit bread and hot muffins.

The Homestead presently has three guest rooms: one downstairs, and two upstairs that open onto a flower-filled porch with views of the old red barn and rolling, wooded countryside. Rooms are furnished with cast-iron or carved oak bedsteads (equipped with *new* mattresses, flowered quilts and matching sheets). Children's school desks, with vases of fresh flowers, serve as night tables. Janice is now renovating the nearby bunkhouse to hold another room with private bath for guests.

A favorite pastime of Homestead guests is helping with the farm chores: feeding the chickens and collecting their eggs, helping to tend the vegetable gardens or harvest the fruit from the trees, petting Janice's Welsh pony and thirty-five-year-old burros. Other guests prefer just to loaf on the porch swing and admire the pastoral setting.

The Fleming Jones Homestead

FLEMING JONES HOMESTEAD, 3170 Newtown Road, Placerville, California 95667. Telephone: (916) 626-5840. Accommodations: three rooms with double beds; one private bath, one shared bath, tub/shower and shower; no telephones; no television. Rates: moderate, breakfast included. No children under 12. No pets. No cards. Open all year.

Getting There: From Placerville, take Highway 50 east to the Newtown Road/Point View Drive exit. At the base of the off ramp, jog to the right to another stop sign and turn left onto Broadway, which runs parallel to the freeway and becomes Newtown Road. The Homestead is on the right just past a pond.

Home of Champion Horses and Blue-Ribbon Baking
THE RUPLEY HOUSE
Placerville

One of the forty-niners who settled in Placerville was John Wesley Rupley of Pennsylvania. His grandson, A. J. Rupley, became a lumber tycoon, married the granddaughter of Fleming Jones and in 1929 built a farmhouse east of Placerville in the Pennsylvania Dutch tradition of his ancestors. Fay Jones Rupley lived here until 1978 when she sold the house to attorney Al Hamilton and his wife Virginia. Al's hobby is raising quarter horses on the ninety-three acres that surround the farmhouse and Virginia's avocations include baking and crafts. Now, since early 1983, they share another interest: running a country inn. "We're not doing this to earn a living," Al comments, "but for fun. You meet such neat people."

On entering the house you immediately become aware of Virginia's activities. A large loom sits in the living room, where the Hamiltons entertain their guests in the evenings with sherry or apple wine before a blazing fire. There's a 1934 slot machine in the corner with nickels provided by the hosts. And set around the lower floors are pieces of etched and stained glass (another one of Virginia's talents). Her handmade quilts adorn many of the walls and one of these heralds good things to come in the morning: Virginia has decorated the quilt with county fair medals she has won for her baked goods—zucchini bread, apple-banana cake, baking powder biscuits and more. These are served for breakfast in the big dining room along with fresh fruit from nearby Apple Hill® and baked eggs, just laid by the Hamiltons' chickens.

The Rupley House has three upstairs bedrooms and two downstairs, one of which (the former family room with a fireplace) is used by the Hamiltons unless they have a full house. They are decorated with antique furnishings and, of course, Virginia's quilts and needlepoint. One might be wary of noise here, because the house is built right alongside busy Highway 50, but double glass windows completely muffle the traffic's din and a glade of sycamore, silver maples and dogwood blocks the highway from view.

In back of the house a patio provides picnic tables and a view of the barn and pastures where Al's horses, cows and pet bull graze. Down the hill are rocks where the area's first settlers—the Indians—ground their acorns and several little streams where there's still some gilt to be found with the help of the Hamiltons' gold pan and shovel.

THE RUPLEY HOUSE, 2500 Highway 50(P.O. Box 1709), Placerville, California 95667. Telephone: (916) 626-0630. Accommodations: five rooms with twin or queen-size beds; one private bath with stall shower, two shared baths with tub/shower; no telephones; television in one room. Rates: moderate, breakfast included. Children under 15 discouraged. No pets. No smoking. No cards. Open all year.

Getting There: From Placerville take Highway 50 east. After the Point View Drive exit you will cross some railroad tracks; the inn is one-half mile beyond on the right.

Where the Vines Have Replaced the Mines
AMADOR COUNTY
Amador City, Sutter Creek and Jackson

Located in the heart of the Mother Lode, this is one of California's smallest counties in both size and population, yet its mines yielded more than half the gold that came out of the entire Sierra foothills. Gold may still be panned in the streams, and many of the old mines are open to the public. But today the commercial interests of the Amadoreans have turned from the mines to the vines. Amador County's Shenandoah Valley produces some of the state's most distinctive Zinfandel. And many of the wineries are open for touring and winetasting.

In Amador County, Highway 49 winds through oak-studded hillsides and the old mining towns of Amador City, Sutter Creek and Jackson. The brick or clapboard buildings, with their second-story balconies covering raised sidewalks, now house antique shops, art and craft galleries, and saloons. A worthwhile side trip from Sutter Creek or Jackson is a visit to the picturesque mining town of Volcano, situated in a valley surrounded by pine-forested mountains above Highway 49.

It would be difficult to become bored in Amador County. Besides shopping, sightseeing, mine and wine touring, and visiting historic museums, you may participate in a host of recreational activities. There are fishing and boating at nearby Lakes Amador, Pardee and Camanche, and rafting on the Mokelumne River. There are hunting, tennis, a nine-hole golf course, and even skiing in nearby Kirkwood Meadows. And on summer evenings the Claypipers Theater presents old-time melodrama. You can also eat well in Amador County. Jackson offers a number of family-style Italian restaurants, such as Buscaglia's, where the food is both hearty and above average.

Getting There: From San Francisco take Highway 580 east through Tracy to Manteca, Highway 5 north to Stockton and Highway 88 northeast to Jackson. Sutter Creek is four miles north of Jackson on Highway 49; Amador City is two miles north of Sutter Creek. This part of the Mother Lode may also be reached by taking Highway 50 to Placerville and proceeding south on Highway 49.

THE MINE HOUSE
Amador City

Over $23 million in gold bullion was removed from the Keystone Consolidated Mines in Amador City before they were finally closed in 1942. The mining company's offices, grinding and assay rooms were located in a two-story brick building on a hillside across the highway from the mines. In 1954 the building, then abandoned and run-down, was purchased by Marguerite and Peter Daubenspeck, who came to California on a vacation, were charmed by Amador City and decided to stay. Originally the Daubenspecks intended to restore the old mine house for a residence; then they decided it would be an ideal inn.

After two years of renovation, the eight rooms were ready for guests. The Daubenspecks furnished the entire building with authentic period furniture, found within one hundred miles of Amador City. And the rooms are handsome, indeed. There are burled-walnut pieces, Empire dressers, commodes topped with Italian marble, rockers, platform rockers, armoires, carved bedsteads, and under each bed an old-fashioned bed warmer. Many of the rooms contain old pitchers and wash basins set on a commode. But these are for show only. The Daubenspecks have added modern wood-paneled baths throughout.

The rooms of the Mine House are named after their original usage. Downstairs is the Mill Grinding Room, where the ore was brought to be ground; the supports that held the shafts for the grinding machinery are still on the ceiling. Next door is the Assay Room, where the ore was evaluated for its gold content. There is a Retort Room, where the gold was smelted into bullion, and a Stores Room that once contained the mining supplies. All the interiors are of painted brick.

The upstairs rooms, however, are the most attractive, with thirteen-foot-high ceilings paneled in redwood. On one side rooms open to a wide balcony overlooking the highway. On the other side they open to a covered patio dug out of the grassy hillside. These rooms originally housed the Keystone Consolidated Mining Company's offices and are appropriately named: Directors' Room, Bookkeeping Room, Keystone Room and Vault Room, which contains the safe in which the bullion was stored until the stagecoach transported it to San Francisco.

There is a swimming pool for guests at the Mine House. No meals are served, but each morning Peter Daubenspeck III or his wife Ann

Marie, who now own the inn, leaves a tray of orange juice and coffee, tea or hot chocolate by each door.

THE MINE HOUSE, P.O. Box 245, Amador City, California 95601. Telephone: (209) 267-5900. Accommodations: eight rooms with one or two double beds; private baths with showers; no telephones; no television. Rates: inexpensive, orange juice and hot beverage included. Children welcome. No pets. No cards. Open all year.

Getting There: The Mine House is on Highway 49 in Amador City.

Mother Inn of the Mother Lode
SUTTER CREEK INN
Sutter Creek

Here, in a century-old, two-story house in the heart of Sutter Creek, California's first bed and breakfast inn was opened nearly two decades ago. Jane Way fell in love with the house, once the biggest in town, on a visit to the Mother Lode in 1966. The house was not for sale, but after months of perserverance she convinced the owners to allow her to buy it and soon her bed and breakfast shingle was inviting travelers to spend the night. Word spread and later many of the visitors included would-be innkeepers who borrowed her ideas and incorporated them into their own places. Sutter Creek is truly the prototype of a California country inn.

Jane, a woman of enormous talent and energy, has dressed up every inch of the inn with a riot of color and charm. The gracious living room, painted a pale aqua, is comfortably furnished with large sofas upholstered in floral print, a hutch filled with antique china, a small piano and a grandfather clock. A chess set and a decanter of sherry by the fireplace are ready for the guests' enjoyment.

But the highlight of a stay at Sutter Creek Inn is breakfast in the country-kitchen/dining room. Walls, partially brick, partially paneled, are hung with copper colanders, an Oriental rug and a collection of guns. Two long, polished plank tables are gaily set with orange mats, gold-rimmed china and a pewter pitcher filled with dried flora. Shuttered windows look out to the lawn and gardens. Jane carries on an animated conversation with guests as she cooks, serves and pours a shot of brandy into the coffee. Her menu is ambitious: fresh fruit,

Sutter Creek Inn

berries or perhaps peaches, just picked from the inn's own trees, along with pancakes full of chopped nuts and apples, corn bread or a soufflé.

Several upstairs bedrooms in the main house have recently been enlarged. But the most desirable rooms are the outbuildings in the rear of the house—the woodshed, carriage house, storage shed and old laundry house, which Jane has extensively remodeled and furnished with flair. Eight of these have fireplaces and four have "swinging beds," actually suspended by cables from the ceiling. This was an idea she picked up in the tropics of Mexico where people often hang their beds to avoid crawling insects and lizards. But if you suffer from motion sickness, you won't need Dramamine; the beds may be stabilized easily.

No two of the rooms are alike, except that they are perfectly appointed down to the tiniest details: books, magazines, a deck of cards, a decanter of sherry. In one you might find a fireplace, in another a Franklin stove, in yet another a sunken bathtub. Some open out to private patios or porches, others into the lovely back garden. Some are furnished in solid Early American maple, others have canopied four-poster beds, still others contain brightly painted wickerware. Jane transforms whatever she finds around the countryside: an old drum topped with a wicker tray for a table, a miner's scale for a planter, a milk can for a lamp base, two water barrels for the base of a bathroom sink. All is visual joy.

Though there is much to see and do in the Sutter Creek area, Jane admits that most of her guests come primarily to relax, to get away from it all. But one diversion unique to this inn is a session of Jane's handwriting analysis, made with the warning: "This might change your life completely." So might a visit to Sutter Creek Inn.

SUTTER CREEK INN, 75 Main Street (P.O. Box 385), Sutter Creek, California 95685. Telephone: (209) 267-5606. Accommodations: seventeen bedrooms with twin, double and queen-size beds; all private baths; no telephones; no television. Rates: moderate, breakfast included; lower rates on week nights. Children discouraged; children under 15 not allowed. No pets. No cards. Open all year except Thanksgiving and Christmas and Christmas Eve.

Where Modern Comforts Mingle with Antique Artifacts
THE HANFORD HOUSE
Sutter Creek

When Ronald Van Anda bought an old Spanish bungalow and antique shop on Sutter Creek's main street, he aspired to mix the old with the new in a structure that would house his antique shop, living quarters and a nine-room inn by 1983. The bungalow is now the nucleus of this complex, its whitewashed beamed ceiling sheltering a homey sitting area and breakfast room. To one side, in a brick replica of a gold rush era building, is the antique store.

In the rear another new brick wing houses the guest rooms. These contain new queen-size beds with, in most rooms, headboards fashioned from antique doors, luxurious modern baths and European or American furnishings that in some cases date back to the eighteenth century. All the rooms are air-conditioned or carpeted. And each contains those often-neglected touches that insure a relaxing stay: four pillows on the bed, reading lamps on each side of the bed, a comfortable couch or two armchairs, plants, fresh flowers and a welcoming bottle of Amador County white Zinfandel. On the top floor of the bedroom wing a large deck commands a panoramic view of the town of Sutter Creek and the surrounding hills. Upstairs there is also a deluxe—and more expensive—unit with a view and a fireplace with gas-burning logs.

For breakfast Ron puts out an ample spread of three juices, melons, apples, oranges, cheese, rolls and coffee. The Hanford House might be a little too modern for die-hard nostalgia buffs, but those who put comfort above all will love it.

HANFORD HOUSE, 3 Hanford Street (P.O. Box 847), Sutter Creek, California 95685. Telephone: (209) 267-0747. Accommodations: nine rooms with queen-size beds; private baths with tub/shower in eight rooms; one room with facilities and tub for the handicapped in bathroom plus wheelchair access; no telephones; no television. Rates: moderate to expensive, Continental breakfast included; discount on week nights. Children over 12 welcome. No pets. Some designated no-smoking rooms. Cards: MC, VISA. Open all year.

A Romantic Place for Romantic Occasions
THE FOXES
Sutter Creek

Next door to Sutter Creek Inn is a 125-year-old house that was renovated for a restaurant called The Brinn House in the mid 1970s. Then Pete and Min Fox bought the place in 1979 to relocate his real estate offices upstairs and her antique shop downstairs. They had no intention of opening an inn, but Min couldn't keep her hands off two unused second-story rooms and transformed them into a romantic Honeymoon Suite furnished with a nine-foot headboard and other handsome period pieces from her shop.

Later Pete's office became the Anniversary Suite, boasting a nineteenth-century Austrian bedroom set of carved wood that includes a ten-foot tall armoire under the high pitched ceiling. A bathroom down the hall was enlarged to house a claw-legged tub set on a platform in a curtained alcove. Even the baths are romantic here. Finally Min turned two of the first-floor rooms into the Imperial Suite. Here a huge 1895 Japanese screen dominates the bedroom which connects to a large living room with a wood-burning brick fireplace and floor-to-ceiling shelves well stocked with books. Min has concealed a color television in a cupboard of this suite ("because I had nowhere else to store it") and admits that the guests—perhaps no longer on a first or second honeymoon—do cheat and use it a lot! Throughout the inn, Min has placed dramatic bouquets of silk flowers. And there are a lot of little

The Foxes

foxes, such as a stuffed furry pair curled up on a gilt Louis XV day bed in the Anniversary Suite.

Pete still maintains his real estate office on the first floor of The Foxes, but Min has given up the antique business. It's now a full-time job running the inn and pampering her guests indulgently. In each suite a little table is set where breakfast is brought on silver service. Min gives her guests a number of choices among juices, hot beverages and four kinds of muffins; she often serves coddled eggs. "But we've done just about everything—sourdough French toast, eggs Benedict, even biscuits and pan gravy at a customer's request," Min recollects. She also likes to know when guests are celebrating a special occasion— honeymoon, anniversary or birthday—so she can plan a special surprise for them. Though nowadays she often knows without being told, as more and more of the honeymooners return for their anniversaries.

THE FOXES, 77 Main Street, Sutter Creek, California 95685. Telephone: (209) 267-5882. Accommodations: three suites with queen-size beds; private baths with stall showers or tub/shower; no telephones; color television in one suite. Rates: expensive, breakfast included; lower rates on week nights. No children. No pets. Smoking discouraged. Cards: AE. Open all year.

The House of One-Hundred Clocks
GATE HOUSE INN
Jackson

It wasn't just the miners who reaped the riches of the Mother Lode. Workers at the mines outside of Jackson used to tote their ore to the Chichizola General Store to exchange it for food, clothing and supplies. With this fortune gleaned from the gold rush, the Chichizola family at the turn of the century built a handsome two-story home next to the store, surrounded by a huge parcel of wooded, hilly acreage that is still owned by their descendants. Frank and Ursel Walker bought the house and opened the doors for bed and breakfast in 1981.

The original floral wallpaper still remains in mint condition in the master bedroom which is cheered by a white tile fireplace. All the light fixtures are the original Italian imports, as is the marble fireplace in the living room. *Fin de siècle* antiques decorate all the rooms, along with fresh flowers, decanters of sherry and the Walkers' collection of over one hundred priceless old clocks. The choice quarters in the house,

144

The Gate House Inn

oddly enough, are the rooms formerly occupied by the Chichizolas' baby and cook, now a suite. The cook's room, paneled in natural wood, has a bank of windows looking over the inn's pretty garden and orchards and a private staircase to the kitchen, today a convenient exit to the inn's lovely swimming pool.

In the garden a grape arbor leads to the summerhouse, once the caretaker's cottage. There's a cast-iron wood-burning stove in the bedroom/sitting room and an immense cedar-paneled bathroom where the Walkers have installed stained-glass windows from the Comstock mansion in Virginia City. Across the lawn from this cottage, a screened-in barbecue area is provided for the guests' use if they tire of the hearty fare of Jackson's famous Italian family-style restaurants, which are within walking distance of the inn. You won't go hungry at breakfast either. Having owned a restaurant in Sutter Creek, the Walkers feed their guests well. The large table in the formal dining room is set with bone china, lace and linens and a rose on each napkin, and promptly at nine o'clock they serve a repast of juice, fresh fruits, pastries, muffins and coddled eggs.

GATE HOUSE INN, 1330 Jackson Gate Road, Jackson, California 95642. Telephone: (209) 223-3500. Accommodations: three bedrooms plus one suite and one cottage with double or queen-size beds; private baths with tub/shower or stall shower; no telephones; no television. Rates: moderate, breakfast included. No children. No pets. Smoking discouraged. No cards. Open all year.

Getting There: Turn off Highway 49 on Jackson Gate Road, just north of the intersection with Highway 88 from Stockton.

A Legacy of the Old South
THE HEIRLOOM
Ione

The Ione Valley, west of Highway 49 in the lower foothills, was the supply center for the boom towns of Amador County during the gold rush. This valley had been settled in the early 1800s by a number of Virginians, most of whom left during the Civil War. One family among these settlers, the Stephenses, left a legacy of the Old South: a brick antebellum mansion adorned with classical columned porticos. This architectural heirloom was later purchased by Patrick Scully, a rancher who owned most of the surrounding valley. In 1980 Patricia Cross and Melisande Hubbs, two women whose children were grown, bought the Heirloom for an inn.

From a nondescript residential area you approach the Heirloom by a long driveway bordered by acacias, eucalyptuses and fruit trees, suddenly encountering a secret garden from another era. A giant gnarled wisteria, graceful magnolias, a brick terrace and a lush lawn nestle up to the gracious old house. A croquet course and hammocks are set up for guests. From the veranda you enter a spacious sitting room appointed with a square piano (once owned by Lola Montez), comfortable couches placed by the fireside, antiques, scattered Oriental rugs, tables equipped with decanters of sherry, dominoes and jigsaw puzzles. A breakfast of fresh fruit, Louisana dark-roast coffee and an entree such as crêpes, quiche or soufflé is served here, on the patio or in one of the four upstairs bedrooms. These are decorated with irresistible charm, using family antiques from the innkeepers' former homes, brass bedsteads with flowered or patchwork quilts and fresh flowers. Two of these rooms open to a broad balcony. One has a fireplace, along with its own private entrance, bath and balcony. A recent addition is an adobe cottage with a wood-burning stove and skylight.

Although the sleepy town of Ione offers few diversions, it's only a short drive from Jackson and Sutter Creek and all the attractions of Amador County.

THE HEIRLOOM, 214 Shakeley Lane (P.O. Box 322), Ione, California. Telephone: (209) 274-4468. Accommodations: five rooms with twin, double, queen-and king-size beds; three rooms share bath, two with private bath; no telephones; no television. Rates: moderate, breakfast included. No children under eight. No pets. No cards. Open all year.

Getting There: From San Francisco take Highway 580 and Highway 205 to Charter Way in Stockton. Take Charter Way to Highway 99, go north to Highway 88 and east to Highway 124, which leads to Ione. Turn left on Main Street, turn right on Preston and left on Shakeley Lane. From Highway 49, take Highway 124 or Highway 88 west.

Even President Grant Slept Here
MURPHYS HOTEL
Murphys

The historic mining town of Murphys was known in its heyday as Queen of the Sierra. It was not gold, however, but the discovery of the Calaveras Big Trees—a forest of giant sequoias in the mountains east of Murphys—that attracted some of the town's most illustrious guests. To accommodate them, flour magnate J. L. Sperry built a luxury hotel in 1855, which after a fire and a succession of owners and names was finally christened Murphys Hotel and designated a historic landmark on both the state and federal registers. Over the years the hotel hosted such disparate luminaries as Black Bart, Mark Twain, Count von Rothschild, John Jacob Astor and Horatio Alger, Jr. Ulysses S. Grant was another visitor, and the bed he slept in still occupies the Presidential Suite.

In the late 1970s a group of investors purchased and restored the hotel with the help of state funds, keeping most of the original furnishings in the nine guest rooms. No closets, televisions or private bathrooms detract from the authenticity of yesteryear, but for those who like these comforts, the new owners constructed a modern twenty-room motel next door. (If you want to be in the old hotel, be sure and specify when you make your reservations.) The downstairs parlor was refurbished with a pot-bellied stove, Oriental rugs and Victorian chairs. Adjacent is an old-time saloon, resplendent with hunting trophies, which offers live music on weekends; a large dining room is in the rear.

Besides hiking in the six thousand forested acres of Calaveras Big Trees, the area offers many attractions: river rafting, tennis, golf, and exploring gold mining museums, natural caverns and caves.

MURPHYS HOTEL, 457 Main Street (P.O. Box 329), California 95247. Telephone: (209) 728-3444. Accommodations: double, queen- and king-size beds; hotel rooms share bath; motel rooms have private bath; no telephones; television and air conditioning in motel rooms only. Rates: inexpensive to moderate. Open to the public for breakfast, lunch and dinner. Children welcome. Smaller pets sometimes allowed. Cards: AE, MC, VISA. Open all year.

Getting There: From Placerville take Highway 49 south to Angels Camp, then head east on Highway 4 to Angels Camp and turn left on Main Street. From Stockton take Highway 4 east.

A Gold Mine of Early Californiana
CITY HOTEL
Columbia

Columbia was one of the most prosperous gold rush towns, with ore taken from its fabulously rich mines valued at over $80 million. Within three years after gold had been discovered in 1850 at Hildreth's Diggings, as it was then called, the town's population had grown to some twenty thousand and ranked as the second largest city in California. In its heyday Columbia boasted forty saloons, one hundred fifty gambling houses, eight hotels, four banks and two volunteer fire companies! Despite their efforts, most of the original frame structures were destroyed in two early fires and the town was almost completely rebuilt in brick.

The Columbians' paranoia about fire has benefited posterity. The durability of these brick buildings caused the state of California to purchase the town in 1945 and restore it as the Columbia Historic State Park. Today, except for an onslaught of tourists, the tree-shaded Main Street with its boardwalks and balconied buildings looks much the way it did in the 1860s. No automobiles are allowed in the town itself, but a stagecoach does lumber through, offering visitors a ride. The old blacksmith shop, harness and saddle shop, carpenter shop and a Chinese herb store are in working condition. And the historic Fallon House Theater comes back to life for six weeks each summer as a repertory playhouse for University of the Pacific students.

One of the old brick buildings restored by the state in Columbia is the City Hotel, with its wrought-iron balcony overhanging the sidewalk of Main Street. Built in 1856, the hotel was ravaged by fire in 1867 and rebuilt four years later.

In the 1940s the state of California acquired the City Hotel as part of Columbia Historic State Park, and after spending $800,000 on restorations and furnishings, opened its nine bedrooms, dining room and saloon to paying guests. The operation of the hotel is unique in California. The young chambermaids in their "granny caps," the waitresses in their long last-century dresses, the waiters and busboys in their black ties are not the college students off on a lark usually found at resort hotels. They are all serious students of the Hospitality Management Program at Columbia Junior College, which operates the hotel as an on-the-job training facility.

The bedrooms have been impeccably furnished with massive burled-wood Victorian bedsteads framing comfortable brand-new

149

City Hotel

mattresses, brass coat racks, marble-topped bureaus. The rooms have half baths, no shower or tub, but the hotel thoughtfully provides each guest with a "bathroom caddy," a basket containing soap, washcloth, shower cap and even terry-cloth shower shoes. The trip down the hall to the shower is made as pleasant as possible here.

Upstairs there is also a homey old-fashioned parlor decorated with flocked paper, Oriental rugs and Victorian settees. There is a small library and games for the guests' use. A Continental breakfast is served here each morning.

Downstairs is the What Cheer Saloon and a gracious high-ceilinged dining room, a serene setting for the magnificently appointed tables set with cut-glass goblets, graceful wineglasses of varying sizes, flowered service plates, small brass hurricane lamps and even silver napkin rings on the sparkling white napery.

The food here is far removed from the mountain-country cooking you might expect to find in the Mother Lode. The City Hotel's kitchen is run by a first-rate chef from San Francisco and his menu would come as no surprise in New York or Paris. But in Columbia? There are escargots and fresh bluepoint oysters baked with a sauce mornay among the appetizers. Bibb lettuce and hearts of palm compose some of the salads. Shrimp bisque, French onion gratinée and vichyssoise compose the choice of soups. Then there is a choice of twenty-four elegant entrées: chicken poached in wine with oranges and mushrooms, veal with apples and cream sauce, chateaubriand with a sauce béarnaise, and a rack of lamb stuffed with spinach are but a few. Dinners are à la carte, expensive, and worth it.

CITY HOTEL, P.O. Box 1870, Columbia, California 95310. Telephone: (209) 532-1479. Accommodations: nine rooms with twin, double and twin double beds; private half baths, community showers; no telephones; no television. Rates: moderate, Continental breakfast included. Open to the public for lunch, Sunday brunch and dinner. Children welcome. No pets. Cards: MC, VISA. Conference facilities for 25 available. Open all year except Christmas and Christmas Eve.

Getting There: From San Francisco, 580 to Tracy, 205 to Manteca; Highway 120 east past Knights Ferry to intersection of Highway 108: Highway 108 east to Sonora; Highway 49 north to Columbia.

A Rambling Adobe from Gold Rush Days
THE GUNN HOUSE
Sonora

Sonora is only four miles south of picturesque Columbia, but a century away in atmosphere. Although some of the old adobe and frame buildings still stand as a testament to Sonora's original Mexican settlers and gold rush past, the town today is a bustling community living in the present. Nevertheless, a bit of the colorful history can be recaptured at the Gunn House.

The house is named for Dr. Lewis C. Gunn, who was lured from Philadelphia via Mexico to the California gold mines. Settling in Sonora he became the first county recorder and in 1850 started the Mother Lode's first newspaper, the Sonora *Herald.* Using Mexican laborers, he built the town's first two-story adobe as home and office. During his ten years of residence in Sonora, Gunn was a controversial figure. Once, protesting his editorial views, angry townspeople burned his printing press in front of his home.

In the early 1960s, Margaret Dienelt bought the house and began an ambitious restoration, adding wings up the steep hillside in back. For nearly two years she searched the area for antiques: "I had to visit people's attics. There were very few antique shops in those days, but as word spread, people started calling me." The twenty-five guest rooms reflect her efforts. They combine handsome period pieces—marble-topped tables, quilted bedspreads, carved-wood chairs and settees—with the modern comfort of private baths, telephones, television and air conditioning.

There is no sitting room, but chairs and tables are scattered around on the covered verandas that surround the building, on little patios scattered here and there and around the oval swimming pool in back. A small barroom with marble-topped tables is the setting for Continental breakfast in the morning; coffee and rolls are replaced by full bar service in the evenings and the public is invited to partake along with hotel guests.

If this sounds like a perfect inn to you, be warned of one drawback. The Gunn House fronts on Sonora's heavily trafficked main thoroughfare. It can be quite noisy, but then maybe this is the perfect inn for those city folk who complain they can't sleep away from the din of traffic.

THE GUNN HOUSE, 286 South Washington, Sonora, California 95370. Telephone: (209) 532-3421. Accommodations: twenty-five

The Gunn House

rooms with twin, double, twin double and queen-size beds; private baths with tub/shower; telephones; television; air-conditioning. Rates: moderate, Continental breakfast included. Full bar service. Children and pets welcome. Cards: AE, MC, VISA. Open all year.

Getting There: Take Highway 108 into central Sonora and turn right on South Washington.

A Great Place for a Family Vacation

WILLOW SPRINGS COUNTRY INN
Soulsbyville

Ben Soulsby was a lucky prospector who struck it rich to the tune of $6.5 million in gold near the tiny town that now bears his name. Considering the enormity of this fortune in those days, he built himself a relatively modest country house, encircled by a wide covered porch. After extensive remodeling by previous owners, this house was opened to guests in 1983 by Karen and Marty Wheeler, who moved here to raise their child in the country.

Just seven miles up the road from Sonora, the inn is surrounded by lawns, gardens, orchards, oaks and rolling hills. Three sides of the old veranda have been closed. These serve as an entry hall, as a large country kitchen with a brick barbecue and cast-iron stove and as a homey living room with a Franklin stove and profusely pillowed rattan couches. The original dining room is now a bedroom, its built-in hutch housing a collection of old books. The old summer kitchen, now wood-paneled and shuttered, holds another two bedrooms. But the nicest quarters of all, off the living room, are furnished with white wicker and a ruffled canopy bed. All the guest rooms have overhead fans, ruffled sheets and pillows (two per person) and bouquets of fresh flowers.

On weekends the Wheelers serve a full breakfast of crêpes or quiche, with two or three kinds of bread and fruit; weekdays (when the rates are reduced), it's fruit and bread only. Pretty little tables for two are set on the enclosed porch adjoining the kitchen. Wine and hors d'oeuvres are offered during the evening social hour.

Willow Springs is a great place for a family vacation. It adjoins the recreational area of the local homeowners' association and the inn's guests have use of the tennis courts, shuffleboard and horseshoe facilities, picnic tables, barbecue pits and a little swimming lake with paddle boats and a tiny beach. A lifeguard is on duty during the summer, so you can leave your kids at the lake while you take in the sights of the southern Mother Lode.

WILLOW SPRINGS COUNTRY INN, 20599 Kings Court, Soulsbyville, California 95372. Telephone: (209) 533-2030. Accommodations: five bedrooms with double and queen-size beds; some private baths, some shared baths, tubs and showers; no telephones, no television. Rates: inexpensive to moderate, breakfast included, lower rates on week nights. Children welcome. Some pets allowed. No smoking. No cards. Open all year.

Getting There: From Sonora take Highway 108 east to Soulsbyville, turn right and then turn left on Kings Court just before the town.

Victorian Replica on an Old Dairy Ranch
OAK HILL RANCH
Tuolumne

On an oak-studded knoll, surrounded by the pine forests of the lower Sierra, stands a Victorian replica that few could distinguish from the real thing. Sanford Grover, a retired college counselor, and his wife Jane, a former schoolteacher, built the four-bedroom house in 1979 as a family home and then decided to turn it into an inn. Although the structure is new, designed by their architect son, the detailings—a mahogany fireplace, redwood doors, an intricate staircase and many of the moldings—were collected by the Grovers for twenty-five years from old houses throughout California and as far away as Canada. They also did all the stripping and refinishing themselves.

The furnishings are period pieces and include a stunning burled walnut secretary and an old pump organ in the living room and a dining room table that seats twenty. Here the Grovers, dressed in turn-of-the-century attire, serve a hearty breakfast, cooked by themselves in the house's spacious country kitchen. A typical meal might be melon, an omelet with bacon, and biscuits with homemade jelly. Other refreshments are offered when it's the gracious and natural thing to do: a cup of coffee or tea for arriving guests or a glass of wine if it's late in the day or a sip of sherry before retiring. "People who stay here are treated as our personal guests," Jane remarks. Two of the upstairs rooms share an adjoining bath, complete with an old claw-legged tub and brass shower rail. A third room, furnished with a canopied bed, opens to a private

Oak Hill Ranch

balcony and shares the downstairs bath with the Grovers. Down the hill from the main house is a small cottage which was once a milking barn for this fifty-five acre dairy ranch. The "cow palace," as it's known, has its own private living room with a large slate fireplace, a bedroom and complete kitchen. With a queen-size sofa bed in the living room and a roll-away bed, it will sleep five persons. Although Oak Hill Ranch is but fifteen minutes away from Sonora, this is peaceful countryside with the quiet broken only by the sounds of cows, roosters and crickets.

OAK HILL RANCH, 18550 Connally Lane (P.O. Box 307), Tuolumne, California 95379. Telephone: (209) 928-4717. Accommodations: three rooms with double or queen-size beds; two shared baths with tub/shower in main house; private bath and kitchen in cottage; no telephones; no television. Rates: inexpensive to moderate, full breakfast included. Children allowed in cottage only. No pets. No smoking. No cards.

Getting There: From Sonora take Highway 108 to Tuolumne Road. From there follow directions on map that will be sent to you when you make your reservations.

Hollywood's Favorite Old West Setting
JAMESTOWN

The gold rush came to Tuolumne County in 1848 when a seventy-five pound nugget was discovered in Woods Creek, which once flowed down Jamestown's Main Street. Hordes of prospectors swarmed to the area, among them Colonel George James, a Philadelphia lawyer and veteran of the Mexican War, who founded and later skipped the town, deeply in debt to suppliers and employees. So embittered were the local folk that they renamed the town American Camp, but the original name of Jamestown was soon revived and later it became a bustling railroad center. Today "Jimtown" is one of the most picturesque sights in the Mother Lode with the balconied facades of the old buildings overhanging raised wooden sidewalks. Movie fans will recognize the typical old west town as the site of *High Noon, Duel in the Sun* and *Butch Cassidy and the Sun Dance Kid*. Another hundred feature films were shot on the line of the Sierra Railway, whose steam-powered locomotives now pull trainloads of tourists through the oak-studded Sierra foothills. The railway depot is in Jamestown's Railtown 1897, now a State Historic Park with a twenty-six-acre roundhouse and shop complex where vintage rolling stock is exhibited. You can even pan for gold near Jamestown today; prospecting expeditions are conducted daily from the old livery stable on Main Street. And your nostalgic visit here is made complete by a stay in one of the town's restored hotels.

Getting There: From San Francisco, take 580 east to Tracy, then go east on 205 to Manteca; Highway 120 east to Highway 108 which leads east to Jamestown.

First and Finest of the Restored Hotels
JAMESTOWN HOTEL
Jamestown

In 1859 the two-story Jamestown Hotel was built and served as a center for the boom town's social life. During this century, a fire, years of neglect and even a stint as a hospital marked the hotel's course. Then in the late 1970s, the Sierra Railway (before it was owned by the state) restored the hotel, giving back its original flavor. In 1981 Larry Moblad, who had owned several hotels in the San Francisco Bay Area, bought the place and continued the improvements. Now there are eight accommodations, mostly suites with a sitting room or two bedrooms with gaily papered walls and antique furnishings. Brass bedsteads, wicker settees and patchwork quilts abound. A bridge leads from a second-floor solarium to a secluded deck.

Downstairs a handsome saloon with swinging etched-glass doors is open to the public as is the attractive dining room for lunch and dinner. In the morning a Continental breakfast of fresh fruit and rolls is served here for guests only. But they will probably want to return for other meals as well. The restaurant's menu is as ethnically eclectic as the miners who came to the Mother Lode. Chinese broccoli beef shares the menu with nachos, veal piccata and hearty steaks, while baskets of puffy hot sopapillas are served with all dinners. It's all delicious.

JAMESTOWN HOTEL, Main Street (P.O. Box 539), Jamestown, California 95327. Telephone: (209) 984-3902. Accommodations: eight units including four suites with sitting rooms and three two-bedroom suites; twin, double and queen-size beds; private baths, tub/showers or stall showers; no telephones; no television. Rates: moderate, Continental breakfast included. Restaurant open for lunch and dinner. Full bar service. Children welcome. No pets. Cards: AE, MC, VISA. Open all year.

Jamestown Hotel

A Ten-Year Restoration Project
NATIONAL HOTEL
Jamestown

The same year the Jamestown Hotel was built—1859—the National Hotel was erected just a half-block down Main Street. Owned by the Carbone family for nearly a century, the National has been continuously operated as a hotel except for a year in the mid-1920s when the old wooden structure was destroyed by fire and rebuilt in concrete. In 1974 the Willey brothers bought the place and, with Stephen Willey as resident manager, started a decade-long restoration which at this writing is not yet complete. With a shoestring budget, Steve did most of the construction work himself. "When we ran out of money, we stopped. When we got some more, we did more work." New plumbing, wiring and air-conditioning were first priorities and the "cosmetics" came last.

When they finally opened the eleven upstairs bedrooms to guests in 1982, many of the amenities like nightstands and reading lamps were missing, but they have been slowly added. "My employees would cheer every time I came in with a new piece of furniture," Steve recalls. "We still have several years to go, but are about ready for the added touches like paintings on the walls." Even without the frills the National is comfortable and clean with modern stall showers in the baths and new queen-size beds with brass steads.

In 1983 the Willeys completed one of the biggest projects: restoration of the facade and old front porch to match photos from the 1800s. Next on the agenda is rebuilding the wooden sidewalks and creating a reception area in the big downstairs saloon, which is resplendent with its massive original bar and an 1882 cash register. It's hard to predict what levels the improvements might reach in the next few years, except that they will go on with Stephen at the helm.

Plans are also underway for redecorating the two downstairs dining rooms which are open to the public for lunch and dinner, serving everything from "gazpacho to escargots." In the morning, hotel guests are served a Continental breakfast of fruit, bread and coffee—along with that morning's *Chronicle*—either in the dining room or under the adjacent hundred-year-old grape arbor: the one thing that's not changed at the National.

NATIONAL HOTEL, Main Street (P.O. Box 502), Jamestown, California 95327. Telephone: (209) 984-3446. Accommodations: eleven rooms with twin and queen-size beds; some private and some shared baths with stall shower, wash basins in rooms without private baths; no telephones; television available on request. Rates: inexpensive, Continental breakfast included. Full bar service. Children over eight welcome. Some pets allowed. Cards: MC, VISA. Open all year.

Queen Cities of the Northern Mines
NEVADA COUNTY
Nevada City and Grass Valley

At the peak of the gold rush Nevada City was the third largest town in California, with a population of twelve thousand. Today with only two thousand residents it's a much quieter place, except for a freeway that unfortunately cuts through its hilly streets. Despite a few misbegotten modern buildings, the town retains much of the character of an 1850s mining community, with picturesque gas lamps along the main street and many of the old buildings intact and restored. History buffs will find much of interest here. The American Victorian Museum, located in a former foundry, houses a collection of historical books, documents, photographs and old mining equipment. More history exhibits are mounted in the gingerbread-trimmed Firehouse No. 1 and at Ott's Assay Office, where the miners reportedly brought a booty of $27 million in ore over the years.

Five miles from Nevada City, in Grass Valley, California's richest mines once produced over $400 million in gold; a mining display with a thirty-one-foot waterwheel may still be viewed. Also open to the public are the homes of the infamous dancer Lola Montez and her young protégée, Lotta Crabtree, who later became nationally renowned as an actress. Four miles from Grass Valley is the semiabandoned town of Rough and Ready, which once tried to secede from the Union in protest of mining taxes.

This area is noted for a number of fine restaurants. Nearby lakes in the pine-forested mountains around the towns offer swimming and fishing. Good cross-country skiing is only twenty-five minutes away and the Sugar Bowl ski area is less than an hour's drive.

Getting There: From San Francisco take Highway 80 through Sacramento to Auburn. From here Highway 49 north leads to Grass Valley and Nevada City. From Reno take Highway 80 west to the intersection of Highway 20.

A Gothic Beauty Complete with Ghost

RED CASTLE INN
Nevada City

This heavily ornamented, four-story brick structure has been cited as one of the best examples of Gothic Revival in the West. The imposing house was built between 1858 and 1860 as a two-family residence by Judge John Williams, who crossed the plains in 1849 and became a prominent businessman, mine owner and civic leader in Nevada City. The judge's son and his family also occupied the house and, according to local lore, young Williams, a lawyer, used to serenade the townsfolk every Sunday afternoon from the top veranda of the Red Castle with impromptu recitals on the trumpet or cornet. Both Williamses, father and son, died before the turn of the century, and the judge's widow operated her home as a boardinghouse for a number of years. Then the house was sold and resold to a succession of owners, who allowed it to slowly decline.

In 1963 James Schaar restored the Red Castle and converted it into an inn. His wife managed it until 1978, when Jerry Ames, a former schoolteacher, and Chris Dickman, a department store display designer, bought the inn. They have redecorated most of the rooms with bright paint or floral wallpapers and an eclectic selection of furnishings. "We decided to make it comfortable rather than stiffly authentic," Jerry comments. They painted the walls of the elegant old parlor ochre and mixed some contemporary pieces—an overstuffed sofa—with a gilt-edged Victorian mirror, Oriental lamps and artifacts. Here and elsewhere in the inn the original pine plank floors and plaster ceiling moldings remain intact.

Eight bedrooms occupy four floors of the inn; all but two have private bathrooms in which old-fashioned wash basins remain, but new stall showers have been added. "I think quaintness should stop short of the bathroom," Jerry laughs. From the spacious, high-ceilinged rooms on the lower floor, lace-curtained French doors open out to the veranda. The middle floor contains "parlor suites," each composed of a tiny sitting room, with barely enough room for a love seat and a little cast-iron, wood-burning stove, and a bedroom almost entirely filled by a double bed. Two garret rooms on the top floor have Gothic windows and share a parlor, a bath and the balcony where Judge Williams's son conducted his concerts a century ago. From here and the lower verandas that surround the house, you look down on terraced, wooded

162

Red Castle Inn

gardens, and across to the picturesque town of Nevada City on the adjacent hillside.

In the mornings, when guests gather for coffee and home-baked breads in the parlor, Jerry likes to talk about the history of the house. "There really is not that much history, but like all old houses, it does have a ghost—supposedly the Williamses' governess—but I haven't met her het." Also in residence with Jerry and Chris are four cats, because, they explain, "Every Gothic building has to have a cat."

RED CASTLE INN, 109 Prospect, Nevada City, California 95959. Telephone: (916) 265-5135. Accommodations: eight rooms with double beds; six rooms have private baths with shower, two rooms share a bath; no telephones; no television. Rates: inexpensive to moderate, Continental breakfast included. Children discouraged. No pets. No cards. Open all year.

Getting There: From Highway 49 take Broad Street exit in Nevada City; turn right to Sacramento Street, turn right again and proceed up hill to first road on the left; make a hard left turn onto Prospect Street.

Genial Hospitality in a Gold Baron's Home
MURPHY'S INN
Grass Valley

Innkeeping is no change of lifestyle for Marc Murphy. His family has owned Murphy's Resort on the Russian River since 1902 and while in school he worked there every summer. After college he went into the real estate and construction business, but when the stately Edward Coleman house came on the market in 1982, he bought it for an inn. Coleman's fortune was derived from the famous North Star and Idaho mines, as well as railroad and timber interests, and in 1866 he built his house to last forever. "It was in excellent shape," Marc recalls, with the original chandeliers, wainscoting and fireplaces in mint condition. There were only three owners before Murphy and they cared for the house with pride.

Nevertheless, with a nod to modern comforts, Marc added private baths for all but one of the seven bedrooms; some with copious double-spigoted showers for two. Several of the bedrooms have tile or marble fireplaces, as does the handsome parlor where decanters of sherry and Courvoisier are set out for the guests to help themselves. After the inn

Murphy's Inn

had been open a year, Marc decided to serve a full breakfast, so he added an addition to house a big cheerful kitchen with dining area. Now he can chat with his guests as he whips up a hearty breakfast that often changes. A typical feast would be fresh fruits, eggs, sausage and hashed brown potatoes, one of his specialties.

Marc has arranged for his guests to have full privileges at the nearby Auburn Valley Country Club which has an eighteen-hole championship golf course; they need only to pay the green fee. He has also put together a wintertime ski package whereby his guests receive a $5 discount on lift tickets at Sugar Bowl, Monday through Friday, as well as $15 off their room rate at the inn.

MURPHY'S INN, 318 Neal Street, Grass Valley, California 95945. Telephone: (916) 273-6873. Accommodations: seven rooms with double, queen or king-size beds, rollaway cots available; six baths with stall shower or tub/shower; no telephones; no television; air conditioned. Rates: moderate, breakfast included. Children welcome. No pets (will recommend local kennels). Smoking discouraged. Cards: AE, MC, VISA. Open all year.

Getting There: From Highway 49 take Marysville/Colfax exit. Turn left on South Auburn, then left on Neal.

Restrained Elegance Near a Mountain Lake
MAYFIELD HOUSE
Tahoe City

High above the Mother Lode, cradled among the peaks of the Sierra Nevada, lies Lake Tahoe: one of the most beautiful lakes in the world and one of California's most popular year-round playgrounds. This two-hundred-square-mile body of blue water is ringed by sandy beaches and forests of pine, cedar, dogwood and aspen. Swimming, boating and waterskiing lure the summer visitors, while excellent skiing—Squaw Valley and Heavenly Valley, for example—attract the winter tourist. The lake is bisected by the California-Nevada border, and all year hordes of gamblers flock to the Nevada casinos, which also offer shows by big-name entertainers on a par with Las Vegas.

Far from the neon glitter of the casinos is the Mayfield House, on the edge of Tahoe City. This sturdy house was built of wood and stones among the pines in 1932 by Norman Mayfield, a contractor. A frequent guest was his good friend Julia Morgan, the architect responsible for the San Simeon castle of William Randolph Hearst. In 1980 the house was converted into an elegant little inn.

Impeccable taste and an eye for detail pervade the inn, from the classical taped music in the living room to the restful rosy-beige and blue color scheme throughout, to thoughtful touches such as providing bathrobes for guests. The living room, with its dark-stained pine paneling, beamed ceiling and large stone fireplace, is furnished with Early American pine tables, chairs and love seats upholstered in blue, kerosene-fired hurricane lamps and an assortment of books and games. The adjoining breakfast room sports a corner hutch and some of the African violet specimens that abound throughout the house. Here a full breakfast is served on pretty blue and white flowered English china: homemade goodies such as Finnish pancakes or Portuguese toast with fruit sauce or cheese blintzes with berry sauce. Or, if you prefer, you may have your breakfast served in your room.

All rooms are appointed with fresh flowers, a selection of books, down pillows and comforters, and original watercolors by Margaret Carpenter. Mullioned windows offer views of the mountains, woods or the golf course across the road. But each room has its distinctive decor. One of the downstairs rooms, the former den of Norman Mayfield, is wood-paneled and decorated with brown, beige and rust plaid drapes. By contrast, the upstairs room where Julia Morgan stayed is all frills, with a blue and white papered gabled ceiling, a white chenille spread and a skirted dressing table. Mayfield's former bedroom asserts its masculinity with paneled walls, a quilted brown velvet spread on the king-size bed and a sitting area with a brown leather couch and chairs.

From Mayfield House it's only a short walk to the beach for summer guests. In winter, skiing at Squaw Valley is about a fifteen-minute drive, but several smaller ski resorts are even closer. The casinos of Tahoe's North Shore can be reached in about fifteen minutes. And good restaurants are plentiful in the area.

MAYFIELD HOUSE, 236 Grove Street (P.O. Box 5999), Tahoe City, California 95730. Telephone: (916) 583-1001. Accommodations: six rooms with twin, queen- and king-size beds; three shared baths; no telephones; no television. Rates: moderate, breakfast included. No children under ten. No pets. Cards: MC, VISA. Open all year.

Getting There: From San Francisco or Reno take Highway 80 to Truckee, turn south on Highway 89 to Tahoe City, turn north on Highway 28 to Grove Street, turn left.

Living Like a Bonanza King
THE SAVAGE MANSION
Virginia City

Gold was found first here on the side of Mount Davidson, but the discovery of silver in 1859 was the big bonanza of the Comstock Lode, one of the richest ore deposits in the world. Over $300 million in precious metals was excavated within twenty years from the deep mines that still lie under the streets of Virginia City. This silver helped to finance the Civil War and to build the city of San Francisco. It also made millionaires of those who exploited the mines: James G. Fair, George Hearst, James Mackay, William Ralston and William Sharon to name a few.

In the 1860s and 1870s, Virginia City was queen of the West, second largest city this side of the Rockies, the richest boom town in America. Palatial mansions studded her barren hills. Extravagant entertaining was the order of the day (heaps of oyster shells and wine bottles still lie around the town). Fortunes in silver passed over the lusty bars of the Bucket of Blood and 109 other saloons. The most glamorous performers of the day played to bejeweled audiences at Piper's Opera House. And in 1872, a twenty-seven-year-old adventurer-prospector started writing of these lively events for the *Territorial Enterprise* under the pseudonym of Mark Twain.

Today only about seven hundred people live in Virginia City and their bonanza is tourism, with one-arm bandits in the old saloons reclaiming the lost silver. Around the town many of the old mansions stand freshly painted, proud of their new prosperity, and open for visitors who want to relive the colorful past.

One of the most splendid high-Victorian mansions to grace these hilly streets is the Savage Masnion. The Savage Mining Company only unearthed some $20 million in silver from its mine—a pittance compared with Consolidated Virginia's big bonanza of $105 million. Yet the Savage Mine made a mark on history as the breakthrough point of the famous tunnel that Adolph Sutro built through Mount Davidson, at a cost of $6,500,000, to drain and ventilate the Comstock mines.

The three-storied Savage Mansion with its mansard roof was built in 1861 to house the mining company's offices on the first floor and the superintendent's family on the upper levels. The house was magnificently furnished, even by the Comstock's opulent standards, and was used to entertain notables of the era. General Ulysses S. Grant was

The Savage Mansion

a guest for two days in 1879 and Thomas Edison spent time in the mansion as well.

After the Comstock's silver was depleted, the Savage Mansion deteriorated along with the rest of Virginia City. Before restoration began in 1960, it was deserted and a veritable wreck with shingles missing from the mansard roof, paint almost totally peeled away and the foundation partly disintegrated. Now in mint condition, with its original furnishings intact, the mansion is run as a bed and breakfast inn by owners Bob and Irene Kugler, who also reside here and conduct tours of the building.

Among the third-floor guest rooms is the one that was occupied by General Grant, furnished as it was then with floral wallpaper, a pot-bellied stove and an awesome bedstead that rises to ceiling height. One of the shared bathrooms retains the plumbing of the 1880s: a toilet with overhead tank and a six-foot-long copper tub. Recently the Kuglers have opened to guests a bridal suite on the second floor and offer use of the formal parlor for weddings. In the morning, coffee and rolls are served in the Victorian kitchen.

SAVAGE MANSION, South D Street, Virginia City, Nevada 89440. Telephone: (702) 847-0574. Accommodations: five rooms with double, two double or king-size beds; three shared baths with tub/shower; no telephones; no television. Rates: moderate, Continental breakfast included. Children discouraged. No pets. Cards: MC, VISA. Open all year.

Getting There: From San Francisco take Highway 580 east to Reno, Highway 395 south to Highway 17 which leads south to Virginia City. From Lake Tahoe, take Highway 50 east through Carson City and Highway 17 north through Gold Hill to Virginia City. Nearest airport: Reno.

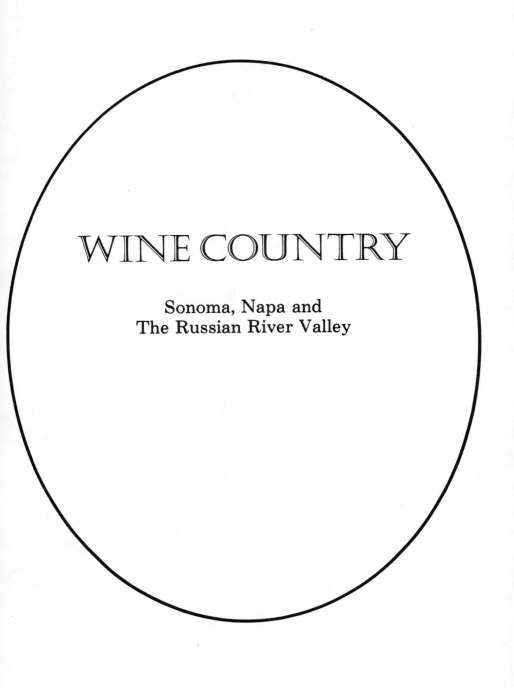

WINE COUNTRY

Sonoma, Napa and
The Russian River Valley

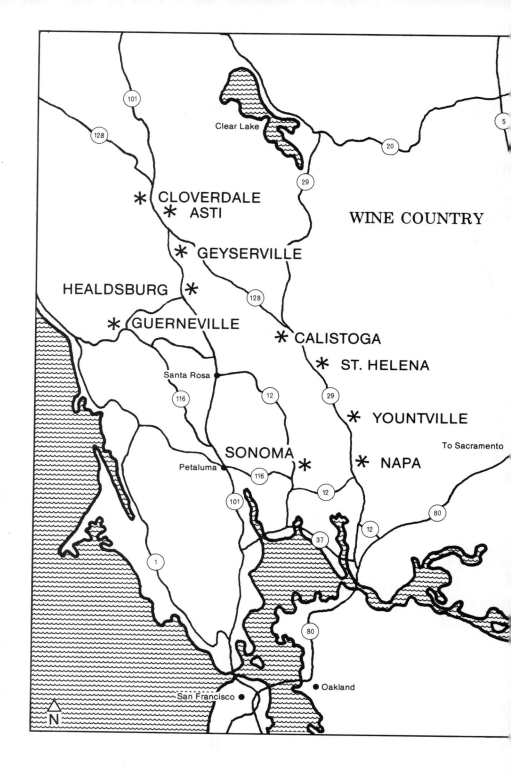

WINE COUNTRY

SONOMA

Sonoma's large tree-shaded plaza was laid out by General Mariano Guadalupe Vallejo in 1835 when he founded Pueblo de Sonoma as Mexico's most northerly outpost against hostile Indians. Twelve years earlier Mission San Francisco Solano de Sonoma had been built there as the northern tip of California's chain of missions. Vallejo built himself a two-story adobe *palacio* on the plaza where his regiment of Mexican soldiers marched daily. The peace was shattered on June 14, 1846, when a band of three dozen armed Americans, acting on their own authority, captured the town, imprisoned Vallejo, and proclaimed Sonoma capital of the Bear Flag Republic. The Bear Flag flew over the Sonoma plaza until the following month, when California became part of the United States.

Sonoma's second important settler after General Vallejo was Colonel Agoston Haraszthy, an Hungarian nobleman who planted his Buena Vista vineyards here in the 1850s and started northern California's winemaking industry. Sonoma has ever since been an important viticultural center. The Buena Vista's old stone cellars are open to the public. Tours are also conducted at the Sebastiani Winery, Hacienda Cellars, and twenty-nine other wineries in the area.

Sonoma is rich in Californiana. The Sonoma State Historic Park maintains the mission, General Vallejo's home and the Toscano Hotel, which are open to visitors. The old barracks, which has headquartered three armies—the Mexicans, the Bear Flag rebels and the Americans— has also been restored. Near Sonoma at Glen Ellen is the last home of Jack London, now also preserved as a state park.

Getting There: From San Francisco take Highway 101 north through San Rafael to Ignacio; there take Highway 37 east to Highway 21, which leads to Sonoma Plaza.

Overlooking the Historic Plaza
SONOMA HOTEL
Sonoma

At one corner of Sonoma's plaza is a three-story hotel. No one knows for certain when the hotel was built, but the lower two stories are probably a century-year-old adobe. The third floor with its high gables was added at a later date circa 1880, when the building housed a dry goods store on the first level and a two-story meeting hall above. About 1920 it was purchased by the winemaking Sebastiani family, who converted the cavernous hall into two floors, partitioned these into seventeen rooms and rechristened it the Plaza Hotel. In 1974 John and Dorene Musilli bought the hotel and redecorated it with antiques. "There's not one reproduction in the place," Dorene points out.

Sixteen of the rooms are furnished with French and English bedroom sets made at the turn of the century. In each room nearly all the pieces match—dresser, armoire, headboard, even chairs. Mattresses were custom-made to fit the odd-size beds, which were covered with quilted flowered spreads. Ruffled organdy curtains and a watering can full of dried flowers and grasses add a homey note to each room.

The seventeenth room has been named the Vallejo Room in honor of the Italianate hand-carved burled walnut furniture that belonged to General Vallejo's sister and is on loan to the hotel from the Sonoma League for Historic Preservation. The bed looks fit for the general himself, with an eleven-foot-high backboard and a bedspread of scarlet velvet.

The Musillis stripped eight coats of paint off the wainscoting in the hotel lobby to reveal the natural dark fir. Here, in front of a large stone fireplace, guests are served a Continental breakfast of juice, croissants from a nearby French bakery, and a choice of teas, coffee or hot chocolate. In 1982 the hotel's bar and restaurant was reopened and refurbished with antiques. In a town already noted for its many fine restaurants, the Sonoma Hotel is winning rave reviews.

SONOMA HOTEL, 110 West Spain Street, Sonoma, California 95476. Telephone: (707) 996-2996. Accommodations: seventeen rooms with twin and double beds; some private baths with tub, community baths with showers; no telephones; no television. Rates: moderate, Continental breakfast included. Restaurant open to the public for lunch and dinner Friday through Tuesday; full bar. Children welcome. No pets. Cards: AE, MC, VISA. Open all year.

Sonoma Hotel

VICTORIAN GARDEN INN
Sonoma

In the 1860s Sonoma was a tranquil town surrounded by prosperous farms and proud houses which relied on enclosed two-story towers topped by windmills for their water supply. In 1983 interior designer Donna Lewis transformed one of these farmhouses into a most romantic and sophisticated inn. The farm lands are long gone and subdivided, but nearly an acre of lush gardens and fruit trees remain, as does the old water tower (now *sans* windmill) which Donna has turned into three charming guest rooms. The top room has ten-foot ceilings and is decorated with a riot of blue and white Marimekko patterns: wallpaper, quilted spread, sheets, shower curtain and even the fabric gathered into shutter frames at the windows all match. For one of the downstairs rooms, Donna has chosen a pink and peach Laura Ashley print for the papers and fabric. In the other lower room a salmon and forest green floral pattern prevails. This room, the biggest and the best, boasts a brick wood-burning fireplace, high knotty-pine ceilings and redwood wainscoting. A forest green sofa assures comfortable seating here, as do wicker chairs in the other rooms.

Just a few steps away from the water tower, separated by a deck and grape arbor, is the old farmhouse with one guest room upstairs. Downstairs in the large living room, decorated in restful tones of beige, Donna offers her guests a nip of wine or sherry before a cheery fire. In the mornings a Continental breakfast is offered in the sunny, plant-filled dining area. Or, if you wish, wicker trays are available to carry your juice, fruit, coffee and rolls to one of the many tables out on the deck and gardens.

The Victorian Garden Inn offers nineteenth-century pastimes such as strolling in the gardens and playing lawn croquet. But it also offers a twentieth-century treat: a dip in the lovely swimming pool behind the house.

VICTORIAN GARDEN INN, 316 East Napa Street, Sonoma, California 95476. Telephone: (707) 996-5339. Accommodations: four rooms with double or queen-size beds and electric blankets; water tower rooms have private baths with shower or tub/shower, one room in main house shares bath with tub/shower; no telephones; no television. Rates: moderate to expensive, Continental breakfast included. No children. No pets. Cards: AE, MC, VISA. Open all year.

Victorian Garden Inn

In the Style of 1910 California

THISTLE DEW INN

Sonoma

Restful, serene and understated are the first words that come to mind when describing this newly opened inn. Located in two single-story cottages just a few doors off the Sonoma Plaza, the Thistle Dew's simple, uncluttered decor in the style of 1910 California is a welcome change from the full-blown Victoriana that has almost become an innkeeping cliché. In the front house, which faces the street, soft classical music fills the air of the living room, where on chilly days a fire burns in a stove set on a brick hearth. Here, as throughout the inn, the walls are white, the fabrics are oatmeal, the carpeting is dark grey and the oak furnishings are of the simple mission style. The spacious dining room houses a long table and buffet where, for breakfast, four or five items are set out, including cheeses and pastries from local shops. Sherries from nearby Sebastiani winery await the guests' evening pleasure. Two bedrooms in this front house share a bath.

An arbor, garden and flagstone terrace separate the front house from the rear one, which also has a small sitting room with a round oak table and brick fireplace. This room is liberally stocked with paperback books, games and puzzles and opens to a wide wooden deck in the rear. Two of the bedrooms in the rear house have private baths; the other two share a bath. Thistle Dew Inn is owned by Jon and Jackie Early who also rent out a country cottage on their property one and one-half miles away.

THISTLE DEW INN, 171 West Spain Street, (P.O. Box 1326), Sonoma, California 95476. Telephone: (707) 938-2909. Accommodations: queen-size and bunk beds; two rooms with private baths, four rooms with washbasins in room and shared baths, stall showers, one bath with tub; television and telephones installed if requested. Children not encouraged. No pets. No smoking. Cards: AE, MC, VISA. Open all year.

Thistle Dew Inn

NAPA VALLEY

This lovely long valley, caressed by gentle mountains, is one of the world's most important winemaking regions. The Franciscan fathers from nearby Sonoma Mission started making wine here in the 1820s, but it was an inferior wine made from their Mission grapes. It was not until some thirty years later, in 1858, that Charles Krug produced the first European-type wine for which the valley is now known. After Colonel Agoston Haraszthy proved that the European *vinifera* grapes would thrive north of San Francisco Bay in his Buena Vista vineyards in Sonoma, French, Italian and German immigrants flocked to the Napa Valley in the 1860s, planting cuttings from Haraszthy's stock.

This viniferous valley stretches north from the city of Napa, an early timber-shipping center and once even a mining town during a silver rush in 1858. The valley ends at the town of Calistoga, whose mineral spas have attracted the weary since Mormon settler Sam Brannan first discovered underground hot springs here in 1859. Towering above Calistoga is the forty-five-hundred foot peak of Mount St. Helena, which Robert Louis Stevenson described as the "Mont Blanc of the Coast Range" after spending his honeymoon in a bunkhouse at the mountain's base in 1880.

One of the most interesting settlements in the valley is Yountville, named after the valley's first white settler, George Yount. In exchange for a favor to his friend, General Vallejo, the Mexican government granted Yount an eleven-thousand–acre tract of land comprising most of the Napa Valley. The old Groezinger Winery in Yountville has been converted to a fascinating complex of shops, galleries and restaurants called Vintage 1870. Next door the train depot and railroad cars house yet more shops. And along the town's picturesque streets there are antique shops, restaurants—and a growing number of country inns.

North of Yountville is Rutherford Square, where outdoor musical productions are presented in the summer months. Just north of here is St. Helena, where a museum containing Robert Louis Stevenson memorabilia is housed in a stone hatchery. Beyond the town is an old grist mill with a waterwheel forty feet in diameter, and Freemark Abbey, another interesting complex of shops.

All through the valley, of course, are the wineries, most of which conduct tours of their cellars and tastings of their bottlings. This is unquestionably the most popular form of recreation in the valley. Space does not permit a description of all the wineries, but one stands out as spectacular over all the others. This is Sterling Vineyards, a recently built Moorish structure on a hilltop in the center of the valley between St. Helena and Calistoga. An aerial tramway whisks visitors to the winery over treetops. Inside, the winemaking operation is explained graphically, allowing visitors to tour the premises at their own pace. Afterwards, sipping wine in the late afternoon on the terrace as the mountains cast their shadows onto the vineyards below is an experience long remembered.

Other forms of recreation in the Napa Valley include aerial gliding and ballooning around Calistoga, and swimming, fishing and boating at nearby Lake Berryessa. The valley also offers a diversity of dining experiences, in settings both elegant and casual: French haute cuisine, nouvelle cuisine and country cooking; Mexican, Italian and Chinese. From a culinary point of view, the Napa Valley has truly come of age.

Getting There: From San Francisco take Highway 101 north through San Rafael to Ignacio; there take Highway 37 east to Highway 21 north to the intersection of Highway 12 which leads east to Napa. From Napa Highway 29 extends north through Yountville, Rutherford and St. Helena to Calistoga.

Country Elegance in a Historic House
LA RESIDENCE
Napa

One of Napa Valley's early settlers was Harry C. Parker, a New Orleans river pilot who came to California during the 1849 gold rush. After working as a merchant in San Francisco and Stockton, he took up farming in Napa and in 1870 built himself a handsome three-story house just north of town. This is no ordinary farmhouse. It is built in the Gothic Revival style, with a columned porch and balcony onto which the large front bedrooms open. Marble or brick fireplaces enhance many of the rooms.

In 1981 Barbara Littenberg transformed the historic house into a charming inn decorated in the style of a nineteenth-century country house with antique armoires, sofas and queen-size replicas of brass and cast-iron beds covered with quilted eyelet or floral spreads. Two years later she constructed a two-story barn behind the house, covered with rustic shingles and cupolas outside, but containing eight comfortable guest rooms within, all with fireplaces, sitting areas and private baths.

181

The furnishings here are English country pine and oak pieces combined with flowered fabrics from France.

She also included a commercial kitchen and dining facilities in the barn, so now you need not leave La Residence in the evening. After a day of wine touring you can enjoy a dip in the hot tub by the flower-filled rear patio, relax with a glass of wine and pâté in the pretty parlor of the main house and then stroll over to the barn for dinner prepared by a professional chef.

LA RESIDENCE, 4066 St. Helena Highway North (Highway 29), Napa, California 94558. Telephone: (707) 253-0337. Accommodations: seven rooms in main house with queen-size beds; private or shared baths with tub/shower; wheelchair access to some rooms, eight rooms in barn with private baths and stall showers; no telephones; no television. Rates: moderate to expensive, Continental breakfast included. No children. No pets. Cards: AE, MC, VISA. Open all year.

Getting There: Take Highway 29 beyond Napa and past Salvador Road; turn right at Bon Appetit Restaurant, where a sign will direct you to the inn, which faces the highway.

True to its Vintage
MAGNOLIA HOTEL
Yountville

Built in 1873 with large stones from the Silverado Trail, this small
three-story hotel has had a checkered history. Originally a traveler paid
a dollar a night for a room, including a barn and feed for his horse. Those
who could afford the luxury of rail travel were met at the Yountville
depot by a surrey sent by the hotel. At one time the Magnolia was
reputedly a brothel, and it is known fact that the cellar was a center for
bootlegging activities during Prohibition. Then for many years the
hotel was boarded up until Ray and Nancy Monte purchased it in 1968
and restored it to an inn of eminent charm and respectability. In 1977
the Magnolia was again sold, to Bruce Locken, former general manager
of the Clift Hotel in San Francisco, and his wife Bonnie. They have
continued the improvement process, adding four luxurious new rooms
with decks and fireplaces in an adjoining building.

Furnishings are from the Victorian era: marble-topped tables with
crystal decanters of port in the bedrooms, antique brass or wooden
bedsteads with crocheted or quilted spreads and everywhere dozens of
handmade dolls and pillows which Bonnie has collected over the years.
Concessions to twentieth-century living have been made, however, with
private tiled baths throughout. Many of the rooms have splendid views
of the vineyards across the road.

Breakfast here, announced by the ringing of a gong at precisely
nine o'clock, is an important event at the Magnolia. Guests gather
around in the restaurant adjoining the hotel, introduce themselves and
share wine-touring tips. Bruce, a skilled raconteur, moves around the
table, telling anecdotes from several decades of hotelkeeping while
replenishing the coffee pot and serving generous platters of food. The
Lockens' system of devising the menu is unique: First-nighters are
served French toast with port-wine syrup, second-nighters get shirred
eggs, third-nighters receive a sherry and mushroom omelet, and so on,
so that no one has the same breakfast two mornings in a row. For a while
Bonnie, a talented cook, opened the restaurant to the public and earned
the Magnolia a few Holiday Travel Awards. Now the Lockens only serve
dinner occasionally or for private parties.

The Magnolia Hotel has several other attractions not offered by
other inns in the Napa Valley. There is a large swimming pool
surrounded by lawns. Here—or in your room if you like—Bruce will

serve you a bottle purchased from his fine collection of Napa wines. And behind the hotel, set in an enclosed redwood deck, is a commodious Jacuzzi pool, which is lighted from under the water at night.

MAGNOLIA HOTEL, 6529 Yount Street, Yountville, California 94599. Telephone: (707) 944-2056. Accommodations: eleven rooms with twin, double, queen- and king-size beds; private baths with shower only; no telephones; no television. Rates: moderate to very expensive, breakfast included. No children under sixteen. No pets. No cards. No smoking. Open all year.

Nineteenth-Century Vintner's Mansion
CHALET BERNENSIS
St. Helena

In 1884 Swiss wine maker John Thoman built a handsome Victorian home for his family next door to his winery in St. Helena. Later the winery and the home were purchased by John Sutter (a relative of the John Sutter on whose land gold was first discovered in California). Today the Trinchero family owns the Sutter Home Winery, while Jack and Essie Doty operate the old Thoman mansion as an inn. When the Dotys first bought the place in 1973, they started an antique shop in the downstairs rooms and later rented the upstairs bedrooms. But as the innkeeping business began to boom in the late 1970s, the sale of antiques took second place, and the lower sitting room with a fireplace and a dining hall became pretty much for their guests' exclusive use. A breakfast of scones, muffins, fruit and juices is served here in the mornings; sherry, coffee and cookies are served in the evening.

The five upstairs bedrooms are small and cozy, furnished with antiques, floral papers, quilted spreads and Oriental rugs. Because old photographs of the Thoman-Sutter house showed an adjacent three-story water tower that no longer existed, in 1979 the Dotys constructed a replica of the tower containing four additional guest rooms. These have fireplaces with old mantels, and private baths.

Chalet Bernensis is surrounded by lovely grounds, planted with roses, palms and beds of ivy. It is a perfect place to picnic, and picnic tables are provided.

CHALET BERNENSIS, 225 St. Helena Highway (Highway 29), St. Helena, California 94574. Telephone: (707) 963-4423. Accommodations: nine rooms with double or queen-size beds; bedrooms in house share two baths, one with tub; private baths with tub or shower in water tower, also air conditioning; no telephones; no television. Rates: moderate, Continental breakfast included. No children. No pets. Smoking discouraged. Cards: MC, VISA. Open all year.

New Life for a Century-Old Hotel
HOTEL ST. HELENA
St. Helena

In 1881, while the Beringers and Krugs were busy expanding their wineries, an elegant two-story hotel opened on St. Helena's Main Street. But as the wineries flourished, the hotel deteriorated, its rooms eventually little better than flophouses, its lower floor occupied by a branch of Montgomery Ward. Almost a century later Santa Barbara developer Carl Johnson bought the hotel and restored it to a degree of luxury it had probably never known before.

Downstairs, shops and a restaurant open onto a flower-filled arcade. Upstairs, a lounge and eighteen guest rooms have been skillfully decorated by Tom Brooks and Linda Daniels, who combined antiques with modern comforts. The hall is papered with a striped and floral pattern of burgundy, tan and brown—setting the color scheme for all the rooms. In the sitting room at the top of the stairs, love seats upholstered in burgundy velvet flank a fireplace; a beautiful old wooden sideboard is set with coffee, tea and fruit breads in the morning. The bedrooms are painted in colors of burgundy, mauve, chocolate brown, dark tan or pale gold; patterned quilted bedspreads and dust ruffles echo these hues. The larger rooms have headboards of brass or carved wood, armoires, lounge chairs and round, cloth-covered tables. The smaller rooms have painted iron headboards and ladderback chairs. Four rooms without private baths have bent-willow headboards and marble-topped commodes with baskets of fresh towels and soap. There's also a suite with a sitting room. All the rooms are richly carpeted; windows are shuttered in white throughout. At the rear of the hotel, overlooking the arcade, is a wide deck with chaises and tables: a restful spot to relax before or after a day of winery touring.

HOTEL ST. HELENA, 1309 Main Street (Highway 29), St. Helena, California 94574. Telephone: (707) 963-4388. Accommodations: eighteen rooms with twin or queen-size beds; fourteen rooms have private baths with stall shower or tub/shower; four rooms share two baths; no telephones; no television. Rates: moderate to expensive, Continental breakfast included. No children. No pets. Cards: MC, VISA. Open all year.

Hotel St. Helena

A Dream Come True
WINE COUNTRY INN
St. Helena

Ned and Marge Smith had long dreamed of opening an inn in the wine country. For several years they spent vacations touring the inns of New England to get ideas and advice. One warning they heeded: "Don't restore an old building, build a new one. There will be fewer headaches and more comforts." The Wine Country Inn, though constructed in 1975, looks as though it has been sitting on its hillock surrounded by vineyards forever. That's the way they wanted it to look. The three-story stone and wood structure with dormered windows and a gabled tower is a composite of ideas borrowed from historic buildings in the valley. Several years later the Smiths added two smaller buildings nearby.

Comfort is the key word here. All rooms are carpeted and have modern baths. The furnishings are antique, from a potpourri of periods, but the old four-poster beds have been widened to queen-size and the brass-framed doubles elongated. The rooms are papered with a floral motif and each is different, but romantic in its own way. Fifteen of the rooms have freestanding fireplaces, seven have patios landscaped for privacy, and twelve have intimate balconies. Some have window seats in alcoves with views of the surrounding countryside.

On the ground floor of the main building is a large, homey common room, equipped with card tables and books on wine. Here in the mornings, at a long refectory table, a Continental breakfast is served of fresh fruits and juices, assorted hot breads and coffee. On warmer days this repast is served on a deck outside.

WINE COUNTRY INN, 1152 Lodi Lane, St. Helena, California 94574. Telephone: (707) 963-7077. Accommodations: twenty-five rooms with twin, double or queen-size beds; private baths, some with tub/shower, some shower only, seven rooms with wheelchair access; no telephones; no television. Rates: expensive, Continental breakfast included. No children under 12. No pets. Cards: MC, VISA. Open all year.

Getting There: From Napa take Highway 29 two miles past St. Helena and turn right on Lodi Lane.

Wine Country Inn

Bedecked with Literary Allusions
BALE MILL INN
St. Helena

North of the town of St. Helena lies Bale Gristmill State Historic Park where a gigantic undershot water wheel next to the highway has long been a valley landmark. Built in the nineteenth century by Dr. Edward Bale to grind the grain of Napa settlers, the mill later became a county picnic ground and fell into disrepair. In 1972 the State of California took over and rebuilt the mill, and the plans are to have the huge wheel turning once again.

Just beyond the mill a two-story roadside structure—originally a railway freight depot and later a tavern—advertises lodgings and antiques for sale. One would never expect to find a charming country inn above the antique store, especially upon entering and climbing the narrow stairs to the second-floor living quarters. But once there— surprise! French doors open from a sun-splashed parlor to a wide deck outfitted with upholstered chaises, an umbrella-topped table and an ancient carriage filled with potted marigolds. The adjacent hillside, banked with clumps of yellow daisies, stretches upwards through an acre of wooded land to a trail that connects the three hundred acres of the Bale Gristmill Park with the Bothe-Napa Valley State Park. Truly a hiker's paradise in the inn's back yard.

But it is not only this sylvan setting that lures guests to the Bale Mill Inn. One of the big attractions is owner Tom Scheibal's collection of authentic antiques—no reproductions here! Each morning he bakes goodies like hot cinnamon bread and almond crescents in a 1906 cast-iron cook stove in the parlor which also contains black wing wicker chairs and a marble baker's table. The bedrooms are decorated according to their namesakes. A Spanish-American war canteen and an African safari helmet are among the memorabilia in the Hemingway room. The Teddy Roosevelt room is bedecked with crossed forty-six-star flags and a large walking stick that inspired one visitor to quip: "Snore softly and sleep with a big stick." Tom has also dedicated rooms to Emily Dickinson (furnished with white wickerware like a New England summer porch), Jack London (featuring old hickory camp furniture) and Captain Quinn (embellished with nautical motifs).

All rooms have overhead fans and four open to private balconies. The baths, however, are not private. Guests share a full bathroom with a claw-legged tub upstairs and a toilet and stall shower located off the entry, one flight down from the bedrooms. Another disadvantage to this otherwise delightful inn is the noise from the highway just a few yards away. Tom, however, is soundproofing these front rooms with double-glazed glass.

BALE MILL INN, 3431 North St. Helena Highway, St. Helena, California 94574. Telephone: (707) 963-4545. Accommodations: five rooms with double beds; two community baths, one with tub, one with stall shower; no telephones; no television. Rates: moderate, Continental breakfast included. Children over ten welcome. No pets. Cards: MC, VISA. Open all year.

Gracious Living in the Vineyards
LARKMEAD COUNTRY INN
Calistoga

Lillie Coit is best known for her devotion to San Francisco's firemen and for the monument she had built for them on Telegraph Hill: Coit Tower. Few people connect her with wine history, but she owned the Larkmead Vineyards south of Calistoga in the 1880s. A later owner was Swiss-born Felix Salmina, who in 1918 built for his son and daughter-in-law a sprawling clapboard Victorian in the middle of his vineyards. The Hans Kornell winery, whose champagne cellars are next door, now owns the grape lands. Gene and Joan Garbarino bought the lovely old house for a second residence and then decided in 1979 to run it as a country inn.

Through fieldstone gates the driveway leads to a wisteria-covered loggia in the rear of the house. Up some stairs is the gracious living room appointed with a Persian carpet, antiques that the Garbarinos have collected in their European travels and a well-stocked library. A fire burns on the hearth evenings and mornings when guests gather for breakfast in the adjoining dining room. The table, which seats ten, is elegantly set with sterling silver and peony-patterned porcelain plates on which Joan artfully arranges grapes and slices of watermelon, oranges, pears, peaches and kiwis—whatever is in season. Then individual baskets of croissants, scones and French rolls are served with crocks of sweet butter and freshly ground coffee.

European etchings and oil paintings grace the dining and living rooms, as well as the four bedrooms. These are named after various wines and command spectacular views of the vineyards. Chablis, dressed up in muted green tones, features an enclosed sun porch off the bedroom, while Beaujolais has private use of the open porch over the loggia. Chenin Blanc is feminine and flowery with draperies, wallpaper and a chaise covered in matching patterns. And Chardonnay has an Art Deco look, with old brass bedsteads that came from a Parisian hotel. Fresh flowers and a decanter of wine are placed in all the rooms.

The Larkmead Inn is surrounded by wide verandas and lawns shaded by sycamores, magnolias and cypress. It's a peaceful haven you will be reluctant to leave. But you don't have to go far for wine touring. Just walk next door to the winery, where Hans Kornell himself or members of his family will explain in detail the process of making bottle-fermented champagnes.

LARKMEAD COUNTRY INN, 1103 Larkmead Lane, Calistoga, California 94515. Telephone: (707) 942-5360. Accommodations: four rooms with twin or double beds; private baths with stall showers; air conditioning; no telephones; no television. Rates: expensive. Continental breakfast included. No children. No pets. No cards. Open all year.

Getting There: Take Highway 29, and north of St. Helena turn right on Larkmead Lane.

A Small, Homey Place
WINE WAY INN
Calistoga

Once a sleepy, slightly run-down resort town, Calistoga is now a lively community with restored hotels, shops and restaurants lining its quaint main street. On the edge of town, at the base of a forested mountainside, is the Wine Way Inn. Built in 1915 as a private residence, the small house still retains a homey feeling, reinforced by the warm hospitality of innkeepers Allen and Dede Good who have owned the place since 1980. A glass of chilled white wine is offered to newly arrived guests who can sit and unwind on the huge overstuffed couch in front of the fireplace in the fir-paneled living-dining area. The rear wall here is entirely covered with cupboards, their leaded glass doors revealing a fine collection of silver, china and pewter. Round breakfast tables are covered with brown and blue checkered cloths, blue underskirts and surrounded by ladderback chairs. Café curtains are at the windows. The morning meal—a choice of three or four breads and pastries, plus orange juice and fruit—is served here or on the immense deck behind the house. Furnished with picnic tables and chaises, this is a great place to relax and stare at the mountain above. Now covered with redwoods and maples, the terraced slopes were once vineyards, the second oldest in the area.

Upstairs, the five bedrooms are small and pretty with gabled ceilings, antiques, and beds covered with heirloom patchwork quilts

that range in age from seventy-five to a hundred years. In the rear a tiny cottage, once a carriage house, with half-timbered walls and a private porch, nestles among the trees.

WINE WAY INN, 1019 Foothill Boulevard (Highway 29), Calistoga, California 94515. Telephone: (707) 942-0680. Accommodations: five rooms with twin, double or queen-size beds; three rooms and cottage have private baths with stall shower; two rooms share bath with tub/shower; no telephones; no television; air-conditioned. Rates: moderate, Continental breakfast included. No children. No pets. Cards: MC, VISA. Open all year.

Vineyards to Rival Nearby Napa
RUSSIAN RIVER VALLEY
From Cloverdale to Guerneville

From its origin in Mendocino County, the Russian River winds over two hundred miles through the lush vineyards of northern Sonoma County and through the redwood-forested coastal mountains to the Pacific. The first settlers here engaged in agriculture and lumber, but in the last quarter of the nineteenth century vineyards began to appear, from Guerneville in the south, where the Korbel cellars were established in 1886, to Cloverdale in the north, home of Italian Swiss Colony since 1887. Until very recently, however, most of the other wineries in this region produced mostly inexpensive wines. Then in the late 1960s, at the peak of California's wine boom, wine makers began to realize that the climate and soil of this area were capable of producing premium grapes to rival those of nearby Napa—particularly in the Alexander and Dry Creek valleys. Today twenty-seven wineries are bottling varietal wines from the vineyards alongside the Russian River, among them such prestigious names as Davis Bynum, Simi, Trentadue and Dry Creek. Many have tasting rooms, winery tours, and picnic areas. (Specific information on these wineries, a map showing their locations, and schedules of forthcoming special events such as fairs, musicals, art shows and barrel tastings, can be obtained from The Russian River Wine Road, P.O. Box 127, Geyserville, California 95441.) The advent of the premium grape in the Russian River Valley was followed inevitably by the appearance of country inns in the river towns from Cloverdale to Guerneville.

Getting There: From San Francisco, Highway 101 passes through Healdsburg, Geyserville and Cloverdale. Guerneville is reached by taking River Road west, just north of Santa Rosa. From the Napa Valley, Highway 29 leads from Calistoga to Geyserville.

Triple-Towered Queen Anne
VINTAGE TOWERS
Cloverdale

At the turn of the century Simon Pinschower, a wealthy merchant, built himself a twenty-room Queen Anne towered Victorian on a quiet side street of Cloverdale. In 1913 two more towers were added. When Tom and Judy Haworth turned the stately old mansion into an inn in 1980, they named it after the three vintage towers: one round, one square and one octagonal. These tower suites are now the choicest of the inn's seven charming guest rooms. And the pick of the lot is Calico Tower, where a spiral staircase winds up to a private balcony. Carousel Tower beguiles with bright colors, circus posters, a children's merry-go-round horse in the corner, and a love seat, upholstered in a tiger print, made from a baby's crib. Wicker Tower lives up to its name with all wicker furniture: headboards on the bed, a love seat and chaise in the fern-bedecked tower area.

The spacious downstairs rooms promise a paradise for readers. Tom Haworth has been collecting books since his childhood, and his library contains fifteen hundred old and rare volumes, mostly concerned with history. But music lovers will be happy here too. There are a piano and a "piano player," a device that is set on the keyboard to bang out tunes from Tom's large collection of player-piano rolls. Nearby an old-fashioned Victrola is stocked with several hundred records.

The wood-paneled dining room has a fireplace and windows looking out to the lawn and rose gardens. Judy serves a hearty breakfast here: perhaps a frittata, with fresh melon and blueberry muffins, or a poached egg on corned-beef hash with dill sauce. On nice mornings guests may breakfast on the wide veranda, where wine is also served on balmy evenings. Across from the veranda is Tom's pride and joy: a gazebo he built himself, in which he occasionally stages concerts for guests and townspeople and which is also a lovely site for weddings.

As if there weren't enough to do in the inn itself and in the surrounding wine country, Vintage Towers provides some very special diversions. Bicycles are available for exploring the town and countryside

195

and the inn's limousine is also available for wine tours. And when time permits, Tom likes to take his guests white-water tubing or rafting on the Russian River or sailing in his boat on Lake Mendocino, some thirty-five minutes away.

VINTAGE TOWERS, 302 North Main Street, Cloverdale, California 95425. Telephone: (707) 894-4535. Accommodations: seven rooms with king-size and four with double beds; private baths with tub, others share bath with tub/shower; no telephones; no television; air-conditioning. Rates: inexpensive to moderate, breakfast included. No children under ten. No pets. No smoking. Cards: MC, VISA.

Getting There: From San Francisco take Highway 101 north to the first stop light in Cloverdale; turn right for one block; then turn left on Main Street.

Turn-of-the-Century Summer Home
THE OLD CROCKER INN
Asti

Henry J. Crocker, a nephew of railroad tycoon Charles Crocker, was president of the West Coast Life Insurance Company and had a serious interest in grape cultivation. In 1897 he built a rustic summer home in the wooded hills above the Russian River wine country. The living room and five bedrooms opened to a small courtyard where Crocker installed the first swimming pool in Sonoma County. A wide veranda encircled the house, offering spectacular views of the Asti vineyards where, at the turn of the century, Pietro Rossi was winning medals throughout Europe and America for his Italian Swiss Colony wines. In 1933 the Crocker heirs sold the property which over the years has been used as a dude ranch, a spa and eventually a restaurant.

Then in 1982 Edward Lyons, former sales manager of the Claremont Hotel in Berkeley, and his wife Deborah bought the old lodge for an inn along with five acres of the surrounding oak and redwood covered hillsides. From the front veranda you enter the oak-paneled living room where an immense brick fireplace soars up to the twelve-foot high ceilings. The adjoining common room is paneled with koa wood and beyond is a curved veranda, now glassed in to shelter a row of koa tables where a Continental breakfast, embellished with eggs or quiche, is served. The dining area is a legacy of the former restaurant,

The Old Crocker Inn

as is a fully equipped commercial kitchen—a boon to the Lyons, for they often hire caterers to provide dinner for their guests or food for small conferences and wedding receptions.

In the bedrooms of the main house, the high wooden ceilings and board-and-batten walls are painted a sparkling white, the wainscotings are papered with a floral chintz and furnishings are simple antiques befitting the woodsy setting. French doors lead to the old veranda. Housed in adjacent outbuildings are four other guest rooms, paneled in redwood car siding, one of which has a wood-burning stove. Across a wide lawn is a little cottage with a bedroom and sitting room. Near the cottage a modern swimming pool has been added to replace Crocker's original pool, which is now covered with a wooden deck.

Besides swimming, there is plenty to do at Old Crocker Inn such as croquet, badminton and hiking in the hills. You'll probably want to check out the wines at nearby Italian Swiss Colony too, as Crocker presumably did in his day—although he wouldn't recognize the place now: Costumed guides conduct daily tours for nearly one-half million visitors a year, supposedly the world's record for wine tourism!

THE OLD CROCKER INN, 1116 Palamino Road, Cloverdale, California 95425. Telephone: (707) 894-3911. Accommodations: ten rooms with queen-size beds; private baths with tub or shower; no television; no telephones. Rates: moderate, breakfast included. Dinner for a minimum party of ten by prior arrangement. Children permitted in cottage only. No pets. Cards: MC, VISA. Open all year.

Getting There: During the summer months only take Highway 101 to the Canyon Road exit south of Cloverdale. Go north on Asti Road to Washington School Road and turn right. After crossing the river, the road turns north and becomes River Road. Turn right on the road leading to the KOA campground; the inn is a mile beyond the campground. During other months of the year or if you are coming from the north, turn off 101 at First Street in Cloverdale; head east across the river and River Road branches to the south. Continue down River Road to the KOA Campground sign.

In Celebration of Victoriana
HOPE-MERRILL HOUSE
HOPE-BOSWORTH HOUSE
Geyserville

For six years Bob and Rosalie Hope operated a resort in Guerneville while Rosalie pursued with a passion her hobby of collecting Victoriana. Then in 1980, when the Hopes moved up the Russian River to the tiny town of Geyserville, her avocation became an important asset in their new vocation: They converted two Victorian houses to inns and restored and furnished them with an authenticity rarely encountered in the current renovation craze.

Their first project was a 1904 Queen Anne cottage built from a pattern book by the Bosworth family, pioneers of the area. Rechristened Hope-Bosworth, the inn is papered with reproductions of Victorian wall coverings, but the furnishings in the cozy parlor, dining room and four upstairs bedrooms are genuine antiques from the era.

The Hope-Merrill House is a stately century-old Italianate that stands on land once occupied by the Geyserville Hotel, a Wells Fargo stage stop. Here the wallpapers are magnificent custom-made replicas of *fin de siécle* patterns that Rosalie especially admired, complete with a frieze around the ceilings. The hall wainscoting is an original Lincrusta Walton pattern, unpainted and in mint condition. The pride of the high-ceilinged formal sitting room is a five-piece Eastlake walnut parlor set, with chairs upholstered in cranberry velvet. Pieces of cranberry glass, cut glass and crystal embellish the room. The dining room is distinguished by Tudor-style furnishings and a massive 1871 cast-iron chandelier with glass chimneys and its original shades.

Also on the first floor is one bedroom with private bath, plus a large enclosed porch with French doors opening to a back deck and a side garden. The four upstairs bedrooms contain some pieces of museum quality, such as an 1865 walnut and burl headboard and an 1850 child's crib. One room is entirely furnished with turn-of-the-century wickerware; another has an antique brass bedstead and an unusual chestnut dresser. Most of the bedspreads are old crocheted or handknit coverlets. Some six dozen vintage photos, prints and paintings cover the walls of the house, and everywhere you look are pieces from Rosalie's collections of Victorian bric-a-brac, plus old books and current publications on the era.

Hope-Merrill House

Homemade preserves and breads with fruit and juice start the day at both Hope houses. Sherry, port and Sonoma County wines are offered in the evening. With advance notice and a minimum party of six, the Hopes will also prepare dinner at the Hope-Bosworth House. But you need not worry about going hungry in Geyserville. Just down the road is Catelli's, a bastion of home-cooked, old-style Italian food. And nearby the Souverain Winery runs a beautiful restaurant set in the midst of their vineyards.

HOPE-MERRILL HOUSE, 21253 Geyserville Avenue, Geyserville, California 95441. Telephone: (707) 857-3945. Accommodations: five rooms with double or queen-size beds; two rooms have private baths with shower or tub/shower three rooms share two baths with shower or tub/shower; no telephones; no television. Rates: moderate, Continental breakfast included. No pets. No smoking. Cards: MC, VISA, Open all year.

HOPE-BOSWORTH HOUSE, 21238 Geyserville Avenue, Geyserville, California 95441. Telephone: (707) 857-3356. Accommodations: four rooms with double or queen-size beds; private and shared baths; no telephones; no television. Rates: inexpensive to moderate, Continental breakfast included. No pets. No smoking. Cards: MC, VISA. Open all year.

Bed, Breakfast and a Jacuzzi Bath
THE GRAPE LEAF INN
Healdsburg

In the heart of the Russian River wine country, is the quiet town of Healdsburg, its side streets lined with trees and Victorian houses, many of which have been turned into inns in recent years. One of the first to offer bed and breakfast was the Grape Leaf Inn, a 1901 Victorian that was converted by airline stewardess Laura Salo and furnished with antiques she had collected in her travels—Austrian headboards, Oriental rugs, brass coat stands.

Real estate broker Terry Sweet bought the inn and furnishings and added another four luxurious units to the previously unused second floor. These have stained-glass dormer windows and skylights set in the pitched roof, private baths with Jacuzzi tubs and full air-conditioning. The lower floor now contains three bedrooms and a large double parlor with a fireplace, lots of books and a dining table by the cafe-curtained windows. You may breakfast here or in a cheerful alcove off the country kitchen. And it is a real breakfast too, with eggs, fresh ground coffees and home-baked breads. In the afternoon, wines from Sonoma County are served in the parlor or out on the wide veranda that shades two sides of the house and overlooks the pretty garden.

GRAPE LEAF INN, 539 Johnson Street, Healdsburg, California 95448. Telephone: (707) 433-8140. Accommodations: seven rooms with twin, double, queen- or king-size beds; private baths with tub/shower, one with wheelchair access; no telephones; no television. Rates: moderate to expensive, full breakfast included. No children. No pets. No smoking. Cards: MC, VISA. Open all year.

Getting There: From Highway 101 take Headsburg Avenue exit to Grant and turn right. Drive two blocks to Johnson.

On the Plaza

HEALDSBURG INN

Healdsburg

When Genny Jenkins took a Sunday drive to Healdsburg with a friend several years ago, she had no intention of buying an inn. But the turn-of-the-century Kruse Building on the town's plaza was for sale and Genny bought it. She leased the lower floor to shops and turned the second story, which originally housed medical offices, into a bed and breakfast hostelry. Before the inn opened in 1982, there were a few problems, like only one bathroom for twelve rooms. Undaunted, Genny added nine baths, giving each of the eight single rooms and the two suites private facilities, many with old claw-legged tubs that Genny had bought over the years thinking she might use them in some restoration project. Baths are a big deal here; she even provides toy ducks.

As you enter the inn by the wide carpeted stairwell, splashed with light from a skylight, you're likely to hear ragtime or baroque music from the well-stocked record and tape collection playing on the phonograph. If it's late afternoon, you'll probably smell corn popping which will accompany your welcoming glass of wine.

The front rooms are light and spacious with bay windows overlooking the wooded plaza, while some of the rear rooms are small and dark, but cozy. All are furnished with antiques, floral quilted spreads and Oriental throw rugs on the carpeting. The sitting rooms of the two-room suites have brass sofa beds with a cot underneath that can be pulled out so two people can sleep in the room. The most spectacular accommodation here is a huge room with skylights along one side (once a photography studio) and a fully equipped kitchen in the corner.

There is no common room at the Healdsburg Inn, but each morning coffee, hot breads and fruit are set out in the pantry for guests to take back to their rooms.

HEALDSBURG INN, Matheson Street (P.O. Box 1196), Healdsburg, California 95448. Telephone: (707) 433-6991. Accommodations: double and queen-size beds, two singles in suites; private baths with shower or tub/shower; no telephones; no television. Rates: moderate, Continental breakfast included. Children over five welcome. No pets. No smoking. Cards: AE, MC, VISA. Open all year.

Getting There: From Highway 101 take second Healdsburg exit to the Plaza and turn right on Matheson.

Even the Nuns Return

THE HAYDON HOUSE
Healdsburg

This 1904 Queen Anne on a quiet side street of Healdsburg exudes the warmth and charm of a well-run country home. You would never guess that three decades of housing a convent, then a boys' home and eventually a rest home had taken their toll on the place. But innkeepers Joanne and Richard Claus painstakingly removed the traces of institutional wear and tear, including the asphalt tiles that covered all the floors. Now the gleaming natural fir contrasts splendidly with pastel Dhurrie rugs, handmade in India. The five second-floor bedrooms are decorated with French and American antiques, custom-made down quilts that match the bed linens, baskets of mixed dried and silk flowers and Laura Ashley prints. Only one room has a private bath, but the others have washstands set in old-fashioned dressers and three have claw-legged tubs with ring showers in the room. The *pièce de résistance* of the Haydon House restoration is a former attic space over the porch, now brightly illuminated by skylights in the sloping roof. A sofa bed in the foyer allows three people to sleep in this spacious area.

Joanne serves a full breakfast at two round tables in the large, sunny dining room. A typical repast would be scrambled eggs, melon, fresh apple cake and bran muffins. In the evening, wine is served in the comfortable double parlor. Haydon House is a place people want to come back to and Joanne says that even the nuns from the convent often drop in to see their former home. One of the Claus' early guests— a landscape designer and her horticulturalist husband—returned with their family once to take over the entire inn, and then proceded to draw up plans for landscaping the grounds that surround the house.

HAYDON HOUSE, 321 Haydon Street, Healdsburg, California 95448. Telephone: (707) 433-5228. Accommodations: five rooms with double or queen-size beds, additional sofa bed in attic room; one private bath, three rooms with tub/showers in rooms, one room with private shower across hall, one and one-half community baths; no telephones; color television in parlor. Rates: moderate, breakfast included. No children under 13. No pets. Cards: MC, VISA. Open all year.

Getting There: From Highway 101 take second Healdsburg exit to the plaza, turn right on Matheson. Drive two blocks to Fitch and turn right. Drive another two blocks to Haydon and turn left.

A Nabob's Palatial Country Home
MADRONA MANOR
Healdsburg

In 1881 one of San Francisco's nabobs, financier John Paxton, spared no costs to build a three-story mansion with a gabled mansard roof on a wooded knoll overlooking the Russian River valley. Even though the manor was only to be a summer home, he lavished it with fourteen-foot high ceilings, ten fireplaces inlaid with brightly painted tiles, floors of Italian mosaic, furnished with massive pieces of carved walnut and mahogany.

When Carol and John Muir (a distant cousin of the naturalist) discovered this country estate a century later, they knew it was the perfect site for the inn they had been dreaming of when Muir had served as a Bechtel executive in Saudi Arabia. Although the mansion needed a lot of repair, the original furnishings were still in place and the Muirs added only the fine Persian carpets they had acquired in their travels. The downstairs music room, where aperitifs are now served in the evening, boasts a magnificent rosewood piano, while an adoining room shelters a huge billiard table. Five guest rooms, each with fireplace and private bath, contain hundred-year-old, ten-foot high four-posters or carved headboards, gigantic armoires and marble-topped dressers. One room has a sunny balcony and a splendid view of Mount St. Helena.

Behind his mansion Paxton had built a Carpenter Gothic carriage house. The Muirs reconstructed its interior, which holds a large common room with fireplace and game tables along with eight guest rooms furnished with carved rosewood tables and chairs that they had commissioned in Nepal for their then non-existent dream inn.

The Carriage House at Madrona Manor

Although the carriage house rooms—with twin or queen-size beds and modern baths—are undoubtedly more comfortable than those in the main house, they lack the opulent, almost museum-like style of the manor rooms. Two other outbuildings have been remodeled as two-room suites, each with its own sitting room, and renovation of four third-floor bedrooms in the main house is in the works.

Yet the sleeping accommodations are only half the story of Madrona Manor. The food reaches a quality that even Paxton, with all his millions, probably never experienced. The dining rooms and kitchen are the domain of the Muirs' son Todd and his sous chef Mark Holmoe, both graduates of San Francisco's Culinary Academy and proteges of Alice Waters at Berkeley's famous Chez Panisse restaurant. They practice the new California cuisine, concocting innovative dishes from the seasonal bounties of Sonoma County, including fruit and vegetables from Madrona's gardens. Breakfast consists of fresh fruits, platters of smoked meats and local cheeses, eggs, hot freshly baked breads and churros—little deep-fried puff pastries served with powdered sugar and marmalade made from dwarf mandarin oranges grown on the estate. The restaurant is open to the public for dinner and features unusual pastas à la Alice Waters, pizzas baked in an oak-burning brick oven, smoked salmon, trout and duck from the manor's own smoke house, and meats, poultry and seafood grilled over mesquite charcoal. Not to be missed when offered is an appetizer of fried Sicilian cheese redolent with garlic and olive oil.

Madrona Manor sits on eight acres of orchards and gardens studded with oaks, redwoods and the palms that Paxton planted a century ago. But the Muirs are adding one luxury that the nabob never dreamed of—a swimming pool.

MADRONA MANOR, 1001 Westside Road (Box 818), Healdsburg, California 95448. Telephone: (707) 433-4231. Accommodations: fourteen rooms and two suites with twin, double, queen- or king-size beds; private baths with tub/shower; no television; no telephones. Rates: expensive, full breakfast included. Restaurant open for dinner with five-course fixed-price meals on Friday and Saturday, à la carte service other nights. Children and pets welcome. Cards: AE, MC, VISA. Open all year.

Getting There: From San Francisco take second Healdsburg exit off Highway 101 and follow Healdsburg Avenue north to Mill Road which becomes Westside Road. From the north take Westside Road exit from Highway 101.

Verandas and Vineyard Views
THE RAFORD HOUSE
Healdsburg

From Healdsburg the Russian River flows west through more vineyards and wooded mountains to the Pacific. Although this is wine country, now, a century ago much of this rich acreage was planted in hops. One of the major hop growers was Raford W. Peterson, who built in the 1880s a spacious house, flanked by broad verandas, on the hillside overlooking his lands. Today the grounds are covered with grapevines and prune trees, and all that remains of the hop ranch are the Victorian farmhouse and the foundation of the hop kilns. In 1980 Alan Baitinger and Beth Foster bought the thirteen-room residence from the Peterson family and converted it into an inn.

Giant palms and gardens rife with roses and other flowers surround the building. Inside, a cheery fire burns on chilly mornings in the dining room, where guests are served a simple Continental breakfast at a long oak table. A big grandfather clock in the corner is a hint of the owners' hobby: Antique clocks of all sizes are found throughout the bedrooms, which are handsomely appointed with turn-of-the-century furnishings. Quaintness, however, ends with the beds (all new mattresses) and baths, which are as modern as tomorrow. Each room has its own distinctive decor and special features. Some have wood-burning fireplaces, others have private patios. Then there is a shared-bath suite of two bedrooms, one light and airy in champagne tones, the other one dressed up in deep burgundy hues with a brass bedstead. A little game room with garden view opens off this room. Raford House is certainly among the best of the many new inns.

RAFORD HOUSE, 10630 Wohler Road, Healdsburg, California 95448. Telephone: (707) 887-9573. Accommodations: seven rooms with double beds; most rooms have private baths with tub/shower; no telephones; no television; wheelchair access to one room. Rates moderate, Continental breakfast included. No small children. No pets. Cards: MC, VISA. Open all year except Christmas.

Getting There: From Highway 101 take River Road exit north of Santa Rosa and drive west seven miles to Wohler Road; turn right.

Wooded Haven on the Russian River
RIDENHOUR RANCH HOUSE INN
Guerneville

As the Russian River nears Guerneville, its valley narrows and the redwoods become denser. Here, next to the Korbel vineyards, is another old ranch house restored as a charming inn. Its history dates back to 1856, when Louis William Ridenhour began to farm 940 acres of the fertile lands on both sides of the river. In 1906 his son, Louis E. Ridenhour, built his home of heart redwood on several acres of the ranch; his daughter Virginia and her husband, former Assistant Surgeon General Justin K. Fuller, continued to live there, enlarging and remodeling the house, until 1977. Martha and Bob Satterthwaite saw the house that year and knew it would be perfect for the inn they had dreamed of starting. After two years' work the Satterthwaites had created a gracious hostelry with the ambience of a private home, a quiet haven well away from the honky-tonk river resorts.

Fireplaces, Oriental rugs, comfortable furnishings and a profusion of greenery and African violets grace the large redwood-paneled living room and adjoining dining room. You can breakfast here, or in the cheerful family kitchen, or out on the patio: a light repast of freshly ground coffee, nut breads or muffins, fresh juices, and fruits (sometimes from the inn's own gardens) cheeses and often hard-cooked eggs. The rest of the day guests are free to help themselves to coffee or tea in the

kitchen, or to pour a glass of chilled white wine from the refrigerator. Decanters of sherry are also found in each room, along with fresh flowers and plants. The two spacious downstairs bedrooms have queen-size beds with Victorian headboards and quilted spreads; each of these has a private bath, and one has a little sitting room with a couch that folds into a bed. Upstairs three cozy little rooms with dormer windows nestle under the eaves, sharing a bath. These have an Early American look with hooked rugs and chenille spreads or handmade quilts. The original touches of Martha Satterthwaite, a former interior designer, are here and there: straw hats on the wall of one room and on another a Japanese kite fashioned from calico fabric. Recently, another two rooms with private entrances have been added on a lower level. Every room of this inn provides sylvan views of surrounding oaks and redwoods or the Korbel vineyards next door. A stroll through these woods and through the gardens informally landscaped with daisies, zinnias, marigolds is a favorite pastime here. Other diversions include a redwood hot tub and a croquet court. The Korbel champagne cellars and secluded river beaches are a short walk away.

RIDENHOUR RANCH HOUSE, 12850 River Road, Guerneville, California 95446. Telephone: (707) 887-1033. Accommodations: seven rooms with queen-size, double or two double beds; four rooms with private baths with tub/shower; three rooms share bath with shower; no telephones; no television; wheelchair access to one room. Rates: moderate, Continental breakfast included. Childred over ten welcome. No pets. Cards: MC, VISA.

Getting There: From Highway 101 take River Road exit north of Santa Rosa and drive west twelve and one-half miles.

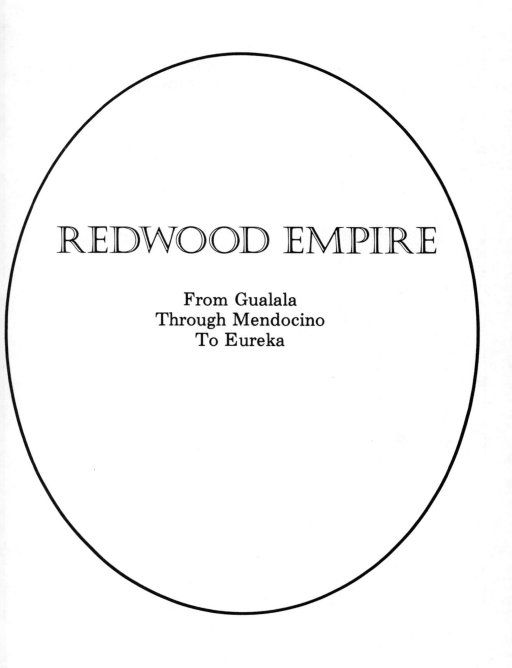

REDWOOD EMPIRE

From Gualala
Through Mendocino
To Eureka

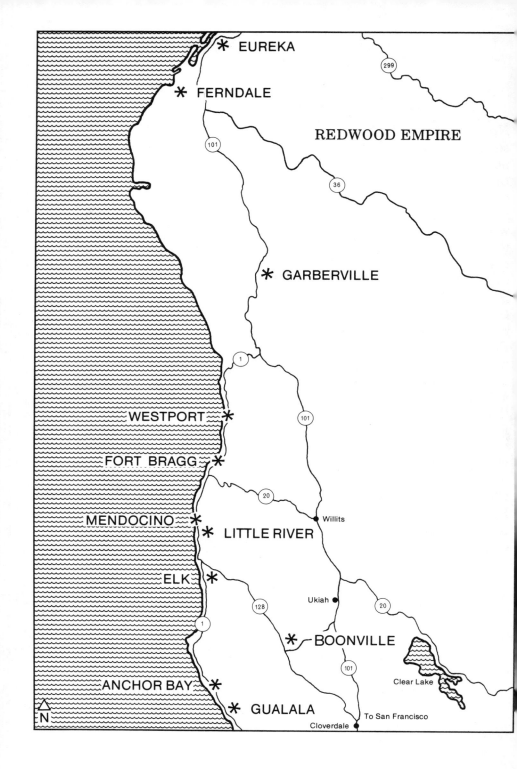

Where Forested Mountains Meet the Sea
NORTH COAST
From Gualala through Mendocino to Westport

North of Jenner, where the Russian River meets the Pacific, Highway 1 soars upwards, switchbacking through mountainous terrain, then stretches north along the craggy coast to Mendocino. This awesome drive through mostly isolated countryside takes you past the reconstruction of Fort Ross, the site of a Russian seal- and otter-trapping settlement in the early 1800s. It also takes you past numerous coves where weathered pilings and abandoned cemeteries are the only testimony to the once-thriving lumber towns that studded the coast in the last century. From the forested mountains that rise from the sea, millions of redwood trees were hewn to build the Victorians of San Francisco.

Getting There: To reach Highway 1 from San Francisco, take Highway 101 north to Petaluma; take Washington Street exit to the road leading to Bodega Bay, then proceed north on Highway 1. For about ten miles north of Jenner this road winds along cliffs high above the ocean; it can be hazardous or closed in bad weather and it can frighten people who are bothered by heights. But this drive is breathtakingly beautiful, and the quickest route to Gualala (allow about three hours from San Francisco).

The shortest route to Mendocino, however, is the inland approach via Highway 128, which takes about three and one-half hours, as opposed to some five hours via Highway 1. Take 101 north to Cloverdale and Highway 128 west to the coast where it intercepts Highway 1 just south of Little River and north of Elk. The best way to tour the north coast is to drive up Highway 1 (you will feel safer because your car is on the inside of the road, away from the cliffs) and return via 128.

Clifftop Stagecoach Stop

OLD MILANO HOTEL

Gualala

A midway stopping point on the rugged stagecoach road that linked the coastal lumber towns was Gualala. Here in 1905 an Italian family built' the Old Milano Hotel, offering overnight rooms and refreshments in a large saloon to the stage passengers. But the demise of the logging boom reduced the hotel's business, and in 1922 new owners converted it into a lodge for anglers seeking the steelhead in nearby Gualala River.

In 1940 the highway was moved inland and the hotel was put out of business, becoming a residence. In the 1950s another set of owners with modern ideas sold off most of the surrounding land, installed large plate-glass windows, lowered the ceilings and tossed most of the Victorian furnishings into the gulch. When Bruce and Theadora McBroom discovered the place in 1977, there was not much left to remind one of the hotel's history.

The McBrooms restored the six upstairs guest rooms, installing new carpeting, wiring, plumbing, insulation and soundproofing. Furnishings are family antiques: big oak armoires, white-painted iron bedsteads, Victorian love seats, old handmade quilts and crocheted spreads. Both of the two community baths have tiled "his and her" showers with dual spigots Recently a downstairs suite was added, with a lace-hung eighteenth-century Angelica Kaufman bed, a sitting room and a private bath. Bowls of flowers from the inn's cutting garden and spectacular views of the Pacific pounding away at the cliffs and cove below add to the romantic setting. The most unusual quarters at Old Milano are in an old caboose next to the hotel. This unit is cozy and comfortable, with walls paneled in sandblasted wood, a potbellied stove and a tiny galley.

Thea papered the parlor walls with a fabric from London: a William Morris nature pattern circa 1860. The chairs are an Eastlake design, and the sofa is the first Riviera bed produced in 1906. The old saloon has been restored as another sitting area, with a huge stone fireplace, chintz-covered sofas, and plants and flowers. Tastings of Mendocino wines take place here in the afternoon. A patio in back is surrounded by flowers, including giant dahlias eight feet high. Walkways lead down to a hot tub on a point overlooking the surf.

You will be confronted by only one problem at Old Milano: Deciding where to have breakfast! The choices are many: in your bedroom, by the fireside in one of the parlors, in the patio or gardens. The bread is homemade, as are the plum preserves and apple butter from the McBrooms' organically grown fruit. But it's no problem deciding where to have dinner: Just up the road at the St. Orres Inn is one of the north coast's finest restaurants.

OLD MILANO HOTEL, 38300 Highway 1, Gualala, California 95445. Telephone: (707) 884-3256. Accommodations: nine rooms with queen-size beds; shared baths with tub/shower in hotel, private baths in suite, cottage and caboose; no telephones; no television. Rates: moderate to expensive, Continental breakfast included. No children. No pets. No cards. No smoking. Open daily from April 1 through Thanksgiving weekend, open weekends only December through March.

Getting There: The hotel is on the ocean side of Highway 1 just north of Gualala.

A Tribute to the Coast's Russian Past
ST. ORRES INN
Gualala

Midway up the coast between Jenner and Mendocino is an astounding piece of architectural sculpture: a miniature Russian palace rendered in hand-carved redwood, with onion-top turrets and stained-glass windows. A relic from the Russian settlers of over a century ago? No. St. Orres Inn is the creation of two young men from Marin County who painstakingly handcrafted every detail.

Eric Black and Richard Wasserman acquired a decrepit garage overlooking the Pacific on property once owned by the St. Orres family who homesteaded this area. For four years they scavenged wood from beaches and old barns, collected pieces of stained glass, sawed, hammered and sculptured their inn, which finally opened in early 1977.

Through a patio and trellis-covered terrace you enter a cozy parlor with oval windows, tapestries on the walls and furnishings of the last century. Beyond is the spectacular dining room over which the domed turret rises some fifty feet. From high above, light filters down from stained-glass clerestories while three tiers of mullioned windows provide glimpses of forest and sea through a cascade of hanging plants.

The French menu at St. Orres changes constantly, but a stand-out dish that's usually present is rack of lamb with a Dijon mustard crust; fresh local seafood is also featured. Mumm's champagne and Russian caviar are available as appetizers, and the desserts are decidedly sinful—try the chocolate decadence. In the morning a complimentary breakfast of fruit, juices, breads and coffee is served to overnight guests. Liquid sustenance is available in the afternoon from a new wine bar located next to a plant-filled solarium.

The most luxurious accommodations are in two new cottages, the Cottage and the Tree House. These have kitchenettes, carpeting throughout, wood-burning stove-fireplaces, queen-size beds and living areas with French doors leading to private decks. The Cottage will house a family of four, as will the rustic Cabin, one of the original buildings on the property that has not been remodeled. The upstairs guest rooms in the inn itself are small and sparsely appointed with furnishings designed and built by Black and Wasserman. Guests share three community baths, labeled "his," "hers" and "ours,"—the last has a large tiled tub and dual shower heads.

St. Orres Inn has its own private beach across the road. In season you can pick abalone from the rocks or fish for steelhead. On weekends there are flea markets and local arts/crafts festivals to be explored.

ST. ORRES INN, P.O. Box 523, Gualala, California 95445. Telephone: (707) 884-3303. Accommodations: eight rooms with double beds share three baths with shower in inn; double bed and private bath in cabin; double and queen-size beds, fireplaces and private baths in cottages; no telephones; no television. Rates: moderate in inn and cabin, expensive in cottages; Continental breakfast included. Open to public for dinner and Sunday brunch. Children welcome in cottages only; no children under six permitted in dining room. No pets. Cards: MC, VISA, for overnight guests only. Open all year.

Getting There: St. Orres is on the inland side of Highway 1 between Gualala and Anchor Bay.

St. Orres Inn

Designed with Privacy and Views in Mind
WHALE WATCH INN BY THE SEA
Anchor Bay

Perched on sheer cliffs some fifty feet above the Pacific, this striking inn of contemporary design offers spectacular views of the ocean and the craggy coast. The main building—originally the second home of owners **Irene and Enoch Stewart**—has a **huge hexagonal living room paneled in redwood and glass** with a freestanding fireplace in the center, its flue soaring up to the high pitched ceiling. A wide deck surrounds the ocean side, with stairways leading down to smaller decks with chairs for two—glorious spots to admire the view on sunny days. But even when rain or fog shroud the coast, this beautiful room provides a convivial spot to relax by the fire. There are plenty of comfortable couches, leather wing chairs, two game tables and a good assortment of books, puzzles, games and taped classical music. Several of the guest rooms are also in this building.

However, if it's privacy you seek, Whale Watch is the place to find it. "We guard our guests' privacy so much, that we don't even water the gardens around the rooms when they're occupied," says innkeeper Aurora Hayes. Thus all the rooms in the outbuildings have their own fireplaces, sitting areas, breakfast tables and decks to enjoy the view. If you wish, you need never see another person at Whale Watch, except Aurora or one of her assistants when they bring around the breakfast trays laden with platters of fresh fruit, croissants or freshly baked bread and brie or yogurt. If you're feeling social however, you can arrange to eat in the main building.

One of these outbuildings has four units, each with a modern electric kitchen, fully equipped down to cookbooks and herbs. Two are suites composed of a bedroom and sitting room with a sofa bed—ideal for two couples. In the spring of 1984 the Stewarts started construction of another two-story cliffside building with eight rooms—all with fireplaces and ultra-private decks, some with Jacuzzi tubs and some with lofts.

Wooden steps scale the perpendicular cliff below the Whale Watch Inn's flower-edged lawns, leading to a sandy sheltered beach where it is warm and calm enough to swim in the summer months. In winter and spring the favorite pastime here is watching the great gray whales swim by in their annual ten-thousand-mile migration between the Arctic seas and the warm waters off Baja California. February through April, when they return with their babies, are the best months to spot them.

WHALE WATCH INN BY THE SEA, 35100 Highway 1, Gualala, California 95445. Telephone: (707) 884-3667. Accommodations: sixteen rooms (after completion of new unit) with twin or queen-size beds; private baths with tub/shower; no telephones; no television. Rates: expensive to very expensive, Continental breakfast included. No children. No pets. No cards. Open all year.

Getting There: The Whale Watch is on the ocean side of Highway 1 just north of Anchor Bay, which is five miles north of Gualala.

Edwardian Showplace from the Logging Era
HARBOR HOUSE
Elk

This stately house was built on the cliffs above Greenwood Landing by the Goodyear Redwood Lumber Company in 1916 to be used as an executive residence and for entertaining business guests. In those days the small port below was heavily trafficked by schooners coming for their rich cargoes of lumber from the nearby Albion forests. In fact the house itself is an enlarged replica of a redwood model house, designed by Louis Christian Mullgardt for the 1915 Pan American Exposition in San Francisco.

When the lumber boom came to an end in the 1930s, Harbor House was converted to an inn, which had become run-down in recent years. Since 1975 the inn has been owned and managed by Patricia Corcoran, a former schoolteacher. Her goal is "to recreate the Edwardian atmosphere which once permeated each redwood board."

The walls, vaulted ceiling and fireplace of the gracious living room are entirely paneled with hand-carved and hand-fitted redwood, still preserved by its original finish of polished hot beeswax. Furnishings are comfortable and eclectic: overstuffed chairs, a large Persian rug, a Steinway piano, Chinese chests and tables, bookcases bulging with reading matter.

There are five spacious bedrooms in the house itself, four with fireplaces, and another four cottages built on the edge of the bluff next to the main building. With paint and flowered wallpapers, antiques, and four-poster beds, Trisha has restored these rooms to their original

219

charm. Some of the cottage rooms have French cast-iron fireplaces set on brick hearths; some have private terraces overlooking the ocean. Harbor House offers the best of two worlds: Guests seeking comfort and companionship usually prefer the main house; those wishing privacy and romance opt for the cottages.

Trisha believes that home-cooked meals, leisurely served, are one of the traditional characteristics of country inns. She and her staff make all the soups, breads, salad dressings and desserts from scratch. Vegetables are from the inn's garden. Breakfast and dinner are served in a spacious dining room with a panoramic view of the Pacific and the large tunneled rocks in the harbor below. The morning meal includes juice, fruit and perhaps shirred eggs, omelets or eggs Benedict. At evening, the entrées may be broiled fresh salmon or veal or chicken or a French beef dish. An excellent selection of local wines is available.

Harbor House is only twenty minutes by car from Mendocino's shops and art galleries. But most guests choose to spend their time exploring the inn's private beach.

HARBOR HOUSE, P.O. Box 369, Elk, California 95432. Telephone: (707) 877-3203. Accommodations: nine rooms with twin, double or king-size beds; private baths with shower or tub/shower; no telephones; no television. **Rates: moderate, full breakfast and dinner included;** lower midweek rates in winter and early spring. No children. No pets. No cards. Open all year.

Getting There: Harbor House is on the ocean side of Highway 1 just north of Elk, which is six miles south of the intersection of Highway 1 and Highway 128.

Restful Retreat in the Sheep Country
THE TOLL HOUSE INN
Boonville

Midway between Elk and Mendocino, Highway 128 heads inland, following the Navarro River through dense redwood groves, then through vineyards and orchards to the little town of Boonville. From here Highway 253 twists over the mountains to Ukiah through hilly pastures which have been sheep grazing territory for over a century. One of the pioneer sheep ranchers was the Miller family and in 1912 they built a house six miles up this road from Boonville. At that time they maintained the road and charged a toll to the loggers who hauled their redwood along this route to inland mills. Thus the Miller home became known as The Toll House.

In 1981 Beverly Nesbitt bought the place for a home and inn. And a gracious and restful home it is. Two pillowy couches by the fireplace invite you to relax in the lovely living room where multipaned windows open to the gardens beyond. Here you have your choice of lazing in a hammock on a shady veranda, sunning on a secluded wooden deck or soaking in a hot tub. At day's end you might want to watch the sun set over the mountains or catch an old movie on television in the glassed-in sun porch. Or, if you want privacy, you can curl up on one of the comfortable day beds that are in each of the guest rooms—in front of a fire in two of the rooms. Beverly has decorated these rooms in a riot of floral prints on the wallpapers, curtains, bedspreads and linens.

The day begins at The Toll House with a big country breakfast in the dining room overlooking the gardens. There's usually fresh-squeezed orange juice and sometimes apples from the inn's old orchard, followed by whatever Beverly feels like cooking: omelets, oatmeal and corn muffins, pancakes or waffles. By prior arrangement dinners are served here too, with the cooking done by the inn's manager, Dina Anzilotti, who studied at San Francisco's Culinary Academy. If you're a twosome, she whips up a casual three-course supper, but for larger groups, it's a Continental feast beginning with appetizers like Greek spanakopeta, followed by soup, entrée (often local lamb), vegetables, salad and a homemade pastry.

The Toll House's remote setting attracts those who want to get away from activity. But if you wish, it's only a twenty-minute drive to Ukiah's fine wineries such as Parducci and Fetzer and only ten minutes to the wineries of Boonville, where you can be assured of a fine meal at the Boonville Hotel.

THE TOLL HOUSE INN, 15301 Highway 253 (P.O. Box 268), Boonville, California 95415. Telephone: (707) 895-3630. Accommodations: three rooms with queen-size bed and day bed plus one room with Murphy bed; two rooms with private bath, two rooms share bath with tub and shower; telephone upon request in one room; television in solarium. Rates: moderate to expensive, breakfast included. No children under ten. No pets. Smoking discouraged. No cards. Open all year.

Getting There: From San Francisco take Highway 101 to Cloverdale, Highway 128 west to Boonville and Highway 253 northeast to Ukiah. The inn is about six miles up this highway.

A Complex of Cottages above a Smugglers' Cove
HERITAGE HOUSE
Little River

In this ivy-covered inn with its many cottages rambling over hillsides and meadows and gardens reaching down to a private beach, L. D. and Hazel Dennen strive to preserve the heritage of the Mendocino coast. Dennen's own roots are implanted in the history of the area. His grandfather, John Dennen, who had come from New England, built the inn's main building as a home for rancher Wilder Pullen in 1876. In the 1890s Pullen advertised that the 160-acre sheep and cattle ranch and the seven-room house were for sale; for the land, buildings and livestock he was asking seven thousand dollars. In the early 1930s neighbors started to eye the former Pullen house with suspicion: Baby Face Nelson was using the cove below the house for his bootleg operations and, before his arrest, had concluded one of his last deals inside the house. As recently as the early 1940s, Chinese immigrants were smuggled into the country here.

In 1949, L. D. Dennen bought the house his grandfather had built and turned it into an inn. Over the years, the Dennens have added cottages on the meadows below the original house, building some and moving others from elsewhere in the countryside. All have names such as Schoolhouse, which the Dennens built with lumber salvaged from the Greenwood School in Elk; the school's sign serves as a headboard and the children's desks as bedside tables. Firehouse, Barbershop, Ice Cream are some other names. Recently the Dennens converted an old water tower, brought down from Mendocino, into a two-story unit with a circular stairway leading from a living room to a balconied bedroom. There are over sixty units altogether now, some with brick fireplaces or Franklin or pot-bellied stoves. All have private baths.

Some years back Dennen acquired an old apple storage house from a nearby farm for seventy-five dollars and rebuilt it next to the 1876 house as a bar. The comfortably furnished adjoining lounge with its walk-in fireplace commands magnificent views of the ocean. Even if you do not stay at Heritage House, you should at least drop by for a drink at sunset. The dining room, with its glass-domed ceiling, also has wonderful views and is open to the public. The menu changes nightly, a typical dinner including egg lemon soup, greens mixed with pine nuts and Smithfield ham and radishes, grilled Pacific snapper with sauce mousseline or roast beef with sauce miroton along with fresh vegetables, fettuccine, and poppy seed bread, ending with a rich torte, fruit and

BUILT 1877 AD

Heritage House

cheese. There is also an extensive selection of domestic and imported wines. Breakfasts are hearty too, and are served on the deck on sunny days. A buffet of fruits, juices and cereals is followed by eggs Benedict (or any style), bacon, ham, sausage and dollar-size hotcakes. Heritage House operates on semi-American plan only; breakfast and dinner are included in the rates. This inn is more formal than most north coast places; jackets and ties are encouraged at dinner.

HERITAGE HOUSE, 5200 Highway 1, Little River, California, 95456. Telephone: (707) 937-5885. Accommodations: sixty-five rooms with twin, double or king-size beds; private baths, some tub/shower, some shower only; no telephones; no television. Rates: expensive to very expensive, breakfast and dinner included. Open to public for breakfast and dinner; full bar service. No children. No pets. No cards. Open February through November.

Getting There: Heritage House is on the ocean side of Highway 1 between Albion and Little River.

A Cozy Home by an Apple Orchard
THE VICTORIAN FARMHOUSE
Little River

Just up the coast from Heritage House, its builder John Dennen constructed a Victorian farmhouse in 1877 as a home for himself and his wife Emma Dora. When Tom and Jane Szilasi bought the building in 1981, they faced an enormous restoration task, even though the place had operated as a bed and breakfast for a year. They tore plastic paneling off the downstairs sitting room and installed wainscoting and wallpaper; the corner fireplace was faced with blue and white Delft tiles. The two upstairs rooms—named the Dennen and Emma Dora rooms—have views of the ocean or adjoining apple orchards, and share a Victorian sitting room that opens to a sheltered deck. Steps lead down to a terraced garden in which Tom has planted over two hundred daffodils. Private entrances from the garden lead to the two lower rooms: The Victorian room has its own sitting room, with a French wood-burning stove and a view of the orchard. The Garden Room has a window looking into a tiny garden that can be illuminated at night; one-way tinted glass allows the guests to admire the garden, but no one can look into the room.

The setting here is Victorian, but the comforts are contemporary. All rooms have queen- or king-size beds with dual-control electric blankets and white quilted spreads. By the window in each room is a tiny round table set with a white eyelet cloth, china plates and cups ready for the morning repast of juice, fruit muffins or bread.

THE VICTORIAN FARMHOUSE, Highway 1, (P.O. Box 357), Little River, California 95456. Telephone: (707) 937-0697. Accommodations: four rooms with queen- or king-size beds; private baths with tub/shower; no telephones; no television. Rates: moderate, Continental breakfast included. No children under 16. No pets. No cards. Open all year.

Getting There: The Victorian Farmhouse is on the inland side of Highway 1 between Heritage House and Little River.

New England-Style Mansion of a Lumber Tycoon
LITTLE RIVER INN
Little River

In 1853 pioneer lumber and shipping tycoon Silas Coombs built an impressive New England–style mansion for his family on a hillside above Little River Cove, bringing much of the furnishings around the Horn from his native Maine. In 1929, as the lumber business diminished, the Coombs family turned the house into an inn, which has been expanded to fifty rooms and is run by Silas's great-grandson today.

The mansion, faithfully maintained in its original style, houses an antique-filled parlor and, upstairs under dormered roofs, four floral-papered bedrooms. There is also a cocktail lounge that affords excellent viewing of the annual migration of the California gray whale, along with the large dining room. The old house is now the nucleus for a complex of garden cottages, a motel-style annex, and a challenging nine-hole golf course on 250 acres where Silas's orchard once stood.

Some of the garden cottages are two-bedroom units, wood paneled and furnished in Early American style. Six have fireplaces; all have sun decks, some private, and views of the gardens or ocean. The annex rooms all have sliding glass doors leading to a balcony with a beautiful view of the cove.

In the early days of the inn, the Coombs family served their guests abalone picked from the rocks in the cove below. Little River Inn still is noted up and down the coast for its rendition of the delicate shellfish,

Little River Inn

when available. Ling cod and sole from local waters, salmon in season, chicken, lamb and steaks along with a delicious cobbler, are other highlights of the dinner menu.

LITTLE RIVER INN, Little River, California 95456. Telephone: (707) 937-5942. Accommodations: fifty-one rooms with double, two doubles, two queen- or king-size beds; private baths, some with tub/shower; no telephones; no television. Rates: moderate to expensive, no meals included. Open to public for breakfast and dinner, full bar service. Children welcome. No pets. No cards. Open all year for lodging; bar and dining room closed in January.

Getting There: The inn is on the inland side of Highway 1 across from the Little River post office.

French Antiques and Contemporary Art
GLENDEVEN
Little River

This handsome three-story house—flanked by cypress trees, lawns and flower gardens—stands on a headland overlooking the bay of Little River. It was built in 1867 by an early settler from Maine, Isaiah Stevens, for his bride Rebecca Coombs, whose family owned the house that later became Little River Inn. When Dutch-born designer Jan de Vries and his wife Janet bought the house in 1977, it had been partially restored, but they lavished improvements on it and will probably never stop.

Jan had been director of the Contemporary Crafts Gallery in Portland, Oregon, and he has skillfully mixed paintings, prints and ceramics from artists of that area with lovely European antiques acquired at auctions. A baby grand piano is their latest addition to the spacious and airy sitting room, where a glass of wine by the fireside awaits guests in the evening. Breakfast is served here or by the wood stove in the kitchen where Janet bakes muffins or coffeecake served with fresh fruits, baked apples and eggs.

In their first years as innkeepers, the de Vries and their two children lived in the rear of the house. Later they restored an adjacent barn for their home and guests now have the run of the inn. The bedrooms are charmingly furnished with Louis XIV or XV bedsteads, flowered quilts, marble-topped tables, dried and fresh flower arrange-

227

Glendeven

ments and bright contemporary paintings. Two of the rooms have their own sitting rooms, one with a fireplace and doors opening to a brick patio. All have views of the bay or gardens. In 1984, next to the barn, the de Vries built another four units with fireplaces and sitting areas.

In seven years Glendeven has grown from a lovely B&B to one of the north coast's most distinguished inns. But the de Vries continually think up extras for their guests. Lately they have instigated a series of midweek events—special dinners, cooking workshops conducted by noted chefs, even field trips to survey the wildflowers and mushrooms that abound in the area. Write ahead for a precise schedule.

GLENDEVEN, 8221 North Highway 1, Little River, California 95456. Telephone: (707) 937-0083. Accommodations: six rooms in main house with queen-size beds (one with extra double bed); four rooms have private baths, two share bath, some with tub/shower, some with stall shower; four rooms in outbuilding with private baths; no telephones; no television. Rates: moderate, Continental breakfast included. Children sometimes accepted. No pets. No cards. Open all year.

Getting There: Glendeven is north of Little River on the inland side of Highway I.

New England Village and a Western Lumber Town
MENDOCINO AND FORT BRAGG

Cabrillo discovered Cape Mendocino in 1542 and named it after Don Antonio de Mendoza, first viceroy of New Spain. But except for its name, nothing about the coastal village of Mendocino is Spanish. Situated on a rocky bluff projecting into the Pacific, the town looks like a movie set of a New England village, reflecting the heritage of its founders. Except for fresh paint, time has not touched the Victorian clapboards, set among windmills, water towers and windswept cypress trees. Behind rise the redwood-covered mountains of the Coast Range.

It was this precious timber that attracted the early settlers to the Mendocino coast. Harry Meiggs, a San Francisco lumberman, brought the first sawmill to Mendocino from the East aboard the brig *Ontario* and the lumber boom began. Others harvested the seafood from these northern waters, and started a fishing industry that still flourishes in the nearby harbor of Noyo. In the late nineteenth century, some thirty-five hundred people lived in Mendocino, which then boasted eight hotels, seventeen saloons and as many bordellos.

Today the population is only eleven hundred, and includes many artists and craftspeople. The entire town has been declared a historic monument so that its character will be preserved. Along Main Street, which faces the sea, and along picturesque side streets, where hollyhocks rise over picket fences, there are seventeen art galleries and crafts shops. Within the area are tennis courts and a nine-hole golf course. The surrounding waters offer deep-sea and stream fishing, as well as canoeing.

Just north of Mendocino—but a continent away in atmosphere—is Fort Bragg, which looks like a typical western town and is still an active lumber center for the Georgia Pacific Company. Fort Bragg is also the departure point for the Skunk railroad, a scenic six-hour journey inland along the Noyo River, through forty miles of redwoods. Advance reservations may be made by writing California Western Railroad, Box 907B, Fort Bragg, California 95437.

All along this coast, a favorite winter pastime is watching the migration of the great gray whales from the Arctic to Baja California and back. From December into April you can spot these thirty-ton mammals by the ten-foot water sprays they eject into the air. But the whale watch culminates during the last two weeks of March when an annual whale festival is conducted in Mendocino and Fort Bragg. An even closer look is possible from charter boats operating out of the port of Noyo. Another favorite pastime—year-round—in this area is eating: A number of excellent restaurants dot the coast from Little River to Fort Bragg.

Turn-of-the Century Ambience
MENDOCINO HOTEL
Mendocino

In 1878, one of the houses on Mendocino's Main Street was bought by San Franciscan Ben Bever; his family and furnishings later arrived by schooner. That fall the *Mendocino Beacon* broke the news that Ben Bever was building an addition to his house and starting a boardinghouse. "It shall be called the Temperance House and no liquor shall be served." Bever's brother Sam joined him in the enterprise, and the name was changed to Central House, later Central Hotel and finally Mendocino Hotel.

During the last five decades the hotel has changed hands frequently. In 1973, San Diego businessman R. O. Peterson bought the hotel and renovated it to a level of luxury that had not existed before. Even in its prime, the hotel had been nothing fancy, just a comfortable hostelry for loggers and traveling salesmen. Peterson retained architect Wayne Williams and his wife Paula, an interior decorator, to invest the hotel with the elegance of the Victorian era. Polished dark woods and wainscotings, Oriental rugs and Tiffany-style glass were installed in the lobby and dining room. A spectacular dome of genuine Tiffany, found in Philadelphia, is suspended over the carved wooden bar. (Temperance most certainly is not the house rule today.) Off the lobby an attractive dining room is open to the public for dinner while breakfast and lunch are served in a plant-filled addition to the hotel.

Upstairs, twenty-six bedrooms have been renovated to mint condition. The decorator strived for an authentic, eclectic ambience that would be found at the turn of the century, combining hand-painted porcelain sinks from France and European armoires with replicated American wallpapers and Victorian brass and carved wooden beds. Many rooms have ocean views and private balconies.

MENDOCINO HOTEL, 45080 Main Street (P.O. Box 587), Mendocino, California 95460. Telephone: (707) 937-0511. Accommodations: twenty-six rooms with twin, double or queen-size beds; some private baths, community baths with showers; no telephones; no television. Rates: moderate to expensive. No children under 14. No pets. Cards: AE, MC, VISA. Open all year.

Honeymoon House Circa 1880
MacCALLUM HOUSE
Mendocino

Lumber magnate William H. Kelley owned much of the town of Mendocino in the 1880s. So when his daughter Daisy married Alexander MacCallum in 1882, Kelley built the young couple a honeymoon house even finer than his own home. The three-story Victorian with gingerbread gables had a wide porch where the MacCallums could sit and watch the lumbermen float their logs down Big River into the Pacific. Daisy matured to become the matriarch of Mendocino, and much of the town's social life revolved around her home.

In 1974 San Francisco stockbroker William Norris and his wife Sue bought the house from the MacCallum family and transformed it into an inn. All of the handsome original furnishings were still intact: Tiffany lamps, Persian rugs, carved footstools, paintings and an enormous library of turn-of-the-century books.

The Norrises started out by refurbishing the bedrooms in the house itself, using flowered Victorian wallpapers and matching curtains. These rooms, however, are rather small and dark—especially those under the eaves in the attic—and the old-fashioned bathrooms are "down the hall." More comfort and privacy is to be found in the out-buildings, which Sue has transformed one by one into sleeping quarters over the years.

The old greenhouse is now a rustic cottage with skylights and a free-standing Franklin stove. It shares an adjoining modern bath with the water tower, now a two-story unit. The old carriage house contains two rooms with stoves and a shared bath. The redwood work shed has been furnished with rattan furniture and the outhouse has been turned into a bathroom. Even the tiny gazebo, once the playhouse of the MacCallum children, is for rent and still contains its child-size chairs.

But by far the most luxurious quarters at MacCallum House are to be found in the Norrises' latest renovation project—the barn. The spacious upstairs unit has its own private deck with a view of the town and the ocean beyond. Under the high pitched ceiling, still sheathed with weathered barn siding, is a loft, and below is a charming sitting room with a massive stone fireplace. One of the bedrooms has a similar fireplace; the other has a spectacular view of the ocean.

From the spring through the fall dinners are served in the book-lined dining room of the main house and cocktails are served in an adjacent bar. A Continental breakfast is served year round.

MacCALLUM HOUSE, Albion Street (P.O. Box 206), Mendocino, California 95460. Telephone: (707) 937-0289. Accommodations: twenty-one rooms with double, two double, queen- or king-size beds; shared and connecting baths, some with tub/shower, some tub only, some shower only, private baths in barn; no telephones; no television. Rates: inexpensive to expensive, Continental breakfast included. Restaurant open to public for dinner April through December, weekends only January through March; full bar service. Children welcome. No pets. Cards: MC, VISA. Open all year.

MacCallum House

A Fireplace and Flowers in Every Room
HEADLANDS INN
Mendocino

Of the many north coast inns that have opened in the 1980s, Headlands is one of the loveliest. The three-story, nineteenth-century shingled house, surrounded by a picket fence and a flower-filled garden, commands unobstructed views of the Big River inlet and the tree-covered mountains beyond. Originally built in 1869 as a barber shop on Main Street, the house was expanded and later served as a saloon and as a hotel annex. In 1893 the building was moved to its present site and bcame a private residence. Over the years, however, time and neglect took its toll and by 1979, when a series of aspirant innkeepers began restoration, the building was completely dilapidated. Today, the former inhabitants would scarcely recognize the place.

Rich champagne-colored carpeting flows throughout the rooms, which are painted and papered in restful tones of beige and white and furnished with English and American antiques. All rooms have wood-burning fireplaces, most have ocean views, and one has Dutch doors leading to a private deck. All are appointed with comfortable couches and chairs, queen- or king-size beds, magazines, plants and flowers—

even in the spacious private baths. A second-floor common room contains games, books and a drafting table for would-be artists. Guests may breakfast here, but most prefer to enjoy in their rooms a tray of freshly baked breads and muffins, juice, coffee, the morning paper, and a fresh flower from the garden. Recently a cottage on the property has been restored for another unit containing a fireplace and a large bath with a six-foot-long sunken tub.

The present Headlands owners—Kathy Casper, Lynn Anderson and Pete Albrecht—took over the inn in 1980. Kathy and Lynn, both former teachers, had been next-door neighbors during a prolonged visit to England and became enthralled with the bed and breakfast idea. Back in the States, they pooled their talents as innkeepers: Kathy is an avid baker, Lynn a dedicated gardener, and Pete a skilled carpenter and handyman. They are also avoiding innkeeper's fatigue by splitting the managerial tasks: Kathy runs the inn half the year and Lynn takes over for the next six months.

HEADLANDS INN, 44950 Albion Street (P.O. Box 132), Mendocino, California 95460. Telephone: (707) 937-4431. Accommodations: six rooms with queen or king-size beds; private baths with tub/shower; no telephones; no television. Rates: moderate, Continental breakfast included. No children. No pets. No cards. Open all year.

In the Spirit of Early America
JOSHUA GRINDLE INN
Mendocino

This lovely old home in Mendocino, like the MacCallum House, was built as a wedding gift—for Joshua Grindle and his bride in 1879 by her parents. Grindle had come to California from Maine to seek his fortune in lumber, but later went into banking. In 1977 Bill and Gwen Jacobson purchased the house for an inn.

The Jacobsons searched northern California for a likely piece of property. Then while vacationing at Heritage House they learned that the old Grindle house was for sale. The house was basically in good shape and, even more important, it had space for a private bath in every room. They added baths, carpeted and redecorated each room. The furnishings are Early American, in keeping with the town's New England heritage.

Joshua Grindle Inn

On the first floor one bedroom is papered with historic scenes of Philadelphia, boasts a handsome maple four-poster, and overlooks a patio shaded by a giant rhododendron tree. Another is decorated with pale yellow woodwork, a peony-patterned quilt on a queen-size bed, and comfortable chairs around a fireplace. An upstairs room has a nautical theme and a fine ocean view. Joshua Grindle's former bedroom, with its dormered windows, is large enough for three, with a queen-size bed and a studio couch. A recently completed saltbox cottage contains two rooms with Franklin fireplaces.

The gracious paneled living room houses a piano and an unusual fireplace decorated with hand-painted English tiles. A decanter of sherry and a bowl of fruit are there for the guests' enjoyment. In the cheerful dining room an antique pine refectory table, a handsome old hutch and a grandmother's clock catch the eye. Here Gwen serves a full breakfast of homemade bread or coffeecake, fresh fruits, eggs, coffee and tea. And if you would like to explore the town during the day, bikes are available for guests' use.

JOSHUA GRINDLE INN, 44800 Little Lake, Mendocino, California 95460. Telephone: (707) 937-4143. Accommodations: seven rooms with double or queen-size beds; some fireplaces; private baths with tub/shower; no telephones; no television; one room with handicapped access. Rates: moderate, full breakfast included. No children. No pets. No cards. Open all year.

Bed and Breakfast in a Victorian Home
WHITEGATE INN
Mendocino

Built as a private home in 1880, this pretty two-story inn on the edge of town overlooks the Mendocino headlands and the bay. Except for an eight-year stint as a hospital, the house served as a residence for a century. Even though Wally and Robbie Clegg now operate it as an inn, they have carefully maintained the feeling of a nineteenth-century private home. The original crystal chandeliers still grace the parlor and former dining room, now a bedroom, and authentic Victorian pieces, some dating back to the 1850s, decorate the rooms. Three of the bedrooms have fireplaces or Franklin stoves and scattered throughout are stunning mirrored armoires, Oriental rugs, plants and flowers.

237

Another fireplace cheers the cozy parlor, which also contains an old organ, books and a decanter of wine. On weekend mornings Robbie treats her guests to the house specialty: cinnamon, apple or walnut waffles. The weekday menu is fruit with yogurt, nut breads and cream cheese. The Cleggs take particular pride in their own blend of coffee and wide variety of teas. Most guests agree that there is no lack of hospitality here.

WHITEGATE INN, 499 Howard Street (P.O. Box 150), Mendocino, California 95460. Telephone: (707) 937-4892. Accommodations: six rooms with twin, double or queen-size beds; two rooms share bath with tub; four have private baths with stall showers; no telephones; no television. Rates: moderate, breakfast included. No children. No pets. No cards. Open all year.

Only a Few Clues to an Unusual Past
THE GREY WHALE INN
Fort Bragg

When John and Collette Bailey bought this three-story building on Fort Bragg's Main Street in 1974, they started a massive remodeling program. Carpeting and private baths were added and the rooms were decorated with comfortable, homey furnishings, quilted bedspreads with matching linens, and paintings by local artists. One would never guess the inn's unusual past: It functioned as a hospital for some sixty years. But a few clues do remain, such as an old examining table in the second-floor lounge, extra-wide doors, a window in the door of the former nursery and an overhead surgery lamp in one of the suites.

Some of the thirteen rooms have natural redwood ceilings or pecky cedar paneling; some have ocean views; others have kitchenettes and will accommodate a family of four; one has a fireplace; another an interior patio. Two glassed-in penthouse rooms have private decks and views of the ocean or mountains. Books and magazines abound in the bedrooms and in a small first-floor sitting room where the Baileys have thoughtfully provided scrapbooks of information on local attractions, restaurants and other inns throughout California.

In the morning, guests are treated to Collette's prize-winning baked goods. She has won six blue ribbons at the Mendocino County Fair for the breads and coffeecakes served at the inn. These are set out for a buffet breakfast along with a choice of juices, a selection of fresh or stewed fruits and most often yogurt or cheese. It's a repast guaranteed to provide vigor for one of this inn's other pluses: guest membership, at a nominal fee, in the Redwood Health Club which has facilities for tennis, swimming and weightlifting.

GREY WHALE INN, 615 North Main Street, Fort Bragg, California 95437. Telephone: (707) 964-0640; toll-free reservations from anywhere in California (800) 382-7244. Accommodations: thirteen rooms with twin, double, queen- or king-size beds; private baths; some kitchens; no telephones; no television; wheelchair access to one room. Rates: inexpensive to moderate, Continental breakfast included. Children welcome. No pets. Cards: AE, MC, VISA. Open all year.

PUDDING CREEK INN
Fort Bragg

Fort Bragg's Main Street should be renamed Bed and Breakfast Boulevard for the many B&Bs that have appeared on it in the last few years. One of the nicest is Gene and Marilyn Gundersen's Pudding Creek Inn, which, along with their country store, occupies two century-old houses connected by an enclosed garden. The houses were supposedly built by a Russian count and in his honor the Gundersens display in the parlor the countess' wedding gown, a photograph of the titled pair and other memorabilia they found in the buildings. The parlor also serves as a breakfast room, but most guests prefer to be served their fruit, coffeecake and coffee in the cheerful old-fashioned kitchen or in the garden, which is a veritable jungle of hanging begonias, fuschias and ferns. Water splashes from a little fountain here and, weather permitting, wine is served here in the evening.

The Gundersens have decorated the bedrooms with Early American and Victorian furnishings, flowered wallpapers and quilted spreads. One of the rooms, named after the count, is paneled with inlaid redwood and has a large stone fireplace, another has a brick fireplace and a third has its own sitting room. But each room in the inn also has its individual touch: an antique spinning wheel in one, a school desk for a night stand in another, and a window box filled with pelargoniums in yet another.

PUDDING CREEK INN, 700 North Main Street, Fort Bragg, California 95437. Telephone: (707) 964-9529. Accommodations: ten rooms with twin, double, queen- or king-size beds; private baths with tub or shower; no telephones; no television. Rates: inexpensive to moderate, Continental breakfast included. Children over 10 welcome. No pets. No smoking, except in garden. Cards: MC, VISA. Open all year.

Getting As Far Away As Possible
DE HAVEN VALLEY FARM
Westport

North of Fort Bragg, Highway 1 takes again to the cliffs—winding around mountains plunging into the sea—and leads to the quaint village of Westport. A mile beyond in splendid isolation is DeHaven Valley Farm, surrounded by forty acres of pastureland stretching down to the ocean. "When I first saw the inn and the setting, I knew that I wanted it," says current owner Gale Fairbrother. "We were meant for each other." Gale, who worked in Sacramento, was inn shopping on the Mendocino Coast at the same time that the old Victorian farmhouse, which had been restored as a B&B in 1974, was looking for a new innkeeper.

The farmhouse is homey and unpretentious. In the parlor, a wall lined with books bids you to curl up for a good read on a comfortable couch by the fireplace; a stereo, well-stocked with tapes, and a piano both wait to be played. Most evenings, while you relax with a glass of wine, you will be enticed by the aroma of good cooking floating from the kitchen. Since DeHaven is so isolated (there's only one small restaurant in Westport), Gale does serve dinner, but only with advance notice. It's a four course feast with home-grown vegetables and everything, including soups and breads, made from scratch. Served at two large round tables in the fireplace-warmed dining room, a typical meal would start with mushroom soup, french bread, and avocado vinaigrette salad, followed by scampi, asparagus tips, and pasta sauced with pesto made from the DeHaven's basil. Desserts are often based on the wild berries that grow rampantly on the grounds. At breakfast, freshly baked breads—gingerbread, muffins, coffeecake—are featured, along with orange juice, platters of fruit and cheese.

Upstairs, five cozy bedrooms, furnished with simple country antiques and fluffy comforters, are tucked under the eaves; dormer windows offer glimpses of the pastures, mountains and sea. Another

De Haven Valley Farm

room opens off the living room and over the kitchen is a two-room suite which has its own fireplace, as does a little cottage in back.

The attraction of DeHaven Valley farm is not the activities offered, but the lack of them. This is a place for people who want to get away from it all—as far as possible. If you become restless, however, Mendocino is about forty minutes by car. Nonetheless, most DeHaven visitors seem content to walk along the beach, to explore the countryside or to browse in the arts and crafts shops in Westport.

DE HAVEN VALLEY FARM, North Highway 1 (P.O. Box 128), Westport, California 95488. Telephone: (707) 964-2931. Accommodations: eight rooms with twin, double, queen- or king-size beds; five rooms share two baths with tub or shower; two rooms have private bath or half bath; no telephones; no television. Rates: moderate to expensive, breakfast included; dinner at extra charge by advance notice only. Children permitted in cottage and suite only. No pets. No cards. Open all year.

Getting There: From Fort Bragg, take Highway 1 to Westport; the inn is 1.7 miles beyond the town on the inland side of the road. From Highway 101, at Liggett take Highway 208 west to Rockport and Highway 1 south to Westport.

The Empress of the Redwood Empire
BENBOW INN
Garberville

In 1926 the Benbow family commissioned San Francisco architect Albert Farr to design a small luxury hotel on the banks of the Eel River in a remote valley surrounded by forests of giant redwoods. Farr created a four-story English Tudor manor house of half-timbered construction: an incongruous sight in this mountain setting. The baronial lobby—with its high coffered ceiling, carved woodwork, massive fireplace of sculptured stone, and French doors leading to a formal terrace—was a gathering place for the elite of the era. John Barrymore, Charles Laughton, President Hoover and Mrs. Eleanor Roosevelt were among Benbow's early guests. But even they would be astounded at the luxuriance of the Benbow today.

In the 1940s this fine old inn slid into a period of genteel shabbiness, despite efforts at improvement by a string of owners.

Nostalgia was almost all it had going for it in 1978 when Patsy and Chuck Watts rescued the aging dowager and transformed it into the empress of the Redwood Empire. Now the lobby is resplendent with carved period furniture, Oriental rugs and an impressive array of antique clocks, paintings and prints, which are found throughout the inn as well. The terrace and gardens are a blaze of color from over three dozen varieties of flowering plants. Upstairs, the Watts installed carved cherrywood paneling in the hallways and thick carpeting throughout and all the bedrooms now have modern tiled bathrooms and a lovely country look from matching floral bedspreads, draperies and wallpaper. A decanter of wine, a coffee pot and a basket of paperback mysteries is provided with the inn's compliments. In the deluxe rooms, a small refrigerator is stocked with fruit juice and white wine.

The second- and third-story rooms of the Benbow have views of the surrounding terrain from large windows or bays. These used to be the choice rooms, but that distinction now belongs to two stories of rooms under the terrace overlooking the river. These once were the bane of Benbow, but in 1983 Patsy and Chuck rebuilt them from the ground up, adding all the accoutrements of the upstairs rooms, plus wood-burning fireplaces in some and private terraces or balconies adjacent to all. A rebuilt cottage offers a Jacuzzi as well.

Despite Benbow's isolation, there's no lack of things to do. The dining room is one of the finest restaurants in the Redwood Empire with a sophisticated menu featuring the likes of Provimi milk-fed veal with a Dijon mustard sauce or Long Island duckling embellished with apricots and Grand Marnier. A juke box is filled with big-band favorites—Glenn Miller, Freddy Martin, Artie Shaw, etc.—and a piano player entertains nightly in the lounge just off the lobby. In another salon, old-time movies from a library of some one hundred classic films are shown each night. And there's always the possibility of a game of chess or a jigsaw puzzle in the lobby. The Watts also stage special events at certain times of the year: a spring dance, a Halloween masquerade ball, a November tasting of Napa Valley wines, a nutcracker Christmas celebration and a New Year's Eve champagne dinner dance.

A plethora of daytime activities is available as well: In the summer the Eel river is dammed into a lake, offering swimming from the inn's private beach, canoeing and paddle boating. Nearby are tennis courts, a nine-hole golf course, fishing, hunting and horseback riding trails. Seven miles south of Benbow is Richardson Grove State Park, one of California's most important redwood preserves and to the north is the Avenue of the Giants, a road that winds through dense groves of sequoias, the world's largest, oldest trees.

Benbow Inn

BENBOW INN, 445 Lake Benbow Drive, Garberville, California 95440. Telephone: (707) 923-2124. Accommodations: fifty-six rooms with twin, queen- or king-size beds; no telephones; color television in terrace rooms; central air conditioning. Rates: moderate to very expensive, no meals included. Dining room open to the public for breakfast, lunch, dinner and Sunday brunch; full bar service. Children over three welcome. Dogs allowed. Credit cards: MC, VISA. Open April 1 to December 1, and December 18 through January 2.

Getting There: Benbow Inn is 200 miles north of San Francisco, two miles south of Garberville, on Highway 101. From the Mendocino coast, Benbow may be reached by Highway 1 to Leggett and then north on 101. The inn will send a car to Garberville airport for guests arriving by private plane.

A Mecca for Lovers of Victorian Architecture
EUREKA AND FERNDALE

Eureka shares its name with California's motto: I have found it! Although it wasn't gold that the city's founders had discovered in 1850, but rather a large bay at the mouth of the Eel River. This was a convenient harbor for ships awaiting a cargo almost as precious as gold: the redwood hewn in the great sequoia groves through which the Eel flows. Ferndale's first settlers were not seeking gold either. They were dairy farmers attracted by the verdant pastureland along the river's broad delta. Today, however, visitors are lured to this area by another kind of treasure, for both Eureka and Ferndale are gold mines of well-preserved Victorian architecture.

The county seat, Eureka is the largest port north of San Francisco and a bustling commercial center for the lumber and fishing industries which are still thriving. Yet the city is preserving its heritage in Old Eureka, a re-creation of the old town along the waterfront. Ferndale, on the other hand, remains a sleepy community little changed from the nineteenth century. Its Main Street is lined with brightly painted Victorian buildings that now house a bevy of shops, arts and crafts galleries, restaurants and the Village Theatre, home of the Ferndale Repertory Company. The entire town has been designated an historical landmark by the state of California and has been dubbed "the Victorian Village."

The drive to this area follows the Eel River from the redwood forested mountains down to the sea. Beyond Garberville you will see a number of turnoffs to the Avenue of the Giants. This is the old road that winds through the dense groves of sequoias, some of which are over three thousand years old and as tall as three hundred and fifty feet. It's worth the detour for the awesome experience of being among some of the world's oldest living things.

Getting There: Eureka is 277 miles north of San Francisco on Highway 101. The turnoff to Ferndale is clearly marked shortly before the highway reaches Eureka.

Southern Hospitality in a Gothic Mansion
THE SHAW HOUSE INN
Ferndale

In the early 1850s, Seth Shaw and his brother Stephen were the first settlers of the rich farmlands south of the Eel River, replacing jungles of twelve-foot high ferns with orchards and cultivated fields. Seth chose a spot on the banks of Francis Creek to erect a gabled carpenter Gothic mansion for his bride and named the estate Fern Dale. But as other farmers populated the area, the town name was contracted to Ferndale. As late as 1980, when most of the other Victorians in the town had been restored to mint condition, the old Shaw house remained empty and neglected, its acre of wooded grounds overgrown with weeds and ferns. Then Velna Polizzi, a native of North Carolina, took over. She renovated the house, moved in her enormous collections of antique furnishings, classic and contemporary paintings, rare china and porcelain, and books, numbering in the thousands, on almost every subject. Then she opened her doors to overnight guests, offering the generous hospitality for which southerners are known.

As you open the gate to the garden, it's likely you'll be welcomed by Amber, Velna's gregarious cat, who will follow you to the library where Velna might offer you a cup of tea or glass of sherry by the fireside. The mansion itself is distinguished by an abundance of bays and coffered ceilings—even under the sloping roof of the second-story gables—and there is a deck overlooking Francis Creek off the dining room. Four of the guest rooms are located upstairs. Two of them have Gothic doors opening to private balconies and a third holds the Shaws' honeymoon

The Shaw House Inn

bed with its handsome six-foot headboard. Another bedroom is reached through double doors off the downstairs parlor. All of the guest rooms have homelike touches: decanters of sherry and water, potpourri, fresh flowers and fruit, dishes of mints, pincushions, music boxes and whatnot.

In the morning Velna sets the Empire table in the formal dining room with sterling silver and pieces of Delft, Chinese and English china for a breakfast that includes fruit compote, hot bread and an entrée such as quiche or whatever else she is inspired to cook. Throughout a stay at Shaw House, Velna will overwhelm you with suggestions on what to do and see in and around Ferndale. If her soft southern accent didn't belie it, you'd think she was a native, she's so well versed in the history of the area.

THE SHAW HOUSE INN, 703 Main Street, Ferndale, California 95536. Telephone: (707) 786-9958. Accommodations: five rooms with twin, double or queen-size beds; two private half baths, one shared bath with tub; no telephones; no television. Rates: moderate, full breakfast included. No small children. No pets. No smoking. No cards. Open all year.

As Flamboyant As a Victorian Can Be
THE GINGERBREAD MANSION
Ferndale

Every architectural geegaw known in the 1890s was lavished on this showplace, its gables and turrets festooned with intricately carved spoolwork, brackets, finials and friezes and painted in flamboyant tones of peach and gold. Flanked by a formal English garden where brick walkways lead through a maze of manicured boxwoods and topiaries, The Gingerbread Mansion makes a stunning sight on this quiet side street of Ferndale. In fact Wendy Hatfield and Ken Torbert were so stunned when they first saw it during a vacation trip in 1981 that they gave up their careers in San Francisco, bought the house and became innkeepers.

The same Victorian spirit pervades the inside of the house as well. The rooms are papered with colorful replicas of Victorian patterns and furnished with period pieces: An Empire couch and Eastlake parlor set in the living room, a Hoosier hutch in the adjoining library with an abundant supply of books, games and puzzles, and carved headboards

The Gingerbread Mansion

in the upstairs bedrooms. The corner bedroom that opens to the porch is the choicest room, although it has a most un-Victorian feature: a mirrored ceiling that reflects the flickers of flame from a Franklin stove. The most spectacular room is the two-hundred-square-foot bathroom where a huge claw-legged tub sits in splendor on a raised platform surrounded by a white rail fence. Green and pink irises on the French wallpaper, a matching stained glass window, hanging plants, a mirrored ceiling and a bidet complete the picture.

Wendy, who was formerly in the travel business, treats her guests with a hospitality as lavish as the gingerbread that adorns the house. Late afternoon tea and cake are served at fireside in the living room, beds are turned down at night and a hand-dipped chocolate placed on the bedside table. Bathrobes are provided for the trip down the hall and trays of coffee and tea are set out upstairs in the morning so guests can have an eye-opener before proceding to the dining room for a breakfast of fruits, cheeses and homemade muffins, breads and cakes. The inn even provides high boots for rainy days and bicycles to explore the town. These are painted the same gold and peach as the house, so the shopkeepers can recognize guests from The Gingerbread Mansion.

THE GINGERBREAD MANSION, 400 Berding Street, Ferndale, California 95536. Telephone: (707) 786-4000. Accommodations: four rooms with twin, double and queen-size beds; two shared baths with tub and shower; no telephones; to television. Rates: moderate, Continental breakfast included. No children under 10. No pets. No smoking. Cards: MC, VISA. Open all year.

Carson's Original House
OLD TOWN BED & BREAKFAST INN
Eureka

In the 1870s lumber baron William Carson had a thriving mill on Eureka's waterfront, now Eureka's Old Town, and lived in an unpretentious two-story house on a hill overlooking the bay. He then hired the noted San Francisco architects, Samuel and Joseph C. Newsom, to design a showplace for a residence, a house that would convince the world of the vast potential of redwood. Carson's house was moved across the street and on its original site the Newsoms erected the most flamboyant Victorian in the west. Its many gables, turrets and towers combine aspects of almost every Victorian style and now this mansion, presently a private club, is Eureka's chief tourist attraction and one of the most photographed buildings in America.

While the mansion was being built, the Carson family lived across the street in the original house, which was later moved one and one-half blocks away. This early Carson residence is now the Old Town Bed & Breakfast Inn, owned by Bob and Agnes Sobrito. They restored the century-old house painstakingly, adding flowered wallpapers throughout. In the gracious living room, a fire burns cheerily for the evening ritual of wine and hors d'oeuvre. Beyond is a formal dining room where breakfast is usually served. But if the inn is not full, Agnes prefers to seat her guests in her cozy kitchen, where she bakes bread and muffins on an old wood stove, a skill she learned as a child. Along with this she serves a hearty morning main course—quiche, omelets, French toast, eggs Benedict, and fresh fruit.

Four of the bedrooms are upstairs under the gabled roof and a fifth is on the main floor. All are furnished with antiques the Sobritos have collected over the years. The baths are equipped with all those little things you're likely to forget when you travel: hand lotion, bath beads, nail polish remover. Even a hair drier is available if you left yours at home. This sort of thoughtfulness is the keynote of the Sobritos' brand of innkeeping. Guests have the run of the house, even use of the laundry

room and the kitchen if they want to fix a spot of tea. Bicycles are available for exploring Eureka so you can peddle past the Carson Mansion down to Old Town with its many galleries and shops.

OLD TOWN BED & BREAKFAST INN, 1521 Third Street, Eureka, California 95501. Telephone: (707) 445-3951. Accommodations: five rooms with twin, double and queen-size beds; three rooms with private baths with stall showers; two rooms share bath with tub; no telephones; no television. Rates: inexpensive to moderate, full breakfast included. Well-behaved children over eight welcome. No pets. No smoking. Cards: MC, VISA. Open all year.

Handcrafted Victorian Circa 1980
CARTER HOUSE
Eureka

Samuel and Joseph C. Newsom, architects of Eureka's famous Carson Mansion, also designed a number of other buildings in the city. One of their admirers is Mark Carter, the son of a local real estate developer, who had helped renovate some Newsom structures owned by his father. When he found an old book of Newsom house plans, he decided to build one from scratch! The house he chose had been built in 1884 for a San Francisco banker named Murphy on the corner of Bush and Jones but was destroyed in the 1906 fire. Now Mark has faithfully re-created it on a hillside in Eureka with views of the bay and of the nearby Carson Mansion from almost every room.

Mark and a carpenter friend, along with two helpers, built the four-story structure themselves, handcrafting the intricate detailings on the wood wainscotings and moldings. "The only old things we used," he confesses, "are a pair of brass hinges and two sinks." They followed the Newsom plans in every respect with only one deviation, a bay window in the entry that splashes the hallway with light. In fact, unlike most Victorians, the entire house has a light and airy feeling of flowing space. Joseph Newsom himself wrote, "The lower portion of the house can be thrown open to form a very fine continuous room." And so it is today with the three parlors distinguished by two marble fireplaces and three large bays. Mark did depart, however, from the Victorian tradition of interior design by painting the walls a stark white and eliminating the frills and clutter associated with the period. The decor is beautifully understated with well-chosen and well-placed antiques, Oriental rugs

253

scattered on the highly polished oak floors, no curtains or drapes to shut out the light, contemporary paintings and ceramics by local artists and baskets of flowers and potted plants strategically set about.

Three guest rooms with high-pitched ceilings occupy the top floor while the other two, as well as the wine cellar, are located at street level on a floor below the parlor. Mark, his wife Christi and their son presently occupy the third floor but plan to move out eventually, turning their rooms over to guests.

Christi is an avid cook. One of her breakfast specialties is a recipe learned in classes with Jacques Pepin: a delicate tart with a ground almond filling topped by very thin slices of apple. This might be accompanied with fresh orange juice, eggs Florentine or Benedict or a smoked salmon platter, and a fruit dish such as kiwi with puréed raspberries or zabaglione with fresh strawberries. In the late afternoon the Carters serve wine with brie and fruit, and at bedtime they offer tea, cookies and assorted cordials. If you're lucky Mark might join you for a chat about Victorian architecture or, if you're really lucky, he might take you for a tour of Eureka's Victorians in his 1958 Bentley.

CARTER HOUSE, Third and L streets, Eureka, California 95501. Telephone: (707) 445-1390. Accommodations: five rooms with double or two double beds; three rooms with private bath with stall shower, two rooms share bath with tub/shower; no telephones; no television. Rates: moderate, breakfast included. No children. No pets. No smoking in bedrooms. Cards: AE, MC, VISA. Open all year.

Carter House

INDEX

257

258

CHILDREN WELCOME

Villa Rosa, Santa Barbara, over 14, 34–35
Vintage Towers, Cloverdale, over 10, 195–196
Washington Square Inn, San Francisco, 86–88
Willows Inn, San Francisco, over 8, 101–102
Willow Springs Country Inn, Soulsbyville, 154–155
Wine Country Inn, St. Helena, over 12, 188–189

SWIMMING POOLS OR BEACHES

Benbow Inn, Garberville, 243–246
El Encanto Hotel, Santa Barbara, 32–34
Gate House Inn, Jackson, 144–146
Gunn House, Sonora, 152–154
Hotel San Maarten, Laguna Beach, 11–12
Inn at Rancho Santa Fe, Rancho Santa Fe, 8–10
La Maida House, North Hollywood, 19–21
Magnolia Hotel, Yountville, 183–184
Mine House, Amador City, 137–138
Mission Inn, Riverside, 24–26
Normandy Inn, Carmel, 70–71
Old Crocker Inn, Asti, 196–197
Pelican Inn, Muir Beach, 110–113
San Ysidro Ranch, Montecito, 27–30
Seal Beach Inn, Seal Beach, 13–14
Ventana Inn, Big Sur, 49–50
Victorian Garden Inn, Sonoma, 176–177
Villa Rosa, Santa Barbara, 34–35
Whale Watch Inn, Anchor Bay, 218–219
Willow Springs Country Inn, Soulsbyville, 154–155

INNS WITH RESTAURANTS

Benbow Inn, Garberville, 243–246
Casa Madrona Hotel, Sausalito, 109–110
City Hotel, Columbia, 149–151
El Encanto Hotel, Santa Barbara, 32–34
Heritage House, Little River, 222–224
Hotel San Maarten, Laguna Beach, 11–12
Inn at Rancho Santa Fe, Rancho Santa Fe, 8–10
Jamestown Hotel, Jamestown, 158–159
La Residence, Napa, 181–182
Little River Inn, Little River, 225–227
MacCallum House, Mendocino, 231–233
Madrona Manor, Healdsburg, 205–207
Mendocino Hotel, Mendocino, 230–231
Mission Inn, Riverside, 24–26
Murphys Hotel, Murphys, 148
National Hotel, Jamestown, 160–161
Olema Inn, Olema, 114–115
Pelican Inn, Muir Beach, 110–113
Pine Inn, Carmel, 62

Rose Victorian Inn, Arroyo Grande, 45–46
St. Orres Inn, Gualala, 215–217
San Benito House, Half Moon Bay, 79–80
San Ysidro Ranch, Montecito, 27–30
Sonoma Hotel, Sonoma, 174–175
Union Hotel, Benicia, 119–120
Union Hotel, Los Alamos, 43–44
Upham, Santa Barbara, 30–31
Ventana Inn, Big Sur, 49–50
Vineyard House, Coloma, 128–130

DINNERS FOR GUESTS
In most cases with advance notice

Archbishop's Mansion, San Francisco, 97–99
Bath Street Inn, Santa Barbara, 38–39
De Haven Valley Farm, Westport, 241–243
Gramma's Bed and Breakfast Inn, Berkeley, 107–108
Harbor House, Elk, 219–220
Hope-Merrill House, Geyserville, 199–201
La Maida House, North Hollywood, 19–21
Magnolia Hotel, Yountville, 183–184
Old Crocker Inn, Asti, 196–197
Old Yacht Club Inn, Santa Barbara, 35–36
River Rock Inn, Chili Bar, 130–131
Toll House Inn, Boonville, 220–221
Victorian Inn on the Park, San Francisco, 93–94

SEA VIEWS
From more than one room

Carter House, Eureka, 253–254
Casa Madrona Hotel, Sausalito, 109–110
De Haven Valley Farm, Westport, 241–243
Doryman's Inn, Newport Beach, 12–13
El Encanto Hotel, Santa Barbara, 32–34
Glendeven, Little River, 227–229
Green Gables Inn, Pacific Grove, 59–61
Harbor House, Elk, 219–220
Headlands Inn, Mendocino, 234–235
Heritage House, Little River, 222–224
Jabberwock, Monterey, 54–56
Little River Inn, Little River, 225–227
MacCallum House, Mendocino, 231–233
Old Milano Hotel, Gualala, 214–215
Parsonage, Santa Barbara, 40–41
Rock Haus, Del Mar, 5–8
St. Orres Inn, Gualala, 215–217
Sandpiper Inn, Carmel, 73–74
San Benito House, Half Moon Bay, 79–80
San Ysidro Ranch, Montecito, 27–30
Spreckels Mansion, San Francisco, 94–97
Venice Beach House, Venice, 15–17
Ventana Inn, Big Sur, 49–50
Whale Watch Inn, Anchor Bay, 218–219

CONFERENCE FACILITIES

GREAT PLACES FOR WEDDINGS

COUNTRY INNS GUIDEBOOKS
In 101 Productions' Series

Country Inns of the Far West: Pacific Northwest $7.95
Country Inns of New England $7.95
Country Inns of New York State $7.95
Country Inns of the Mid-Atlantic $7.95
Country Inns of the Old South $7.95
Country Inns of the Great Lakes $4.95
Country Inns Cookery $6.95

If you cannot find these books in your local bookstore,
they may be ordered from the publisher:
101 Productions, 834 Mission Street, San Francisco CA 94103
Please add $1.00 per copy for postage and handling.
California residents add sales tax.

TO ORDER: Indicate quantity for each title above and fill in form below.
Send with check or money order to 101 Productions.

NAME _____

ADDRESS _____

CITY_____ STATE_____ ZIP_____

JACQUELINE KILLEEN is a fourth-generation Californian who has been traveling around the state since the 1930s and writing about it since 1968, when her first book *101 Nights in California* was published. She is also co-author of *Best Restaurants of San Francisco and Northern California* and of *Country Inns Cookery,* as well as another cookbook, *101 Secrets of California Chefs.* She was a restaurant critic for *San Francisco Magazine,* contributor of the San Francisco restaurant section to *Fodor's San Francisco* and has written articles on California for a number of national magazines.

ROY KILLEEN, an architect, not only contributed the drawings for this book but also much technical advice about furnishings and the style of the buildings. He was formerly a project architect with Anshen and Allen of San Francisco and, like many of the innkeepers, has renovated a number of Victorian buildings. He also has designed 101 Productions' Mini-Mansion® series of historical architectural models and illustrated a number of 101 books.